The Poli
of Apocal,.

Rabbi Dan Cohn-Sherbok is Professor of Judaism at the University of Wales, Lampeter. He is the author of over fifty books including the acclaimed: *The Palestine-Israeli Conflict: A Beginner's Guide*, co-authored with Dawoud El-Alami, also available from Oneworld Publications.

The Politics
of Apocalypse

The History and Influence of Christian Zionism

Dan Cohn-Sherbok

ONEWORLD

OXFORD

The Politics of Apocalypse

Oneworld Publications Limited
(Sales and Editorial)
185 Banbury Road
Oxford OX2 7AR
England

Oneworld Publications
(US Marketing Office)
www.oneworld-publications.com

ISBN-13: 978–1–85168–453–3
ISBN-10: 1–85168–453–0

Cover design by Mungo Designs
Typeset by SNP Best-set Typesetter Ltd., Hong Kong
Printed and bound in Great Britain by Biddles Ltd, King's Lynn

Contents

For Lavinia

Acknowledgements

I would like to acknowledge my indebtedness to a number of important works which provided information as well as source material for this book:

Michael Pragai, *Faith and Fulfilment: Christians and the Promised Land*, London, Vallentine Mitchell, 1985;
Stephen Sizer, *A Promised Land*, 2002 (unpublished Ph.D. thesis);
Stephen Sizer, *Christian Zionism: Road-Map to Armageddon*, IVP, 2005;
Kelvin Crombie, *For the Love of Zion: Christian Witness and the Restoration of Israel*, London, Hodder & Stoughton, 1991.

Preface

There's a new religious cult in America. It's not composed of so-called 'crazies' so much as the mainstream, middle- to upper-middle-class Americans. They listen – and give millions of dollars each week – to the TV evangelists who expound the fundamentals of the cult. They read Hal Lindsey and Tim LaHaye. They have one goal: to facilitate God's hand to waft them up to heaven free from all trouble, from where they will watch Armageddon and the destruction of Planet Earth. This doctrine pervades Assemblies of God, Pentecostal, and other charismatic churches, as well as Southern Baptist, independent Baptist, and countless so-called Bible churches and megachurches. At least one out of every ten Americans is a devoted member of this cult. It is the fastest growing religious movement in Christianity today.[1]

This vision of Rapture and Tribulation places the State of Israel centre stage. Not only do millions of Christians worldwide pray for the rapture of righteous Christians and the end of the world, they are committed to the return of the Jewish people to their ancient homeland. This, they believe, will be the fulfilment of biblical prophecy. When God's people Israel return to the Holy Land to establish their own state, everything will be in order for the countdown to the end of history. Although from a secular perspective these beliefs appear incredible, large numbers of dedicated Christians, often of a fundamentalist background, are convinced that God's plans for humanity are being fulfilled. For these individuals, such a millenarian eschatology provides a framework for understanding current events in the Middle East.

Throughout the United States and elsewhere, popular ministers preach Armageddon theology, and polls indicate an increasingly large number of Christians accept such an eschatology. A 1984 Yankelovich poll, for example, showed that 39 percent of the American people said that when the Bible speaks of the earth being destroyed by fire, this meant that we ourselves will destroy the earth in a nuclear Armageddon.[2]

Popular preachers not only draw huge audiences, but also raise large amounts of money such as Pat Robertson who built the Christian Broadcasting Network (CBN) in Virginia Beach, which annually collects up to $97 million in clear, tax free profit. Within the CBN, he also founded the Family Channel, the nation's seventh largest cable network, featuring Robertson's show, *The 700 Club*. In 1997 Robertson sold the Family Channel to Fox Television for $1.9 billion.[3]

Books dealing with Armageddon are best sellers, such as Hal Lindsey's *The Late, Great Planet Earth* which has sold more than 25 million copies. In the late 1990s evangelist Tim LaHaye's *Left Behind* series of books dealing with the rapture of born-again Christians sold nearly three million copies.[4] The Dallas Theological Seminary, the most influential seminary teaching Christian Zionism, graduated many of the pastors now preaching Armageddon Theology in nearly 1000 Bible churches.[5] The popularity of Armageddon theology extends from ordinary believers to the highest level of government. The former Secretary of Defence, Casper Weinberger, for example, remarked in 1982 concerning Armageddon: 'I have read the Book of Revelation and yes, I believe the world is going to end by an act of God, I hope – but everyday I think that time is running out.

Armageddon or Apocalypse Theology – with its central focus on the re-establishment of the Jewish people in their ancient homeland – is not a new development. Rather, such Zionist aspirations have deep roots in the past. The aim of this volume is to trace the Christian preoccupation with Israel from its emergence during the Reformation until the present day. Divided into 17 chapters, this work provides a detailed account of the thought of early Puritans, prophetic and revivalist premillennial theologians, nineteenth- and twentieth-century Christian Zionists who promoted the creation of a Jewish state, and contemporary writers who envisage Israel as a focus for the final days. Throughout, the evolution of Christian Zionism will be placed within the context of the development of Jewish Zionism and the creation of the state of Israel. Armageddon theology – with its Zionist presuppositions – has become a major movement shaping world events: this volume is designed to provide a first point of entry into this fascinating world of religion and politics.

Chronology

1884	First Conference of Hibbat Zion
1891	Arab protests against Zionist settlers in Palestine
1894–5	Alfred Dreyfus falsely charged with espionage
1896	Publication of *The Jewish State* by Theodor Herzl
1897	First International Congress of Zionists
1903	Persecution of Jews in Kishinev
1904	Beginning of Second Aliyah
1908–9	Arab opposition to Zionist settlements intensifies
1909	Publication of the Scofield Bible
1914–18	First World War
1915–16	Sykes–Picot agreement
1917	Balfour Declaration
1919	Chaim Weizmann leads Zionist delegation at Paris Peace Conference
1919–23	Third Aliyah
1920–1	Arab anti-Jewish riots in Palestine
1924–32	Fourth Aliyah
1929	Arab riots in Jerusalem, Hebron and Safed
1930	Passfield White Paper seeks British disengagement from the Jewish National Home aspects of the Balfour Declaration and the British Mandate
1931	Irgun established
1933–5	Fifth Aliyah
1937	Peel Commission recommends partition of Palestine
1939	Conference at St James' Palace White Paper repudiates partition and favours an independent Palestine state
1932–42	Co-operation between British forces and Jews in Palestine
1944	Assassination of Lord Moyne in Cairo
1945	President Truman supports the demand for a large number of immigrants to Palestine
1946	President Truman endorses partition of Palestine and the creation of a Jewish state
1947	General Assembly votes for partition of Palestine into a Palestinian and Jewish state
1948	David Ben-Gurion declares the State of Israel Arab armies attack Israel
1949	Israel concludes armistice agreements with Egypt, Lebanon and Syria
1950	Beginning of immigration to Israel of Jews from Arab countries
1954	Increased *fedayeen* attacks on Israel

1956	Israel attacks in Sinai
1957	Israel announces intention conditionally to withdraw from Sinai
	Palestine Liberation Party (Fatah) founded
1958	Relations between Israel and the United States strengthened
1964	Palestine Liberation Organization (PLO) founded
1967	Six Day War
1968	Golda Meir becomes Prime Minister
1970	Publication of *The Late Great Planet Earth* by Hal Lindsey
1973	Egypt and Syria launch war against Israeli forces
1977	Sadat goes to Jerusalem
1982	Israel invades Lebanon
1985	Palestinian intifada begins in the Occupied Territories
1985	First International Christian Zionist Congress
1991	Gulf War
1994	Baruch Goldstein murders Palestinian Muslims
1995	Rabin assassinated
1998	Wye River agreement between Netanyahu and Arafat
2000	Palestinian uprising
2001	Ariel Sharon elected Prime Minister of Israel
	Terror attack on the World Trade Centre
2002	Israel mounts operation 'Defensive Wall'
2005	Yassser Arafat dies

1
Christians and the Restoration
of the Jewish People

According to early Christianity, the Jewish people were expelled from the Holy Land and destined to wander the earth because of their rejection of Christ. This was to be their eternal destiny. With the Reformation, however, there was a renewed interest in the Hebrew Bible and the fate of the Jewish people. Amongst the Puritans in particular, various writers called for the return of Jewry to its ancestral home prior to the Second Coming. In the eighteenth and nineteenth centuries Christian scholars and theologians published essays and tracts concerning the future of the Jewish nation. Influenced by previous millenarian convictions, these figures were convinced that the Holy Land was given by God to the Israelites for a perpetual inheritance. Alongside these writers who proposed practical schemes for the creation of a Jewish homeland in Palestine, other thinkers emphasized the eschatological aspects of this plan.

Early Christians and the Jews

In 70 CE the Temple in Jerusalem was destroyed by the Romans and Jews were led into captivity. The Roman conquest of Judaea brought about enormous destruction and the enslavement of thousands of Jews. Nevertheless, reconstruction began immediately and the Jews continued as the largest population in the country. Though the Romans heavily taxed the Jewish community, they recognized Judaism as a lawful religion, and exempted Jews from emperor worship and other religious duties.

During this period it appears that the Sadducees and Essenes disappeared. In their place the Pharisees became the dominant religious group led by Rabban Johanan ben Zakkai, who escaped from Jerusalem during the siege. In the town of Yavneh near the Judaean sea coast he assembled a group of distinguished Pharisaic scholars. There these sages engaged in the development of the legal tradition. Under Johanan ben Zakkai and later in the century under Rabban Gamaliel II, the rabbinic assembly summarized the teachings of the earlier schools of Hillel and Shammai. In addition, they determined the canon of Scripture, organized the daily prayers, and transferred to the synagogue some of the observances of the Temple.

At the end of the third century CE, the emperor Diocletian inaugurated reforms that strengthened the empire. Under his reign the republican veneer of Roman rule was replaced by an absolutist structure. An elaborate system of prices, offices and occupations was introduced to halt economic decline. In addition, Diocletian introduced measures to repress the spread of Christianity, which had become a serious challenge to the official religion of the empire. Diocletian's successor, Constantine the Great, reversed his predecessor's hostile stance and extended official toleration to Christians in 313.

By this stage Christianity had succeeded in gaining a substantial number of adherents among the urban population. Eventually Constantine became more involved in Church affairs, and just before his death he himself was baptized. The Christianization of the empire continued throughout the century, and by the early 400s, Christianity was fully established as the state religion. When Christianity became the dominant religion of the Roman empire, Judaism was relegated to a position of legal inferiority. Imperial laws of the middle of the fourth century prohibited conversion to Judaism as well as intermarriage between Jews and Christians. The official stance of the Church was to attempt to bring Jews to the true faith. Judaism was allowed to continue, however, because the existence of the Jewish people was seen as a testimony to the truth of Scripture. According to Church teaching, the Jews would eventually recognize Jesus' messiahship and sovereignty.

Despite such denigration of Judaism and the Jewish people, Christians during this period went on pilgrimages to the Holy Land. Few of these adventurers viewed Jesus as a Jew, yet they were anxious to follow his footsteps in the land where he lived, ministered and died. In the Middle Ages the Crusaders came from all over Europe to free Jerusalem from the Muslim infidels. These and later travellers embodied an ongoing fascination with the land where Christianity had emerged. With the Reformation, the rediscovery of the Bible as the inspired Word of God led to an increased interest in the Holy Land. Amongst Puritan theologians in particular the Jewish nation was viewed as having a central place in God's providential plan.

In a petition of 1649 to Cromwell's Parliament, for example, two English Puritans, Joanna and her son Ebenezer Cartwright, who were living in Amsterdam, called for the repeal of the act of Parliament that banished Jews from England. By reading the Bible in English, they learned that Palestine was the ancestral home of the Jews and the goal of the divinely promised return. The Kingdom of God on earth was for all nations, they believed, and this would occur when the people of Israel were restored to Jerusalem. To fulfil this divine promise, they sent their petition:

> With and amongst some of the Izraell race called Jewes, and growing sensible of their heavey out-cryes and clamours against the intolerable cruelty of this our English Nation, exercised against them by that... inhumane... massacre... and their banishment ever since... that by discourse with them, and serious perusall of the Prophets, both they and we find, that the time of her call draweth nigh... and that this Nation of England, with the inhabitants of the Nether-lands, shall be the first and readiest to transport Izraells sons and daughters in their ships to the land promised to their fore-fathers, Abraham, Isaac and Jacob, for an everlasting inheritance.[1]

Such a notion was based on a millenarian concept which interpreted the Bible literally and concluded that the Second Coming was at hand. It was widely believed that Jesus would resume his rule from Jerusalem for a thousand years. These millenarians anticipated not only the return of the Jews to their ancestral home but their subsequent conversion to Christianity as a precondition for the Second Coming. Among the pamphlets promoting these ideas was a tract by the sixteenth-century theologian Thomas Brightman who prophesied in his *Apocalypsis Apocalypseos*, 1585, the overthrow of the Antichrist who was identified with the Papacy in Rome. This was to be followed by the dissolution of the Turkish Empire and 'the calling of the Jews'. The Jewish people, he believed, would become a Christian nation and return to Palestine to restore their kingdom. Calculations concerning the occurrence of these events were a central feature of such theological speculation. According to Brightman, the prophecies in the Book of Daniel provided a framework for determining when the restoration of the Jews would take place.

Other authors, such as the sixteenth-century theologian Giles Fletcher, who served as Queen Elizabeth's ambassador at the court of Ivan the Terrible, argued that the Tartars near the Caspian Sea were the Ten Lost Tribes of Israel. These rediscovered tribes were identified with the Kings of the Orient who would re-establish the Kingdom in the Holy Land. With their encouragement, other tribes of dispersed Israel – the scattered children of Judah and Benjamin – would leave their places of residence and join the ten tribes in re-establishing a Jewish commonwealth in the Holy Land.

Another theologian Thomas Draxe published a treatise in 1608 in which he contended that it was a marvellous act of God that the Jews, who were dispersed throughout the world, should still continue as a distinct religious body, keeping their laws, rites and ceremonies. However, he was anxious that they embrace the Christian faith. Yet, he failed to mention that Jewish religious practices are grounded in the dream of a return to their ancestral home.

Unlike Draxe, Sir Henry Finch was a staunch advocate of Jewish restoration in the Holy Land. Having served as a member of parliament, Finch was also a jurist of renown. In 1615 he published his *Explanation of the Song of Songs* and several years later his major work: *The World's Great Restoration or Calling of the Jews, [and with them] all the Nations and Kingdoms of the Earth, to the Faith in Christ.* In this work of pre-Zionist Christian literature, Finch encouraged the Jews to reassert their claim to the Holy Land. In his view, the Jews would become a world-wide empire. According to Finch, Christian monarchs will pay homage to them. Yet the Jewish community will eventually convert to Christianity. Biblical prophecy, he argued, should be understood literally:

> Where Israel, Judah, Zion and Jerusalem are named [in the Bible] the Holy Ghost meant not the spiritual Israel, or the Church of God collected of the Gentiles or of the Jews and Gentiles both... but Israel properly descended out of Jacob's loines. The same judgment is to be made of their returning to their land and ancient seats, the conquest of their foes... The glorious church they shall erect in the land itself of Judah... These and such like are not allegories, set forth in terrene similitudes or deliverance though Christ (whereof those were types and figures), but meant really and literally the Jews.[2]

Not surprisingly, Finch was bitterly criticized for his views: King James in particular resented his suggestion that he should pay homage to the Jewish community. Finch's work was considered libellous, and its author and publisher were arrested and imprisoned. To make amends, Finch expressed contrition for his unadvised views and was released.

Elsewhere, other thinkers similarly expressed respect for the Jewish tradition and advocated the return of the Jewish nation to their ancient home. In Ireland, John Toland published in 1714 *Reasons for Naturalizing the Jews in Great Britain and Ireland on the Same Footing with all Other Nations.* As a deist, Toland believed in the universal law of nature and the continuity of human character. Like others, he viewed the Jewish nation as direct descendants of the ancient Israelites who continued the traditions of their ancestors.

The Dutch pietist Holger Paulli maintained that the Jewish return to the Holy Land was a precondition for the Second Coming, and worked for the establishment of a Jewish monarchy in Palestine. To advance this aim, he published books and pamphlets which he sent to the kings of England and France, encouraging them to conquer Palestine so that the Jews could establish a homeland there. In 1695 he went to England to interest William III in this scheme. Referring to Scripture he addressed the King as a Cyrus of his age: 'Cyrus the Great and the Almighty's Instrument thanks to whom the true Phoenix, the last Temple, shall be born from the ashes of Herod's Temple.'[3]

Eighteenth- and Early Nineteenth-Century Thinkers

In the eighteenth century a number of Christian scholars and theologians published essays and tracts which dealt with the future of the Jewish nation. The Anglican Bishop Richard Hurd, for example, argued in 1772 that despite their dispersion and continued persecution, the Jewish people had remained distinct, surviving as a separate group. This, he stated, was not an accident: 'All this hath something prodigious in it which could be none other but that what He had spoken through His prophets of their destiny in the Latter Days when He would gather them to their ancient land and to Himself in true faith.'[4]

Several years earlier Dr Thomas Burnet arrived at a similar conclusion. Referring to the place that Jewry will have in the Kingdom of the Messiah, he was convinced that the Bible had clearly made the promises of the Messiah and his kingdom first to the Jews. From the very beginning, he wrote, the land of Canaan was given by God to the Israelites for a perpetual inheritance. Therefore they have a just title to the land. The time for the promised restitution of Israel, he continued, was bound to arrive and then the Jews would revive again the land of their forefathers. There is no promise more often repeated in Scripture, he declared, than that which concerns the preservation and future restoration of the Jews.[5]

At the same time the Christian writer Joseph Eyre published *Observations upon the Prophecies relating to the Restoration of the Jews.* What was sworn to Abraham, he stated, was that the land upon which he stood should be given to him and his seed forever. Quoting from Ezekiel 36–37, he rejected any allegorical interpretation of these prophecies. 'How can the Churches of the Gentiles or Christians in general become one nation in the land upon the mountains of Israel?' This, he declared, is the 'longest ... prophecy ... concerning the future restoration ... and if there were no other in the whole Scriptures ... this ... prophecy would be sufficient to ascertain the future restoration of the Jews and the Ten Tribes.'[6]

The evangelist Edward Witaker also argued along similar lines. In 1784 he published a dissertation on the final restoration of the Jews. In this work he emphasized the necessity to adhere to the literal meaning of Scripture. All the prophets, he argued, when speaking of a future restoration refer to God's covenant with a people, not with individuals. Paul's statement 'all Israel shall be saved' was consonant with these promises. Hence, he maintained that it was expressly declared that the restoration will be national. This will be a literal restoration which will take place on earth, since God promised to Abraham 'all the land which thou seest.' (Gen. 12:14). Such a promise was absolute and everlasting.[7]

In 1795 Charles Jerram, a divinity student at Cambridge, won a prize for an essay dealing with the future restoration of the Jewish people. According to Jerram, the foundation on which all biblical promises of a future Jewish restoration rested was the covenant God made with Abraham. The promise to give all the land of Canaan for an everlasting possession (Gen. 17:8) was absolute and unlimited. Hence the title of the Jews to the land of Palestine was inalienable. Due to this covenant the Jews were given a just claim to Canaan. If the grant of the Almighty maker and governor of the universe, he wrote, can constitute a legal title to an everlasting possession, the claim of the Jews to the land of Palestine will always be reasonable and just.[8]

In the light of such conviction about the future return of the Jewish people to the land of their ancestors, a number of Christian organizations were established which fostered this scheme. The Christadelphians were founded by John Thomas in the first half of the nineteenth century. Born in London, he settled in Brooklyn, New York in 1830. There he created his group as an independent ecclesia and preached on the application of biblical prophecies to current and future events. Rejecting orthodox views of the Trinity, their theology was millenarian, focusing on the hope of a worldwide theocracy based in Jerusalem.

In his treatise, *Elpis Israel*, Thomas argued that the restoration of the Jewish nation to its ancestral land could be realized with the political assistance of Great Britain. From the outset, Christadelphians were ardent supporters of the idea of the return of the Jews to the Holy Land; this, they believed, was essential to a fulfilment of God's purposes. Long before the emergence of Jewish Zionism as a political movement, Christadelphians gave practical assistance to Jews, such as the Hibbat Zion movement in Russia, who viewed the Holy Land as a place of refuge.

Other practical steps were envisaged by Christian leaders such as George Gawler, a senior commander at the Battle of Waterloo and later the first Governor of Australia. When he returned to England in 1841, he encouraged Jewish settlements in *Eretz Israel*. In 1849 he accompanied Sir Moses Montefiore on a journey to the Holy Land. On this trip, he persuaded Montefiore to invest in Jewish agricultural settlements in the country. In an article published in 1860, he wrote: 'I should be truly rejoiced to see in Palestine a strong guard of Jews established in flourishing agricultural settlements and ready to hold their own upon the mountains of Israel against all aggressors. I can wish for nothing more glorious in this life than to have my share in helping them do so.'[9] Gawler's efforts were continued by his son John Cox Gawler, who proposed a comprehensive plan for Jewish settlement in the Holy Land. This tract was translated into Hebrew and persuaded a group of Jews to leave Jerusalem to found the village of Ptah Tikvah.

During this period another supporter of such schemes was the English novelist Mary Ann Evans who wrote under the pseudonym of George Eliot. In *Daniel Deronda*, she put these words into the mouth of her hero Mordecai:

There is a store of wisdom among us to found a new polity, grand and simple, just like the old, a republic where there is equality of protection, an equality which shone like a star on the forehead of our ancient community and gave more than the brightness of Western freedom amid the despotism of the East. Then our race shall have an organic centre, a heart and brain to watch and guide and execute; the outraged Jew shall have a defence in the court of nations, as the outraged Englishman or American. And the world will gain, as Israel gains. For there will be a community in the van of the East which carries the culture and the sympathies of every great nation in its bosom. Difficulties? I know there are difficulties. But let the spirit of sublime achievement move the great among our people, and the work will begin.[10]

Later in the novel, Daniel Deronda predicts what such a commonwealth will mean for the Jewish nation:

The idea that I am possessed with is that of restoring a political existence to my people, making them a nation again, giving them a national centre, such as the English have, though they, too, are scattered over the face of the globe. That is a task which presents itself to me as beauty. I am resolved to begin it, however feebly. I am resolved to devote my life to it.[10]

Reflections on the Millennium

Pre-eminent among Christian thinkers who stressed the eschatological aspects of the creation of a Jewish homeland in Palestine was Charles Haddon Spurgeon, one of England's foremost preachers in the nineteenth century. In numerous sermons he expressed his premillennial views. Reflecting on earlier millennialist thought, he prophesied future calamities. 'There are sanguine brethren,' he wrote,

> who are looking forward to everything growing better and better and better, until, at last this present age ripens into a millennium. They will not be able to sustain their hopes, for Scripture gives them no solid basis to rest upon... Apart from the second Advent of our Lord, the world is more likely to sink into pandemonium than to rise into a millennium... We look to the darkening down of things; the state of mankind, however improved politically, may yet grow worse and worse spiritually.[11]

Opposed to liberalist tendencies, Spurgeon adopted a literal biblical hermeneutic. In his view Christ's reign would be on earth. In his view, God did not separate the Jewish people from the Church. Rather, he argued that the Church and Israel would be united spiritually and face tribulation together. The millennial kingdom on earth would thus be made up of both Jews and Gentiles. Nonetheless, he believed that there would eventually be a restoration of Israel, and therefore supported the activities of the British Society for the Propagation of the Gospel Amongst the Jews.

This body was a nonconformist equivalent of the Anglican London Society for Promoting Christianity Amongst the Jews. Established in November, 1842 in Regent Square, London, it was supported by Robert Murray M'Cheyne and Andrew Bonar and worked alongside the Church of Scotland's Mission to the Jews. In an address delivered to the Society in 1864 concerning the restoration and conversion of the Jews, Spurgeon stated:

> There will be a native government again; there will again be the form of a body politic; a state shall be incorporated, and a king shall reign. Israel has now become alienated from her own land. Her sons, though they can never forget the sacred dust of Palestine, yet die at a hopeless

distance from her consecrated shores. But it shall not be so forever...
'I will place you in your own land' is God's promise to them... They
are to have a national prosperity which shall make them famous... If
there be anything clear and plain, the literal sense and meaning of this
passage – a meaning not to be spirited or spiritualised away – must be
evident that both the two and the ten tribes of Israel are to be restored
to their own land, and that a king is to rule over them.[12]

This theme was a central feature of his preaching. Reflecting on the
chronology of these eschatological events, he wrote:

> It is certain that the Jews, as a people, will yet own Jesus of Nazareth,
> the Son of David as their King, and that they will return to their own
> land, and they shall build the old wastes, they shall raise up the former
> desolations, and they shall repair the old cities, the desolations of
> many generations... For when the Jews are restored, the fullness of the
> Gentiles shall be gathered in; and as soon as they return, then Jesus
> will come upon Mount Zion with his ancients gloriously, and the
> halcyon days of the millennium shall then dawn; we shall then know
> every man to be a brother and a friend; Christ shall rule with univer-
> sal sway.[13]

Like Spurgeon, other thinkers wrestled with the role of the Jewish
people in these millennial events. In 1826 Henry Drummond, a
city banker, politician and High Sheriff of Surrey, opened his
home at Albury Park in London to a group of about 20 Christian theologians to discuss the nature of biblical prophecy regarding the
Second Coming. In the same year Edward Irving, Lewis Way and
James Hatley Frere founded a society to investigate prophecy. At
Drummond's suggestion their meetings were subsumed within those
which were taking place at Albury. These gatherings were convened
to examine biblical texts to ascertain the degree to which biblical
prophecies had been fulfilled in the life of Christ and the history of
the Church. About two-thirds of those who were present were
Anglicans; others were from the Moravian Church, the Church of
Scotland, and nonconformist branches, as well as Lady Powerscourt.
   According to Irving, these conferences were a prophetic parliament and a school of the prophets. His notes record a series of shared
principles. Discussing the nature of the first conference, he stated,
there was perfect unanimity:

1. That the present Christian dispensation is not to pass insensibly
   into the millennial state by gradual increase of the preaching of
   the gospel; but that it is to be terminated by judgements, ending

in the destruction of this visible Church and polity, in the same manner as the Jewish dispensation has been terminated.

2. That during the time that these judgements are falling upon Christendom, the Jews will be restored to their own land.
3. That the judgements will fall principally, if not exclusively, upon Christendom, and begin with that part of the Church of God that has been highly favoured, and is therefore most deeply responsible.
4. That the termination of these judgements is to be succeeded by that period of blessedness to all mankind, and even to the beasts, which is commonly called the millennium.
5. That a great period of 1260 years commenced in the reign of Justinian, and terminated at the French Revolution and that the vials of the Apocalypse began then to be poured out; that our blessed Lord will shortly appear and that therefore it is the duty of all who so believe to press these considerations on the attention of all men.[14]

At the conference in 1827, there were detailed discussions of the return of the Jews to Jerusalem, the Second Advent, and the times and seasons of the current period. The next year the conference focused on speculation concerning the restoration of the Jews. In the same year, Irving published a major study: *The Last Days: A Discourse on the Evil Character of These Our Times, Proving Them to be the 'Perilous Times' and the 'Last Days'*. In his work Irving stressed that he would live to see the final battle of Armageddon, the Second Advent and the beginning of the Millennium:

> The times and fullness of the times, so often mentioned in the New Testament, I consider as referring to the great period numbered by times... Now if this reasoning be correct, as there can be little doubt that the one thousand two hundred and sixty days concluded in the year 1792, and the thirty additional days in the year 1823, we are already entered upon the last days, and the ordinary life of a man will carry many of us to the end of them. If this be so, it gives to the subject with which we have introduced this year's ministry a very great importance indeed.[15]

In Irving's view, the Second Advent would take place in 1868.

The Albury Conferences gained wider recognition through a quarterly journal, *Morning Watch*, published by Drummond. At this time the Catholic Apostolic Church emerged out of Irving's circle of followers, who were called Irvingites by their critics. In 1834 Irving died on a preaching tour of Scotland, leaving the Catholic Apostolic

Church in Henry Drummond's hands, and the hope of the restoration of Israel to others. From 1830 to 1833 prophetic conferences continued to be held near Dublin under the sponsorship of Lady Powerscourt. The Powerscourt conferences focused on a pessimistic interpretation of world events and the Second Coming. Unlike the Albury meetings, which included only about 40 individuals, the Powerscourt conferences drew together about 400 evangelicals from throughout Britain. Subjects discussed at these conferences included the nature of the Antichrist, the relationship between the Hebrew Bible and the New Testament, the prophetic nature of the biblical books, and the role of the Jews in God's providential plan.

2

The Development of the Doctrine
of Jewish Restoration

In the early decades of the nineteenth century, Christian thinkers wrestled with the scheme of divine redemption. Influenced by the reflections of Edward Irving, John Nelson Darby envisaged the Church and Israel as having distinct roles in the unfolding of God's scheme of salvation. His views, however, were opposed by more conventional thinkers of the age. Paralleling the development of Christian Zionism in Britain, there was a deep interest in the history of the ancient Israelites in the New World. Drawing on Scriptural sources, the early American pioneers understood themselves in the light of the experiences of the Hebrew nation. Scriptural themes also shaped the experiences of later religious sects. The Puritan interest in the restoration of the Jews in their ancestral home and the eventual acceptance of Jesus as Messiah led to the creation of the London Society for Promoting Christianity Amongst the Jews (LJS). Throughout the nineteenth century this group had a profound impact on the growth of Christian Zionism.

Premillennial Dispensationalism

In 1826 Edward Irving translated a work by Manuel Lacunza, a Spanish Jesuit, who wrote a book under the pseudonym of Juan Josafat Ben-Ezra, allegedly a converted Jew: *The Coming of the Messiah in Glory and Majesty.* Lacunza interpreted the Book of Revelation as describing apocalyptic events which were imminent; Irving added a 203-page preface in which he gave his own prophetic speculations about the end of the world, predicting the apostasy of Christendom, the eventual restoration of the Jews, and the imminent return of Christ. Irving's premillennial and prophetic views had a profound influence on those who attended the Albury and Power-scourt Conferences including John Nelson Darby.

Ordained in the Church of Ireland in 1825, Darby shared the pessimistic view expressed by Irving and others. The Church, he declared, was in ruins. This was not primarily the result of denominational division, but because the entire nature and purpose of the Church had become perverted. Previously, Christian eschatology was optimistic about the future, inspiring worldwide missionary activities. Darby, however, was deeply troubled by current events. In a lecture given in Geneva in 1840, he stated:

> What we are about to consider will tend to show that, instead of permitting ourselves to hope for a continued progress of good, we must expect a progress of evil; and that the hope of the earth being filled with the knowledge of the Lord before the exercise of his judgement, and the consummation of this judgement on the earth, is delusive. We are to expect evil, until it becomes so flagrant that it will be necessary for the Lord to judge it.[1]

Previously Irving had used the term 'dispensation' to contrast God's dealing with Israel and the Church. Darby similarly employed the same term to designate a series of failed attempts by humankind to find acceptance with God:

> The detail of history connected with these dispensations brings out many most interesting displays... But the dispensations themselves all declare some leading principle of interference of God, some condition in which He has placed man, principles which in themselves are everlastingly sanctioned of God, but in the course of these dispensations placed responsibility in the hands of man for the display and discovery of what he was and the bringing in their infallible establishment in Him to whom the glory of them all belonged. In every instance, there was a total and immediate failure as regarded man, however the patience of God might tolerate and carry on by grace the dispensation in which man has thus failed in the outset; and further, that there is no instance of the restoration of a dispensation afforded us, though there might be partial revivals of it through faith.[2]

Paralleling Lacunza's conviction concerning the apostasy of Christendom and the eventual restoration of the Jews and finally the imminent return of Christ, Darby taught that Israel would soon replace the Church, rather than the Church having replaced Israel. In his view, the Church was merely one more dispensation that had failed, and only a small remnant would be saved. This remnant, he argued, would be taken from the ruins of the Church. Hence, there could be no future earthly hope for the Church, and it would soon be replaced in God's purposes by a revived Israel:

> The Church has sought to settle itself here, but it has no place on the earth... (Though) making a most constructive parenthesis, it forms no part of the regular order of God's earthly plans, but is merely an interruption of them to give a fuller character and meaning to them (the Jews).[3]

Adopting a literalist interpretation of Scripture, Darby perceived the covenantal relationship between God and Abraham as binding forever. The promises made to the Jewish people were unfulfilled and would find their eventual consummation in the reign of Jesus Christ on earth during the millennium. In an article in *Christian Witness*, he wrote:

> There are two great subjects which occupy the sphere of millennial prophecy and testimony – the Church and its glory in Christ, and the Jews and their glory as a redeemed nation in Christ – the heavenly people and the earthly people. The habitation and scene of the one being the heavens; of the other, the earth.[4]

Adopting a literalist approach to the Bible, Darby argued that all the prophecies concerning Israel that had not been fulfilled would apply to future events:

> Revelation 12 presents to us the last great object of prophecy... the combat which takes place between the last Adam and Satan. It is from this centre of truth that all light which is found in Scripture radiates. This great combat may take place either for the earthly things... and then it is in the Jews; or for the Church... and then it is in the heavenly places. It is on this account that the subject of prophecy divides itself into two parts, the hope of the Church, and those of the Jews.[5]

This eschatological scheme provided the foundation for later dispensational doctrines in which the Church was understood as a parenthesis to God's continuing covenantal relationship with the Jewish nation. For Darby, the Jews will serve as the primary instrument of God's rule on earth during the millennium. According to Darby, the Lord will empty the land of its inhabitants and give it all to Israel. Then, he believed, the Jews will rule on earth in league with Satan: 'The government of the fourth monarchy will still be in existence, but under the influence and direction of the Antichrist; and the Jews will unite themselves to him, in a state of rebellion, to make war with the lamb . . . Satan will then be displayed, who will unite the

Jews with this apostate prince against heaven . . . a remnant of the Jews is delivered and the Antichrist destroyed.[6]

Hence like Irving, Darby formulated two stages to Christ's imminent return. First, Christians would meet Christ in the air and be raptured from the earth. This would be known as 'the rapture of the saints.' Then the Anti-Christ would arise. His rule would finally be destroyed by the appearance of Christ on earth. Concerning rapture, he wrote:

> The Church's joining Christ has nothing to do with Christ's appearing or coming to earth. Her place is elsewhere. She sits in Him already in heavenly places...
>
> We go up to meet Christ in the air. Nothing is clearer, then, than that we are to go up to meet Him, and not await His coming on earth; but that this coming to receive us to Himself is not His appearing is still clearer...
>
> This is the rapture of the saints, preceding their and Christ's appearing... so that at their rapture He has not appeared yet... This rapture before the appearing of Christ is a matter of express revelation, as we have seen from Colossians 3:4.[7]

Darby stated that the tribulation would end seven years after the rapture when Jesus would return to Jerusalem to set up his kingdom over which he would rule for 1000 years. This notion of a pretribulation rapture had a profound influence on later Christian writers who similarly were convinced that the faithful would meet Christ in the air, and that God would guide the course of history to its ultimate fulfilment through the Jewish people re-established in their ancient homeland.

Within Brethren circles, Darby's views were challenged by various thinkers. B.W. Newton, his chief assistant in Plymouth, for example, argued that Darby's views were a departure from biblical orthodoxy. For Newton and others, Darby's elevation of Israel above the Church was a heresy. In their view, the Church in Scripture was made up of both Jews and Gentiles who are one in Christ. According to Newton, there will be a millennial reign in which Israel will be restored under the same covenant as the Church, not one in which, as Darby claimed, national Israel will be restored and the Church excluded. Darby's response to such opposition was to charge his critics with sectarianism and excommunicate them. Darby led the Exclusive Brethren, whereas Newton became the leader of the Open Brethren; later Darby's Exclusive Brethren split into three factions.

From 1862 onwards, Darby's influence over Brethrenism in Britain waned and he began to focus his ministry on North America, making a number of journeys in the ensuing years. During this time he exerted a considerable influence on such evangelical leaders as James H. Brookes, Dwight L. Moody, William Blackstone, and C. I. Scofield as well as the emerging evangelical Bible Schools and Prophesy Conferences. As a result, Darby's new form of millennial teaching had a profound impact on the development of evangelical thought in America, giving rise to a dispensationalist movement with institutional permanence.

Early Christian Zionism in America

When the Declaration of Independence was adopted on the 4th of July 1776, a special committee consisting of Benjamin Franklin, Thomas Jefferson and John Adams was given responsibility for designing a seal for the nation. Inspired by the Bible, the committee proposed a seal which showed pharaoh sitting on an open chariot, with a crown on his head and a sword in his hand passing through the divided Red Sea in pursuit of the Israelites. Rays from a pillar of fire beamed down on Moses who is portrayed standing on the shores extending his hand over the sea causing it to destroy the Egyptian forces. Around this picture were the words: 'Rebellion to Tyrants is Obedience to God'. Although the Great Seal of the United States was subsequently altered, it has always carried the thirteen stars, symbolizing the colonies, arranged in the shape of the star of David. Similarly, the Liberty Bell in Philadelphia had inscribed on it a verse from the Book of Leviticus: 'And proclaim liberty throughout the land unto all inhabitants thereof'. This ideal of liberty and equality, which was exported to the colonies from England and Holland, was directly linked to Scripture.

In addition, the settlers were anxious to link the New World to the Holy Land by giving their settlements biblical names. The following are representative examples:

1. *Salem, Massachusetts.* Originally known by the Indian name of Naumkeag, it was renamed Salem from the Hebrew word meaning peace.
2. *Bethlehem, Pennsylvania.* Named on Christmas Eve, 1741 by Moravian missionaries who had come from Germany.
3. *Sharon.* Towns with this name are found throughout the United States. The name is associated with the blossoming gardens of the plain of Sharon, celebrated in the Song of Songs.

4. *Zion.* This name was given to villages and parks in the United States such as Zion National Park in Utah.

5. *Nazareth, Pennsylvania.* Located near Bethlehem, Pennsylvania, a pilgrimage takes place there every Christmas. Celebrants walk between these two towns just as thousands of years before Mary made her way from Nazareth to Bethlehem to comply with the Roman census regulations and give birth to her child.

6. *Jericho, New York.* This township on Long Island was settled by the Society of Friends. They changed the original Indian name to Jericho because to them it was settled first, just as Jericho on the Jordan had been settled first by the Tribes of Israel when Joshua entered the Promised Land.

7. *Rechoboth, Delaware.* This town was founded by Methodists in 1872. It provided a permanent camp meeting ground and seaside resort where the Sabbath was strictly observed.

Alongside such designations with biblical connotations, the early settlers frequently gave biblical names to their children such as Abigail, Isaac, Jacob, Ichabod, Sarah, Rachel, Joshua and David.

As in England, the Puritan colonists viewed the Bible as their principal spiritual authority. Like the ancient Israelites, they regarded themselves as God's chosen people, and they transplanted the imagery of the Hebrew tribes entering Canaan into their physical environment and thought patterns. Like the Hebrews, they had entered the Promised Land and embraced a new covenant binding them to God. Children's books related Biblical stories to their experiences. John Bunyan's *Pilgrim's Progress* was as popular as the Bible. *The New England Primer*, published in 1649, combined the alphabet with spelling instructions, catechisms, the Ten Commandments, the Old and New Testaments, and verses for religious training. Echoing biblical themes, children were to learn the alphabet through religious associations:

A – In Adam's fall we sinned all
J – Job feels the rod yet blessed God
Q – Queen Esther comes in royal State to save the Jews from dismal fate
R – Rachel doth mourn for her first born
S – Samuel anoints whom God appoints
U – Uriah's beauteous wife made David seek his life.[8]

For these early settlers, biblical history was a constant inspiration as they faced hardship and physical difficulties. In addition, codes of law, such as the *Cambridge Platform* and *The Book of the Laws and Liber-*

ties Concerning the Inhabitants of the Massachusetts of 1648 provided a framework for daily life. The codifiers emphasized the biblical antecedents for their work:

> So soon as God had set up political government among his people, Israel, he gave them a body of laws for judgement both in civil and criminal causes. These were brief and fundamental principles... For a commonwealth without laws is like a ship without rigging and steerage... Therefore... the Lord bestowed upon his peculiar people... that God was nearer to them, and their laws were more righteous than other nations.[9]

Among Christian sects, the Mormons exhibited a profound interest in biblical history. Tracing their history to 600 CE, believers maintain that at that time descendants from the House of Joseph came to America. Their historical record, kept on metal plates, was delivered to the prophet Joseph Smith, who translated them into English. This record – The Book of Mormon – was published in 1830. Under his guidance, the Church grew in numbers; eventually they migrated west and founded their 'Zion' in Utah. The river there was named the Jordan. In their view, the similarity in topography was not accidental; God was continually present in their wanderings.

For the Mormon community, the return of the Jews to the land of their ancestors was a central principle. As the Book of Mormon records:

> And I will remember the covenant which I have made with my people; and I have covenanted with them that I would gather them together in mine own time, and I would give unto them again the land of their fathers for their inheritance, which is the land of Jerusalem, which is the Promised Land unto them forever, saith the Father.[10]

In this regard, Joseph Smith had numerous visions about the fulfilment of biblical prophecy. In his view, the restoration of the Jews to Palestine must precede the coming of the Messiah. In pursuit of this aim, he sent one of the Church's elders, Orson Hyde, on a mission to the Holy Land to dedicate the land for the coming ingathering of the Jews. In Jerusalem, Hyde ascended the Mount of Olives where he prayed:

> to remove the barrenness and sterility of this land, and let springs of living water break forth to water its thirsty soil. Let the vine and olive produce in their strength, and the fig tree bloom and flourish. Let the land become abundantly fruitful... Let it again flow with plenty to feed the returning prodigals who come home with a spirit of grace and sup-

plication; upon it let the clouds distil the virtue and richness, and let the fields smile with plenty. Let the flocks and the herds greatly increase and multiply upon the mountains and the hills; and let Thy great kindness conquer and subdue the unbelief of Thy people. Do Thou take from them their stony heart, and give them a heart of flesh; and may the sun of Thy favour dispel the cold mists of darkness which have beclouded the atmosphere.[11]

In 1873 a visitation was sent to Palestine. Again this mission was charged with dedicating the land to the return of the Jewish nation. A ceremony was held on the Mount of Olives, as one of the members of this trip, George A. Smith, reported back to the Church:

They [the few Jews they met in Jerusalem] express a firm belief in the redemption of Israel and the Return of the Ten Tribes. They say there are no springs here now, but used to be in the days of Israel's prosperity, and there will be again.[12]

In the early part of the twentieth century, Mormon publications enthusiastically supported Jewish immigration, as a report of February 1921 noted:

Jerusalem is rebuilding rapidly. Palestine resounds to the hum of Hebrew industry, while her hills smile under the fields of ripening grain planted by the amicable hands of descendants of both Judea, Esau and Ishmael. In the heart of every Latter-Day Saint there are singing praises which begin with prophecy and end with praise.[13]

Once the State of Israel was founded, Mormon elders visited Jerusalem and in it was decided to set apart the place on the Mount of Olives where Orson Hyde had prayed. There a grove was to be planted, centred around a stone memorial on which a bronze plaque was placed with Hyde's prayer in English, Hebrew and Arabic to illustrate the Mormon Church's belief in the return of the Jews to their ancient homeland.

Alongside the Mormons, Seventh Day Adventists were similarly influenced by biblical teaching. One of the central tenets of their faith was the observance of the original Hebrew Sabbath as the weekly day of rest. Even though they did not support a Jewish return to the Holy Land, they believed in the conversion of the Jews prior to the Second Coming. Other Adventist sects, however, set up independent groups which subscribed to the belief that the Advent would bring about the establishment of the Kingdom of God not in Heaven, but on earth. In this Kingdom, they stated, the Jews would have an elevated position as the Chosen People who will enjoy Divine Grace, and then repent and recognize Jesus. These sects were sympathetic to Zionist aspirations, and later regarded the State of Israel as the fulfilment of biblical prophecy.

One of these groups, the Church of God formed in 1888, was located in Oregon, Illinois. A central principle of this group is the belief in the restoration of the nation of Israel. In the current ingathering of exiles, they see the fulfilment of God's plan. Another group is the Church of God (Seventh Day) which was initially organized in Starberry, Missouri and now has a centre in Denver, Colorado. Their bimonthly publication, *The Bible Advocate*, asserts that modern Israel is the fulfilment of biblical prophecy. A number of other adventist sects hold similar beliefs, uniting in the conviction that the political developments of our time take place in accordance with a Divine scheme. The Jews of today, they believe, are instruments in God's hand on the threshold of the Last Days of Judgement.

First Steps to Restoration

The Puritan interest in the restoration of the Jews in the ancestral home and the eventual acceptance of Jesus as Messiah led to the creation of the London Society for Promoting Christianity Amongst Jews (LJS). Throughout the nineteenth century this group had a profound impact on the growth of Christian Zionism.

This body was largely the initiative of a single figure: Joseph Frey, who was born in Franconia in 1771. The son of a rabbi, he came to faith in Jesus in 1798 and afterwards went to train with the London Missionary Society (LMS). Initially he intended to serve as a missionary in Africa, but changed his mind once he came into contact with poor Jews in the East End of London. Instead, he asked the LMS to support him in his missionary activities in London.

In the beginning he preached the gospel at the Calvinist Methodist Chapel in Jewry Lane, Aldgate. Soon, however, he proposed the creation of a meeting house where Hebrew Christians could be taught a trade as well as a boarding school for Jewish children. Although the LMS directors were unwilling to fund such efforts, Frey and a small group of others formed a society for the purpose of visiting and relieving the sick and distressed, and instructing the ignorant. The idea was that this society would be an auxiliary of the LMS. But the parent society was unhappy with this suggestion, and Frey and his companions formed an organization. Founded in 1809, the London Jewish Society (LJS) received considerable support from distinguished figures including William Wilberforce and Charles Simeon. In 1813 the Duke of Kent became Patron of the Society, and the vice-presidents of the society included the Duke of Devonshire, seven earls, five viscounts and various members of parliament.

Early in the history of the LJS, it was recognized that Jewish believers needed a place of their own to worship, and the Society leased the old French Protestant Church in Spitalfields which they renamed 'The Jews' Chapel'. These believers formed an association, the 'Benei Avraham' which met on Friday evenings and Sunday mornings. In time, however, the society faced financial difficulties with the construction of its new headquarters called 'Palestine Place'. When a chapel was built, denominational conflict between Anglicans and non-Anglicans occurred concerning the form of worship in the Jews' Chapel. Eventually non-Anglicans withdrew and the LJS became an institution of the Church of England.

When Sir Thomas Baring became president of the LJS, he found that the society was deeply in debt. To meet this crisis, Lewis Way, a barrister and Fellow of Merton College, Oxford, donated £10,000 and further sources were later raised to clear the society's debts. When the Napoleonic Wars ended in 1815, Way viewed the time as ripe for pursuing the cause of the Jewish nation. For Way, civil emancipation in Europe and the restoration of a homeland in Palestine were central goals. Appealing to heads of Europe at the congress of Aix-la-Chapelle in October 1818, Way argued on behalf of the Jewish people. Appealing to prophetic passages in Scripture, he maintained that exiled Israel would return to their ancient homeland.

For Way, such longing for the return of the Jews and their conversion was of central importance, and their conversion laid the groundwork for the systematic preaching of the gospel to Jews in Europe, Asia and Africa. Influenced by Edward Irving and Joseph Wolff, Way wrote a series of articles under the pseudonym Basilicus concerning the restoration of the Jews and the imminent return of Christ in the LJS journal, *The Jewish Expositor* between 1820 and 1822. During this period he also published a pamphlet, *The Latter Rain*, in which he urged Christians to pray for Jews; this was vital, he argued, because biblical prophecies have a primary and literal reference to the Jewish people. Through these efforts Way generated evangelical support for Zionism by promoting a futurist eschatology which envisaged the exiled Jewish community returning to their promised homeland.

By the end of the nineteenth century, the LJS supported stations in 46 places outside Britain. Such outreach was accompanied by the growth of the LJS in Britain, where LJS workers travelled throughout the country, taught in churches about the Jewish roots of Christianity, and attracted followers such as Rabbi Michael Solomon

Alexander, who eventually became an Anglican priest and in 1841 was appointed the first Anglican bishop in Jerusalem.

The development of Christian Zionism within Anglican circles at this time was also shaped by Charles Simeon, who was dedicated to the work of the LJS. He, too, looked for a full and imminent restoration of God's chosen people. In pursuit of this aim, he went on preaching tours on behalf of the LJS, speaking on Jewish evangelism and the restoration of the Jewish people. Based on his reading of Scripture, he was convinced that the Jews would return to Palestine as Christians. The future restoration of the Jews and their union with the Gentiles in one universal Church, he believed, would take place together or in near connection. In this respect, he differed from both Irving and Darby, believing that the millennium had already commenced. For this reason, Simeon was energetic in seeking to convert Jews to the Christian faith; through their conversion, he maintained that they would act as evangelists so that 'God will shortly interpose to bring all the nations to such a unity in religious faith and practice as has never been seen upon earth.'[14]

Another figure, Joseph Wolff, who had studied under Charles Simeon at Cambridge, set out to explore Palestine. A German Jew who had converted to Roman Catholicism and then to Anglicanism, Wolff was preoccupied with the discovery of the Ten Lost Tribes. In March 1822 he entered Jerusalem, where he distributed New Testaments and other Christian literature and spoke to those Jews who were prepared to listen. The following year Wolff took up residence on Mount Zion, evoking the hostility of the Jews of Jerusalem. One of those whom he encountered declared: 'It was never seen at Jerusalem that a Jew should come there as for the purpose of persuading them [the Jews of Jerusalem] that Jesus is the Messiah.'[15] Despite such difficulties, Wolff believed that there was a feeling of excitement among the Jews, and concluded that this should be his life's task.

In May 1823, Lewis Way and the Rev. W.B. Lewis sailed for Lebanon with a letter of recommendation from Sir Sidney Smith, the commander of the British fleet that had defeated Napoleon at the Battle of Acre in 1799. Way presented this letter to the Emir of Lebanon who allowed these missionaries to enter the country. Way and Lewis brought 10,000 Bibles with them, which they distributed to those whom they visited. While these missionaries were in Lebanon, considerable opposition was aroused concerning their activities. Remarking on these events, Way wrote: 'I am therefore not surprised that on the landing of 10,000 Bibles on the shore of the Holy Land, there should be persons ready, as if prepared to prevent their distribution, or counteract their efficacy; and such was the case.'[16]

Still in Lebanon, Way became ill and was forced to return to England. Opposition to his scheme stemmed from both Islamic and Jewish circles. Muslim Law forbade the building of new places of worship for either Christians or Jews. As far as the Christian community was concerned, the established churches opposed the creation of a Protestant presence in Jerusalem. The Jewish community, too, were fearful about missionary activity and closed ranks to protect themselves. Reaction from the established authorities was also intense. In January 1824 the Pope issued a bull forbidding Roman Catholics to receive and read any of the 10,000 Bibles, and Turkish authorities issued a decree forbidding the distribution of Christian literature in the Levant.

Determined to overcome these difficulties, Lewis realized that the Protestant Christians as well as Jews in Jerusalem could only be protected through the establishment of a British consulate. Regarding the Jewish community in the Holy Land, he wrote:

> The Jews at Jerusalem... are liable to be stopped by the lowest fallah of the country, who... may demand money of them as a right due to a mussulman, and this extortion may be practised on the same poor Jew over and over again in the space of 10 minutes.[17]

Lewis soon left Jerusalem and was replaced by Dr and Mrs George Dalton who arrived in 1824 to set up medical work in Jerusalem. In 1826 a Danish-born LJS trained missionary, John Nicholayson, arrived to minister to German-speaking Jews of the city.

3

Jews and Christians
in the Holy Land

Alongside the development of Christian eschatology, travellers to the
Holy Land recorded their experiences, and such figures as Lord
Shaftesbury provided practical schemes for the establishment of a
Jewish homeland in Palestine. Such plans predated the emergence of
Jewish secular Zionism at the end of the century. In Palestine, Chris-
tian missionaries sought to bring Jews to the Christian faith. Through
the efforts of the Dutch missionary John Nicolayson, steps were taken
to establish an ongoing Protestant religious presence in the Holy
Land. Unlike early Christian Zionism with its emphasis on the return
of the Jewish people prior to the Second Advent, Jewish religious
Zionism was rooted in the belief that the Messiah had not yet come.
Rather than adopting a passive attitude toward the messianic age, a
number of Jewish thinkers argued that the Jewish community must
create a homeland in anticipation of messianic redemption.

Christian Travellers and the Holy Land

Many Christian pilgrims who journeyed to Palestine were anxious to
record their experiences. As a consequence, a variety of travelogues
were produced over the centuries. In the middle of the seventeenth
century, for example, *A Pisgah Sight of Palestine* was written by Dr
Fuller. In Hebrew *pisgah* refers to a high point; in Scripture, Pisgah
was the top of Mount Nebo from which Moses viewed the Promised
Land. Drawing on this imagery, Fuller produced a fulsome account
in which he described animal and vegetable life in detail and sought
to correct various misapprehensions about the Holy Land. Of 'the
desert', he wrote:

> sounds hideous to English ears; it frights our fancies with apparitions
> of a place full of dismal shades, savage beasts and doleful desolations;

whereas in Hebrew, it imports no more than a woody retiredness from publick habitation; most of them in extent not exceeding our greater parks in England, and more alluring with the pleasure of privacy, than affrighting with the sadness of solitariness.[1]

Another travelogue was written about 50 years later by Nathaniel Crouch: *Two Journeys to Jerusalem*. This work was reprinted various times during the century and contained a special chapter written under the pen-name Robert Burton, 'Memorable Remarks upon the Ancient and Modern State of the Jewish Nation'. In this work he discussed why such a barren land could have supported the prosperous population of Biblical and Roman as well as Byzantine times. In his view, the ancients practised careful cultivation and computed that one acre of good land would feed four souls for a full year, allowing two pounds, six ounces of bread a day. He then calculated the area of the old kingdom of Judaea as 3,365,000 acres, deducting half the land as uncultivatable, and concluded that it would suffice to support at least one man to an acre. Like other visitors, Crouch observed the general barrenness of the country. As with others, he noted that the stretch of land between Jaffa and Jerusalem was desolate owing to continuous wars and ravages. Yet, he emphasized, in biblical times this area was described as a land flowing with milk and honey. Crouch's work also contained the account of fourteen English travellers from the Levant Company in Aleppo who passed through the area around Caesarea and the Sharon Plain south of Haifa. They too stressed that this area was now ruined and inhabited by a company of savage Arabs. Nearly a century later another group of Englishmen from Aleppo toured the country; one of their members, Richard Tyron reported that the land had gone to rack and ruin and now appeared to be under a curse.

In the middle of the next century, the Ottoman Empire became increasingly unstable, giving rise to renewed interest in the country by foreign powers. The first Christian statesman who expressed concern about those Jews resident in the land was Lord Palmerston, the British Foreign Secretary. In 1840 he wrote to the British Ambassador in Constantinople, asking the Ottoman regime to encourage Jewish settlement:

> There exists at the present time among the Jews dispersed over Europe, a strong notion that the time is approaching when their nation is to return to Palestine... It would be of manifest importance to the Sultan to encourage the Jews to return and to settle in Palestine because the wealth which they would bring with them would increase the resources of the Sultan's dominions; and the Jewish people, if return-

ing under the sanction and protection and at the invitation of the Sultan, would be a check upon any future evil designs of Mehemet Ali [of Egypt] or his successor... I have to instruct Your Excellency strongly to recommend [to the Turkish Government] to hold out every just encouragement to the Jews of Europe to return to Palestine.[1]

At this time the London *Times* ran an editorial concerning a plan to plant the Jewish people in the land of their ancestors. According to the *Times*, this scheme was under serious consideration, and the editorial praised Lord Ashley (later Lord Shaftesbury) for his practical statesmanship. Ashley was quoted as canvassing Jewish opinion concerning their return to the Holy Land. He was concerned to know whether they were willing to go and when they would be ready; he also sought to gain information regarding the likelihood of their investing in this project assuming that the Sultan would assure that law, justice and safety were secure.

As a driving force of this scheme, Lord Shaftesbury was a person of resolute faith and conviction. Born into the aristocracy, he was related to Whig Prime Ministers of the day. Offered various cabinet posts, he wished to remain above party and politics and devote himself to welfare work. In his view, the Jews were God's ancient people, and he was convinced that the return of the Jews was linked to the Second Coming. On the basis of biblical prophecy, he believed that the restoration of the Jewish nation in Israel would usher in the final days.

During this period, Turkish–Egyptian relations reached an impasse, and Lord Palmerston concluded a treaty which established a British Consulate in Jerusalem. Lord Ashley supported this initiative and he persuaded Palmerston to issue instructions to the newly appointed Vice-Consul:

> It will be part of your duty as British Vice-Consul in Jerusalem to afford protection of the Jews generally and you will take an early opportunity of reporting... upon the present state of the Jewish population in Palestine.[2]

In his Diary Lord Ashley wrote:

> Young has just been appointed her Majesty's Vice-Counsul in JERUSALEM! What a wonderful event it is! The ancient city of the people of God is about to resume a place among the nations, and England is the first of Gentile kingdoms that ceases to 'tread her down'.[3]

When another travelogue was published by Lord Lindsey, *Letters from Egypt, Edom, and the Holy Land,* Lord Ashley wrote a review in which he discussed the restoration of the Jewish nation in Palestine under British influence. It was, he stated, a time when the persecution of the Jews would cease and an upsurge of interest in the Holy Land would revive among Christians. In the London *Times* of 9 March 1840, such interest was expressed in the restoration of the Jews. His article stated an opportune time had now arrived for Protestants to support the creation of a Jewish presence in Palestine.

Later in the year Lord Ashley presented a formal document to Palmerston for the recall of the Jews to their ancient land. As Lord Ashley noted, the Jewish people believed that the time was near for the deliverance, and that there should be a Four Power guarantee for the return of the Jewish nation. Their industry was prodigious, he explained, and they would return at their own expense. It would be highly advantageous to the Sultan, he told his ambassador in Constantinople:

> that the Jews who are scattered throughout other countries in Europe and Africa, should be induced to go and settle in Palestine, because the wealth and habits of order and industry which they would bring with them would tend greatly to increase the resources of the Turkish Empire and to promote the progress of civilisation therein.[4]

However, when the Whig government was defeated, these plans failed to materialize due to a lack of political support.

Alongside these political aspirations, Christian missionaries championed the cause of Jewish restoration to Palestine. In their view, the prophecies concerning the Second Coming were linked with feelings of guilt concerning the Church's harsh treatment of Jewry through the centuries. As a result, a group of 320 Christians issued a special memorandum to Lord Palmerston concerning the Jewish nation:

> Your Memorialists beg leave... to remind your Lordship that the land of Palestine was bestowed by the Sovereign of the Universe upon the descendents of Abraham as a permanent and inalienable possession nearly 4000 years ago, and that neither conquests nor treaties among men can possibly affect their Title to it. He has also decreed that they shall again return to their country and that the Gentiles shall be employed as the means of their restoration.[5]

Following the Damascus ritual murder trial of 1840, Colonel Charles Henry Churchill, who represented Britain and supported the Jews of Damascus, emphasized the importance of the restoration of the Jewish community. Addressing Sir Moses Montefiore, he stated: 'I cannot conceal from you my most anxious desire to see your countrymen endeavour once more to resume their existence as a people. I consider the object to be perfectly obtainable.' But, he pointed out, it would be necessary for Jews to embark on this project themselves, and further that European powers assist them in this scheme.[6]

Missionary Activity in Jerusalem

When the Dutch missionary John Nicolayson arrived in Jerusalem, he sought to establish a mission station in the country. During the year he was married to Dr Dalton's widow and embarked on missionary travels throughout the Middle East. At the same time, Joseph Wolff arrived in Jerusalem, and distributed the Scriptures to the Jewish community and also established a school. In the summer of 1831 Nicolayson returned to Jerusalem. In November a war broke out between the Turkish Pasha of Acre and the Egyptian leader, Mehemet Ali; by 1832 the Egyptians had conquered Acre, Damascus and Aleppo. In January 1833 Nicolayson wrote to the Egyptians, asking permission to allow missionaries to settle in the Holy Land.

Even though the Egyptians were willing, a number of local Christian communities were opposed to the interference of these Protestants. According to Nicolayson the Armenians and the Roman Catholics had combined their forces to thwart such plans. Open hostility was commonplace. When Nicolayson visited the Church of the Holy Sepulchre on the Saturday before Easter, for example, he was critical of the scene of fire appearing spontaneously from the tomb of Jesus at the Centre of the Church and then spreading throughout the building to candles held by those assembled:

> It anything especial need be urged in favour of a missionary settlement in Jerusalem, this and other similar perversions and mockeries of the truth and of sacred things, furnish a most urgent plea. It is impossible to witness the thousands who flock together here on this occasion as wholly given to idolatry, so blindly led to the service of dumb idols, and all of this in the name of Christianity, without feeling one's spirit stirred within one.[6]

In the same year Nicholayson rented a house near the Jewish quarter, thereby becoming the first permanent Protestant missionary in Jerusalem. The following year a revolt by local peasants against the Egyptian government occurred. Nicholayson was seized and he was about to be killed when he was recognised by a local Arab and spared. In February 1835 the LJS declared that it was now ready to construct a church in Jerusalem. With the help of Lord Ashley, Sir Thomas

Baring, the LJS President, contacted Lord Palmerston, who instructed the British consul-general in Egypt and the ambassador in Constantinople to obtain permission for the building of the church.

At the LJS Annual General Meeting in May 1835, Nicholayson stressed that the Gospel would never be effective in Palestine without a place of worship. Despite these efforts, there were considerable difficulties. Islamic law ruled out the building of a church. Hence, Colonel Campbell, the British consul in Cairo, encouraged the British government to set up a consulate in Jerusalem. Lord Palmerston agreed to appoint William Tanner Young as vice-consul and sent him with instructions to protect the Jewish community in the city. When Young arrived, the Chief Rabbis greeted him with enthusiasm. Interaction between the LJS and the Jewish population increased as a result of this initiative. However, when a young rabbi made a public confession of his faith in Jesus, Jews in the country were shocked. The rabbi was compelled to divorce his wife, and he went into exile.

Following the establishment of a consulate, Nicholayson sought to purchase property for the church. In 1838, the LJS commented:

> Mr. Nicholayson had succeeded, after many delays and difficulties in purchasing two adjoining premises... in the name of a respective native of the country – Mr Nicolayson not having then obtained permission to purchase in his own name. The premises thus purchased, are situated on Mount Zion, exactly opposite the castle of David, near the gate of Jaffa, and on the very confines of the Jewish Quarter.[7]

Soon Nicholayson made plans for the creation of a mission house and chapel. The LJS sent out two more Hebrew Christians, Mr Gerstmann and Mr Bergheim, to re-establish medical work. Several Jewish families came to the mission, and three rabbis were instructed by Mr Pieritz, one of the Hebrew Christians on the staff. In 1839 the baptism of the family of Simon Rosenthal caused further consternation within the Jewish population. Regarding this event, Nicholayson wrote:

> I had then the happiness of baptizing this whole family, as the first Israelitish family, that, in all probability has been baptized in this city since the early Christian times – thus grafted in again into their own olive tree, thus laying once more the first living stones of a Hebrew–Christian Church at Jerusalem, on the same apostolic foundation first laid here on the great first day of Pentecost.[8]

When Consul Young arrived in Palestine, he surveyed the Jewish population and observed to Palmerston that there were two parties in the country. The first, he wrote, is the Jew to whom God gave the land as a possession; the other is the Protestant Christian who is his legitimate offspring. Although he regarded Great Britain as their guardian, he stated:

> Still, the Jew in Jerusalem is not estimated in value, much above a dog – and scarcely a day passes that I do not hear of some act of tyranny and oppression against a Jew – chiefly by the soldiers, who enter their houses and borrow whatever they require without asking any permission – sometimes they return the article, but more frequently not. In two instances I have succeeded in obtaining justice for Jews against Turks – But it is quite a new thing in the eyes of these people to claim justice for a Jew – and have good reason to think that my endeavours to protect the Jews, have been – and may be for some little time to come, detrimental to my influence with other classes – Christians as well as Turks – If a Jew... were to attempt to pass the door of the Church of the Holy Sepulchre, it would in all probability cost him his life...[9]

As Young expected, his interventions were resented by the local authorities as well as the Muslim community. Nonetheless, he continued with his activities. By the end of 1839 it appeared that the construction of the church could begin, and on 17 December Nicolayson laid the foundations for a temporary chapel and mission house. Building commenced later in February. By the end of June Nicholayson wrote that the German carpenters had arrived. Mr Hillier, a professional surveyor/architect as well as a Messianic Jewish assistant were employed to construct the church, but Hillier died of fever after completing a survey. Despite this setback, by July 1840 the structure began to take shape.

This project was interrupted by the Damascus Affair: in March 1840 a French Capuchin monk Padre Tomaso disappeared in Damascus after visiting a Jewish area; later the Jews were accused of murdering him and using his blood for a Passover meal. The French Consul had extracted a false confession from a Jew about the murder, and the Jews of Damascus suffered a serious pogrom. Fearing further assault, the rabbis of Jerusalem called upon Nicolayson and Pieritz, one of the Hebrew Christians on the LJS staff, for help. On 18 March Pieritz set off for Damascus to defend the Jewish community. Commenting on this crisis, Nicolayson observed that this was the first time that the Jewish population in Palestine had prayed for the success of a converted Jew and a missionary.

In support of the Damascus Jews, Nicolayson sent a letter with Pieritz in which he expressed his outrage at the blood libel accusation. Similarly in England over fifty Hebrew Christians signed a statement in which they repudiated the charge:

We, the undersigned, members of the Jewish nation, having lived till manhood in the belief and customs of modern Judaism, but having now, through the grace of God, become members of the Christian Church, do hereby solemnly protest that we have never, directly or indirectly, heard of, much less known, the practice of killing Christians, or using Christian blood, and that we believe this charge, so often brought against them formerly, and now lately revived, to be a foul and Satanic falsehood.[10]

As the representative of British Jewry, Sir Moses Montefiore travelled to Constantinople in support of his coreligionists to meet with the Sultan. On 21 April 1841 Palmerston sent a dispatch to a British consular representative in the Ottoman Empire, encouraging him to look out for further acts of injustice against Jews living in the Ottoman Empire.

The Origins of Jewish Religious Zionism

Pre-eminent among such figures was Yehuda hai Alkalai, born in 1798 in Sarajevo to Rabbi Sholomo Alkalai, the spiritual leader of the local Jewish community. During his youth he lived in Palestine, where he was influenced by kabbalistic thought. In 1825 he served as a rabbi in Semln in Serbia; in 1834 he published a booklet entitled *Shema Yisrael* in which he advocated the establishment of Jewish colonies in Palestine, a view at variance with the traditional Jewish belief that the Messiah would come through an act of divine deliverance. When in 1840 the Jews of Damascus were charged with blood libel, he became convinced that the Jewish people could be secure only in their own land. Henceforth, he published a series of books and pamphlets explaining his plan of self-redemption.

In his *Minhat Yehuda* he argued on the basis of Scripture that the Messiah will not miraculously materialize; rather, he will be preceded by various preparatory events. In this light the Holy Land needs to be populated by Jewry in preparation for messianic deliverance. 'This new redemption will', he wrote,

be different; our land is waste and desolate, and we shall have to build houses, dig wells, and plant vines and olive trees. We are, therefore, commanded not to attempt to go at once and all together in the Holy Land... the Lord desires that we be redeemed in dignity; we cannot, therefore, migrate in a mass, for we should then have to live like Bedouins, scattered in tents all over the fields of the Holy Land. Redemption must come slowly. The land must, by degrees, be built up and prepared.[11]

For Alkalai, redemption is not simply a divine affair – it is also a human concern requiring labour and persistence.

This demystification of traditional messianic eschatology extended to Alkalai's advocacy of Hebrew as a language of communication. Traditionally, Hebrew was viewed as a sacred language; it was not to be profaned by daily use. Alkalai, however, recognized the practical importance of having a single language for ordinary life in Palestine. He wrote:

> I wish to attest to the pain I have always felt at the error of our ancestors, that they allowed our Holy Tongue to be so forgotten. Because of this our people was divided into seventy peoples; our one language was replaced by the seventy languages of the lands of exile. If the Almighty should indeed show us his miraculous favour and gather us into our land, we would not be able to speak to each other and such a divided community could not succeed.[12]

It would be a mistake, he continued, to think that God will send an angel to teach his people all seventy languages. Instead the Jewish people must ensure that Hebrew is studied so that it can be used in ordinary life: 'We must redouble our efforts to maintain Hebrew and to strengthen its position. It must be the basis of our educational work.'[13]

How can this process of redemption be accomplished? Alkalai stressed the importance of convening an assembly of those dedicated to the realization of this goal. Thus he asserted that the redemption must begin with efforts by Jews themselves. They must 'organize and unite, choose leaders, and leave the lands of exile. Since no community can exist without a governing body, the very first new ordinance must be the appointment of the elders of each district, men of piety and wisdom, to oversee all the affairs of the community.'[14]

Reinterpreting the concept of the Messiah ben Joseph, he argued that this assembly of elders is in fact what is meant by the promise of the Messiah, the son of Joseph. For Alkalai, the process of deliverance follows a different sequence from what is depicted in traditional sources. The organization of an international Jewish body is, he believed, the first step to the redemption because out of this organization will emerge a fully authorized assembly of elders, and from the elders, the Messiah, son of Joseph, will appear. The vision of this first messianic figure should thus be understood as a process involving the emergence of a political leadership among the Jewish nation that would prepare the way for divine deliverance. According to Alkalai, it is not impossible for Jews to carry out this project. The sultan, he maintained, would not object to such an aim since he knew that his Jewish subjects were loyal.

Another early pioneer of Jewish religious Zionism was Zwi Hirsch Kalischer, the rabbi of Thorn in the province of Posen. In 1836 he expressed his commitment to Jewish settlement in Palestine in a letter to the head of the Berlin branch of the Rothschild family: 'The beginning of the redemption will come through natural causes, by human effort and by the will of the governments to gather the scattered of Israel into the Holy Land.[15]

Such a conviction did not actively engage Kalischer until 1860, when a society was organized in Frankfurt on the Oder to encourage Jewish settlement in Palestine. After joining this group, he published a Zionist work, *Derishat Zion*, which appeared in 1862. In this treatise he advocated the return of Jews to their native soil. The redemption of Israel, he argued will not take place miraculously. 'The Almighty, blessed be his Name, will not suddenly descend from on high and command his people to go forth. Neither will he send the Messiah from heaven in a twinkling of an eye, to sound the great trumpet for the scattered of Israel and gather them into Jerusalem. He will not surround the holy city with a wall of fire or cause the holy Temple to descend from heaven.'[16] Instead the redemption of Israel will take place slowly, through awakening support from philanthropists and gaining the consent of other nations to the gathering of the Jewish people into the Holy Land.

This view, Kalischer maintained, is inherent in Scripture. Thus the prophet Isaiah declared:

> In days to come Jacob shall take root, Israel shall blossom and put forth shoots, and fill the whole world with fruit... In that day from the river Euphrates to the Brook of Egypt the Lord will thresh out the grain, and you will be gathered one by one, O people of Israel. And in that day a great trumpet will be blown and those who were lost in the land of Assyria and those who were driven out to the land of Egypt will come and worship the Lord on the holy mountain at Jerusalem. (Isaiah 27:6, 12–13)

According to Kalischer, this passage implies that not all of Israel will return from exile at once, but instead they will be gathered by degrees.

The coming of the Messiah must, he believed, be preceded by the creation of a Jewish homeland. It is not enough to wait for miracles; instead Jews must act to bring about this event. Kalischer was aware that there were many Jews who would refuse to support those who are poor in the Holy Land. Such an attitude, he stated, was an argument put forward by Satan since the people of Palestine have risked their lives to become pioneers. 'In this country,' he wrote, 'which is strange to them, how could they go about finding a business or occupation, when they had never in their lives done anything of this kind? Their eyes can only turn to their philanthropic brethren, of whom they ask only enough to keep body and soul together, so that they can dwell in that Land which is God's portion on earth.[17]

For Kalischer, practical steps must be taken to fulfil this dream of resettlement. What is required is that an organization be created to encourage emigration, and to purchase and cultivate farms and vineyards. Such a programme would be a ray of deliverance to those who are now languishing in Palestine due to poverty and famine; this situation would be utterly changed if those able to contribute to this effort were inspired by the vision of a Jewish homeland. An advantage of this scheme would be to bring to fruition those religious commandments that attach to working the soil of the Holy Land. Even those Jews who supervised the labourers would be aiding in the working of the land and would therefore have the same status as if they had personally fulfilled these commandments. But beyond this, Kalischer was convinced that Jewish farming would be a spur to messianic redemption. The policy of active participation in the cultivation of the soil would not divert the people from the task of divine service; rather such labour would add dignity to God's Torah. By working the land, Jews would be dedicating themselves to bringing about the advent of the messianic age.

4

Christian Zionists and Jewish Secular Zionism

When Turkey regained control of the Holy Land, Lord Ashley sought to bring about the realization of biblical prophecy. Through the intervention of Lord Palmerston, plans were formulated for the return of the Jewish nation to its ancient homeland. Simultaneously a bishopric was established in Jerusalem: under the leadership of Michael Solomon Alexander, a Jewish convert to Christianity, a small group of Hebrew Christians worshipped together in the holy city.

Alongside Christian aspirations for the return of the Jewish people to their homeland and their conversion, other writers expressed their interest in the eventual reestablishment of a Jewish commonwealth in the Holy Land. From the Jewish side, secular Zionists in the middle of the nineteenth century advocated a return of the Jewish nation on secular grounds. In their view the belief in the Messiah was a pious hope with no foundation. Instead of waiting for messianic redemption to take place, they encouraged fellow Jews to return to the Promised Land to solve the problem of Jew-hatred.

War and Jewish Mission

When Britain, Russia, Prussia and Austria met in London in July 1840, they made an alliance with Turkey for peace in the region. The terms demanded the withdrawal of Egypt from Turkey. When this proposal was rejected, Britain was in effect at war with Egypt, and the British consul in Jerusalem was compelled to leave although Nico-layson remained in his post. At the same time Syria revolted against its Egyptian rulers and war broke out throughout the region. In September a British fleet captured Beirut and then proceeded southward, capturing Sidon and Acre. The Egyptian ruler then fled the country.

These events encouraged Lord Ashley to seek the return of the Jewish people to their ancient homeland and he appealed to Lord Palmerston, the Secretary of State for Foreign Affairs. In his diary on 24 July 1840 he wrote:

> Anxious about the hopes and prospects of the Jewish people. Everything seems ripe for their return to Palestine: 'The way of the kings of the East is prepared.' Could the five Powers of the West be induced to guarantee the security of life and possessions to the Hebrew race, they would now flow back in rapidly augmenting numbers. Then by the blessing of God I will prepare a document, fortify it by all the evidence I can accumulate, and, confiding to the wisdom and mercy of the Almighty, lay it before the Secretary of State for Foreign Affairs...
>
> August 1 – Dined with Palmerston. After dinner left alone with him. Propounded my scheme, which seemed to strike his fancy; he asked some questions, and readily promised to consider it... Palmerston has already been chosen by God to be an instrument of good to His ancient people; to do homage, as it were, to their inheritance, and to recognise their rights without believing their destiny...
>
> August 24 – Palmerston tells me that he has already written to Lord Ponsonby, to direct him to open an intercourse with Rothschild Pasha at Constantinople respecting protection and encouragement to the Jews...
>
> Sept. 25 – Yesterday began my paper for Palmerston containing, in full, the propositions for the recall of the Jews to their ancient land.[1]

On 11 August 1840 Palmerston wrote a dispatch to Ambassador Ponsonby expressing his support for such a plan on economic, rather than religious, grounds:

> There exists at present among the Jews dispersed over Europe a strong notion that the time is approaching when their nation is to return to Palestine; and consequently their wish to go thither has become more keen, and their thoughts have been bent more intently than before upon the means of realizing that wish. It is well known that the Jews of Europe possess great wealth... It would be of manifest importance to the Sultan to encourage the Jews to return to, and to settle in, Palestine; because the wealth which they would bring with them would increase the resources of the Sultan's dominions; and the Jewish people, if returning under the sanction and protection and at the invitation of the Sultan, would be a check upon any future evil designs of Mehemet Ali or his successor.[2]

The outbreak of war caused the LJS to review its plans for Jerusalem. In early 1841 Nicolayson went to England to meet with the LJS committee which resolved to send more staff to the Holy Land and expand its activities. In addition once the Turks returned to power in Palestine, steps were taken with the support of the King of Prussia to establish a Protestant bishopric in Jerusalem. On 11 November 1841, Michael Solomon Alexander was consecrated at Lambeth Palace as the first Protestant Bishop in Jerusalem. Overjoyed at this event, the LJS recorded its enthusiasm:

> The first time after the lapse of many, many centuries, an apostle to the circumcision, himself a Hebrew of the Hebrews, destined for the land of Israel, and appointed to the Holy City, received his commission... What the friends of Israel longed, and prayed, and laboured for, was not simply the conversion of a few individuals, but the resuscitation of the Jewish people, the resurrection of the Jewish Church.[3]

In January 1842 Alexander arrived in Jerusalem and began his ministry. From the beginning he set about consolidating the Church. In February 1842 he held his first ordination; the candidate was John Muhleisen of the CMS. Subsequently he welcomed a family of Hebrew Christians to Jerusalem; in October he held his first confirmation: all with one exception were of Jewish origin. Within the first year he officiated at a wedding between two Hebrew Christians. This was followed by the ordination into the deacon's orders of E.M. Tarkover. Commenting on these changes, he noted:

> It is deeply interesting to observe that, by the day's solemnities the nucleus of a Hebrew Christian Church in this city is now complete in all its offices, as well as functions... May it grow into a great tree of life, under whose branches the dispersed of Israel shall find shelter, and whose fruits shall be for the healing of the nations.[4]

By the end of the year the Jewish–Protestant Church numbered 15 Hebrew Christians. Not surprisingly, Jews in the area were alarmed by this development. A deputation of Jews from Tiberias enquired whether the report they had heard was true, namely that fourteen rabbis of Jerusalem had embraced Christianity. In Jerusalem the local Jewish community avoided coming into contact with these missionaries. Eventually three rabbis confessed belief in Jesus and two were baptized at a special Hebrew morning service. Counsel Young recognized the hardships faced by the Hebrew Jewish community in the light of these developments:

> When a Jew in Jerusalem embraces the Christian faith many impor-
> tant considerations are involved. If the party is married a divorce is
> arranged, until the wife becomes a convert also... The children are also
> claimed by the Jews until they arrive at years of discretion. Their family
> and friends mourn for the convert as though he were dead, and the
> widow and children become dependent on the congregation.[5]

In these early years the LJS established other institutions to care for
the Hebrew–Christian community including a School for Industry
opened by Alexander in 1843; the Hebrew College for the training
of Hebrew Christian missionaries was opened by the Bishop in the
same year; a Bible Depository was opened by Alexander in 1844, and
was initially staffed by Rabbi Judah Lyons; and the LJS committee
also directed the opening of schools for Jewish children. In 1865,
Alexander died on a trip to Cairo; his remains were brought back
to Jerusalem, where they were buried.

As we noted, in the quest to bring Jewish believers to Christ,
England had played a pivotal role. Earlier in the century, a group of
41 Jewish believers established the Beni Abraham association at
Jews' Chapel. These Jewish Christians met for prayer every Sunday
morning and Friday evening. In addition, they daily visited any sick
member to pray and read the Bible to him. In 1835 the group became
known as the Episcopal Jews' Chapel Abrahamic Society; its aim was
to visit Jewish converts and inquirers. The Hebrew Christian Prayer
Union, founded in 1882 by Dr H.A. Stern, also sought to unite Jewish
Christians in spiritual fellowship. Every Sunday, prayer was offered
privately by each member and there were general worship meetings
as well. From 1883 to 1890 its membership increased from 143 to 600.
In addition, other branches were established in Germany, Norway,
Romania, Russia, Palestine and the United States.

In 1865 an attempt was made by Dr C. Schwartz, minister of
Trinity Chapel, Edgware Road, London, to unite all Jewish Christians
with the creation of the Hebrew–Christian Alliance. At its first conference held in May 1865 eighty Jewish Christians met together,
convinced that this was the first gathering of converted Jews to be
held since the days of the early Church. The next year a public
meeting was held at King Street, St James. At this gathering it was
resolved that although the members of the Alliance belonged to different churches, they were united in Christ. As such, they declared
before the Jewish community that they had found in Jesus the
Messiah to whom the Law and the prophets bear testimony. It was in
his blood, they stated, that they had found peace, and looked for his
coming in glory as the hope of Israel.

Further Plans for Jewish Settlement

In the United States, Manuel Noah, an American Jew, composed a tract dealing with the state of the Jewish nation and later formulated a plan for a city of refuge on Grand Island in the Niagara River, New York. This city was to be named Ararat, and he consulted three ex-Presidents of the United States. In 1825 President Adams wrote a letter of support to Noah:

> I really wish the Jews again in Judea, an independent nation, for, as I believe, the most enlightened men of it have participated in the amelioration of the philosophy of the age; once restored to an independent government and no longer persecuted, they would soon wear away some of the... peculiarities of their character.[6]

Following the Damascus Affair, a German Lutheran Dr C.F. Zimpel published a work, *Israelites in Jerusalem*. He had visited Jerusalem where he was impressed by the Jewish community; he argued that it was necessary to bring about the return of the Jews to the place that belonged to them, Palestine. The Jews, he wrote, should be summoned to become once again a farming people. It was God's purpose, he believed, that they should not be shackled to the various countries through the possession of land but should always remain the inhabitants of their ancient homeland which God had promised them.

Zimpel settled in America, where he promoted his plan to establish Jewish farming villages in Palestine. In 1865 he went to Palestine, and after his return appealed to Christians as well as Jews to liberate the country from Turkish rule. Later he advocated the construction of a network of highways connecting the Mediterranean Sea to the Dead Sea by way of Jerusalem, including Bethlehem, Hebron, Tiberias and Nazareth. In his view, such a route would stimulate trade and commerce. The return of the Jewish nation to its ancestral home, Zimpel believed, would be a realization of biblical prophecy, and at the same time would solve the problem of Jewish persecution.

In Britain, practical steps were undertaken to restore the Jews to Palestine. In 1844 the Revd Samuel A. Bradshaw wrote *Tract for the Times, Being a Plea for the Jews*, proposing that Parliament should allocate four million pounds for the restoration of Israel, with another million to be collected from the Church. The same year a committee was established in London to create a British and Foreign Society for Promoting the Restoration of the Jewish Nation to Palestine. In his opening address, T. Tully Crybbace urged England to secure from Turkey the entire territory of Palestine from the Euphrates to the Nile, and from the Mediterranean to the desert.

Another plan was advocated by Colonel George Gawler who believed that the Jewish people should advance their claim to Palestine. This portion, he stated, belongs to the God of Israel and to his national people.

During this period Laurence Oliphant, an officer in the British Foreign service, held various Foreign Office posts, worked as a reporter, and was a member of Parliament. Subsequently he went to a New England religious community to live the life of a humble Christian. Later during the Russo-Turkish war he became increasingly interested in the Holy Land. Supported by letters of recommendation from Lord Beaconsfield and Lord Salisbury, he went to Palestine in 1879 by way of Romania, where he witnessed a series of pogroms. After surveying Palestine, he sought to persuade the Sultan in Constantinople to grant lands to the Jewish nation under a charter for settlement. On the basis of his travels, he maintained that Jews should be settled first in the area east of Jordan and in biblical Gilead. Further, he recommended that a tract of one million and a half acres be granted, which was to be connected by a new railroad to a port to be built at Haifa and later one at Akaba and the Suez Canal. Although this scheme was nearly accepted by the Turkish Cabinet, Sultan Abdul Hamid rejected it, assuming it was a British ploy.

In his book, *Land of Gilead*, he explained his plan in detail:

> The restoration of the Jews to Palestine has been so often urged upon sentimental or Scriptural grounds that now, when it may possibly become the practical and common-sense solution of a great future difficulty, a prejudice against it exists in the minds of those who have always regarded it as a theological chimera, which it is not easy to remove. The mere accident of a measure involving most important international consequences, having been advocated by a large section of the Christian community, from a purely biblical point of view, does not necessarily impair its political value. On the contrary, its political value once estimated on its own merits and admitted, the fact that it will carry with it the sympathy and support of those who are not usually particularly well-versed in foreign politics is decidedly in its favour.[7]

Undeterred by the presence of Bedouins in the land and lacking concern for their situation, he commented: 'They have very little claim to our sympathy, having laid waste to the country, ruined its villages and plundered its inhabitants until it has been reduced to its present condition.[8] Not only did he foresee the creation of agricultural settlements, he envisioned the regeneration of the Dead Sea. In

1881, when the Jewish community faced increased persecution in Russia, Oliphant formed a group of Christians in London to help advance his plan to build Jewish villages in Gilead. In addition, he advised Jewish organizations who sought to save Jews from Russian persecution. Later Oliphant remained in Haifa and engaged in religious activities. Like other Christian Zionists as well as Jewish settlers in the Holy Land, his overriding preoccupation was with the restoration of the Jewish people in their ancient homeland.

In the United States William E. Blackstone, a Christian evangelist missionary, published *Jesus is Coming* in 1878. A devout biblical scholar, his views were grounded in millenarianism. In his work, which was translated into various languages, he envisaged the Jewish restoration to Palestine as the fulfilment of biblical prophecies related to the Second Advent. Commenting on Israel's survival through the centuries, he wrote:

> And their wonderful preservation, as a distinct people, through all the persecutions, vicissitudes and wanderings of the past eighteen centuries down to the present moment, is a standing miracle, attesting the truth of God's word, and assuring us of his purposes in their future history.

> Said Frederick the Great to his chaplain: 'Doctor, if your religion is a true one, it ought to be capable of very brief and simple proof. Will you give me an evidence of its truth in ONE WORD?' The good man answered, 'Israel.'

> Other nations come and go, but Israel remains. She passes not away. God says of her: 'For a small moment have I forsaken thee; but with great mercies will I gather thee. In a little wrath I hid my face from thee for a moment; but with everlasting kindness will I have mercy on thee, saith the Lord, thy redeemer. (Isa. 54:7–8)[9]

In March 1891 Blackstone presented a petition – 'Palestine for the Jews' – containing the names of over four hundred prominent Christian and Jewish figures to President Harrison. The petition advanced this solution:

> Why not give Palestine back to them [the Jews] again? According to God's distribution of nations it is their home, an inalienable possession from which they were expelled by force. Under their cultivation it was a remarkably fruitful land, sustaining millions of Israelites, who industriously tilled its hillsides and valleys. They were agriculturalists and producers as well as a nation of great commercial importance – the centre of civilization and religion.[10]

Later he continued to promote this scheme, eventually encouraging President Wilson to support the creation of a Jewish homeland for the Jewish nation.

Early Secular Zionism

In Arab lands Jews had flourished for centuries. Yet, in European countries, Jewry had been subject to oppression and persecution. Modern Secular Zionism – fuelled by the emergence of European nationalism during the nineteenth century – arose in response to such suffering. In the middle of the nineteenth century, Jewish writers such as Moses Hess argued that Jews must establish a state of their own if they were to escape from anti-Semitism. Born in Germany, Hess published his first philosophical work, *The Holy History of Mankind, by a Young Spinozist* in 1837. By 1840 he had settled in Paris, where he was active in social circles; in 1842–3 he served as the Paris correspondent of the *Rheinische Zeitung*, edited by Karl Marx. In 1862 he published *Rome and Jerusalem*, a systematic defence of Jewish nationalism. In this work, he explained that, after twenty years of estrangement from Judaism, he had returned to his people.

Anti-Jewish sentiment, he explained, is unavoidable. Progressive Jews think they can escape from Judaeophobia by recoiling from any Jewish national expression, yet the hatred of Jews is inescapable. No reform of the religion is radical enough to avoid such sentiments, and even conversion to Christianity cannot relieve the Jew of this disability. 'Jewish noses', he wrote, 'cannot be reformed, and the black, wavy hair of the Jews will not be changed into blond by conversion or straightened out by constant combing.'[11] For Hess, Jews will always remain strangers among the nations: nothing can alter this state of affairs. The only solution to the problem of Jew-hatred is for the Jewish community to come to terms with their national identity.

According to Hess, the restoration of Jewish nationalism will not deprive the world of the benefits promoted by Jewish reformers who wish to dissociate themselves from the particularistic dimensions of the Jewish heritage. On the contrary the values of universalism would be championed by various aspects of Judaism's national character. Judaism, he contended, is the root of the modern universalist view of life.

What is required today, Hess asserted, is for Jewry to regenerate the Jewish nation and to keep alive the hope for the political rebirth of the Jewish people. According to Hess, a Jewish renaissance is possible once national life reasserts itself in the Holy Land. In the past the creative energies of the people deserted Israel when Jews became ashamed of their nationality. But the Holy Spirit, he wrote, will again animate Jewry once the nation awakens to a new life. The only question remaining is how it might be possible to stimulate the patriotic sentiments of modern Jewry as well as liberate the Jewish masses by means of this revived national loyalty. This is a formidable challenge, yet Hess contended that it must be overcome. Although he recognized that there could not be a total emigration of world Jewry to Palestine, the existence of a Jewish state would act as a spiritual centre for the Jewish people and for all humanity.

The Russian pogroms of 1881 had a profound impact on another early Jewish Zionist, Leo Pinsker, driving him from an espousal of the ideas of the Enlightenment to the determination to create a Jewish homeland. Born in Tomaszow in Russian Poland in 1821, Pinsker attended a Russian high school, studied law in Odessa, and later received a medical degree from the University of Moscow. Upon returning to Odessa, he was appointed to the staff of the local city hospital. After 1860, Pinsker contributed to Jewish weeklies in the Russian language and was active in the Society for the Spread of Culture among the Jews of Russia. However, when Jews were massacred in the pogroms of 1881, he left the Society, convinced that a more radical remedy was required to solve the plight of Russian Jewry. In 1882 he published *Autoemancipation*, a tract containing similar themes to those found in Hess's writings. He subsequently became the leader of the new Hibbat Zion movement, and in 1884 convened its founding conference.

In *Autoemancipation*, Pinsker asserted that the Jewish problem is as unresolved in the modern world as it was in former times. In essence, this dilemma concerns the unassimilable character of Jewish identity in countries where Jews are in the minority. In such cases there is no basis for mutual respect between Jews and non-Jews. 'The Jewish people', he wrote, 'has no fatherland of its own, though many motherlands; it has no rallying point, no centre of gravity, no government of its own, no accredited representatives. It is everywhere a guest and nowhere at home.'[12]

Among the nations of the world, Pinsker asserted, the Jews are like a nation long since dead: the dead walking among the living. Such a ghostly existence is unique in history.

The fear of the Jewish ghost has been a typical reaction throughout the centuries, and has paved the way for the current Judaeophobia. This prejudice has through the years become rooted and naturalized among the peoples of the world. Such Jew-hatred has generated various charges against the Jewish people: throughout history Jews have been accused of crucifying Jesus, drinking the blood of

Christians, poisoning wells, exacting usury and exploiting peasants. Such accusations are invariably groundless – they were trumped up to quiet the conscience of Jew-baiters.

Unlike other peoples, the Jew is inevitably a stranger. Having no home, he can never be anything other than an alien. He is not simply a guest in a foreign country; rather he is more like a beggar and a refugee. The Jews are aliens, Pinsker stated, who can have no representatives because they have no fatherland. Since they have none, because their home has no boundaries behind which they can entrench themselves, their misery also has no bounds. It is a mistake, he continued, to think that the legal emancipation of Jewry will result in social emancipation. This, he contended, is impossible. The isolation of the Jew cannot be removed by any form of official emancipation since the Jew is eternally an alien.

Such natural antagonism between Jew and non-Jew has resulted in a variety of reproaches levelled by both parties at one another. From the Jewish side, appeals to justice are frequently made to improve the condition of the Jewish community. In response, non-Jews attempt to justify their negative attitudes by groundless accusations. A more realistic approach, however, would involve the recognition that the Jewish people have no choice but to reconstitute themselves as a separate people.

The Jewish struggle to attain this goal has an inherent justification that belongs to the quest of every oppressed people. Although this endeavour may be opposed by various quarters, the battle must continue – the Jewish people have no other way out of their desperate position. There is a moral duty to ensure that persecuted Jews wherever they live will have a secure home. In this respect, it is a danger, Pinsker stated, for Jews to attach themselves only to the 'Holy Land'. What is required is simply a secure land for the Jewish nation.

For Pinsker the present moment was a decisive time for the revival of national aspirations. History appears to be on the side of world Jewry in its longing for a national homeland. Even in the absence of a leader like Moses, the recognition of what Jewish people need most should arouse a number of energetic individuals to take on positions of responsibility. Already, he noted, there are societies that are pressing for the creation of a Jewish nation. They must then invoke a national congress and establish a national directorate to bring to fruition these plans: 'Our greatest and best forces – men of finance, of science, and of affairs, statesmen and publicists – must join hands with one accord in steering toward the common destination.'[13]

In conclusion, Pinsker contended that the Jews are despised because they are not a living nation. It is an error to believe that civil and political emancipation will raise Jewry in the estimation of other lands. Instead the only proper remedy for the Jewish problem is the creation of a Jewish nationality, of a people living on its own soil. Jews must reassert their national self-respect, and cease to wander from one exile to another. At present there are forces helping to bring about this vision, and the international Jewish community must work towards this end. No sacrifice, he stated, will be too great to reach the goal which will assure that the Jewish nation's future is secure.

5

Protestants, Travellers
and Settlers

Owing to the co-operation that existed between Britain and Prussia concerning Protestantism in the Holy Land, the King of Prussia was given the responsibility of nominating a new Bishop on the death of Bishop Alexander. His nominee, Samuel Gobat, was a Swiss-born German-speaking Anglican minister working with the Church Missionary Society. Unlike Alexander, he was not Jewish, nor had he worked among Jewish people. As a result, the nomination was opposed by a number of LJS supporters. Despite such resistance, Gobat was eventually welcomed by the LJS and the Archbishop of Canterbury and was consecrated at Lambeth Palace as Bishop of the Church of England and Ireland in Jerusalem. During this period, Christian travellers were filled with hope for the revitalization of the Holy Land. Profoundly influenced by their reading of Scripture, they believed that through intensive labour Jewish settlers could reclaim the land and transform the country into a land flowing with milk and honey. Previously, only a small Jewish population resided in the Holy Land, however, with the emergence of the Zionist movement an influx of immigrants substantially increased the size of the Jewish community in Palestine.

Protestant Christianity in Jerusalem

During this period, the LJS was actively engaged in missionary activity in Jerusalem under the leadership of Nicholayson. The Society had fifteen full-time workers in the Holy Land, of whom nine were Hebrew Christians. In 1846 eight Jews were baptized, including the wife of one of the three rabbis who had confessed the faith in 1842. Not surprisingly, the Jewish inhabitants of Jerusalem were alarmed by such apostasy. In the same year Consul James Finn and his wife arrived in Jerusalem. Consul Finn was anxious to assist in promoting Christianity amongst the Jews, and his wife was equally keen to engage in missionary endeavours.

With the arrival of Bishop Gobat, missionary activity was understood more broadly. Initially Gobat sought to establish schools for Jewish children; he later desired to draw Gentiles to Christ as well. In 1847 he appointed a young Melkite as a scripture reader among the Greek Christians and opened a school for both Jews and others. In time Gobat gathered a small group of Arab Christians whom he employed as scripture readers among the Arab Christian population.

At this time Finn was involved in an attempt to rescue Russian Jews from persecution; he proposed that Russian Jews, who had lost their nationality, should be transferred to British protection. This proposal encouraged Russian officials to believe that the whole of the Jewish population in Russia would emigrate to Palestine, and steps were taken to facilitate this process. The Finns were also involved in other initiatives concerning the Jewish population. In 1849 they founded the first Jewish farm run using modern methods; they also established the Jerusalem Literary Society. This small society was a forerunner of the Palestine Exploration Fund which sponsored mapping and topographical research.

In 1849 Sir Moses Montefiore made another trip to Jerusalem and took steps to improve Jewish living conditions to protect them from the LJS. However, this initiative did not deter the consecration of Christ Church, Jerusalem, which took place on 21 January 1849. The next year the Ottoman government recognized Protestantism as a religious community. With the legalization of Protestantism, the building of a Protestant Church, and the establishment of a Protestant bishopric, missionary activity increased.

By 1852 there were over 80 adults and 40 children who attended the Church, of whom 37 adults and 25 children were Jewish in origin. The following year Nicolayson introduced an Arabic service for Arabic-speaking Jews as well as the Arab Protestants who attached themselves to Christ Church. By 1856 there were Hebrew, English, German, Arabic and Spanish services. With Nicolayson's death in 1856, the Revd Henry Crawford became Head of Mission. By 1862 there were over 50 adult Jewish believers and 50 Jewish children who attended the Church.

After 1850 the major British concern in Palestine was the Church Missionary Society (CMS). In May 1851 a CMS missionary conference was held in Jerusalem under Bishop Gobat's direction; it was decided to begin active missionary work, primarily among Eastern Christians. The same year a CMS mission was opened, and Gobat and

CMS worked together, building schools throughout the region. In reaction to these initiatives, the Rothschild family sent Dr Albert Cohen to assist the Jewish community by developing Jewish institutions in Palestine. Responding to this Jewish scheme, the LJS wrote:

> In reference to Mr Cohen's visit, it is a fact well worth stating, that the methods taken by him on that occasion to relieve the Jews, and render them as far as possible independent of your Society's benevolent efforts, were almost wholly confined to the setting on foot [of] institutions similar to those already established by your missionaries.[1]

In 1854 Cohen also established the Mayer Rothschild Hospital in Jerusalem; when the LJS founded the Bikhur Holim hospital three years later, local rabbis placed guards near the hospital to report any Jews who entered the mission premises. As more Jews came to Jerusalem and settled outside the walls of the Old City, Finn proposed to help these settlers. 'The commonest impulse of humanity', he stated:

> would have led us to try some means of succouring a people so lamentably devoid of resources among themselves... the best idea that suggested itself was that of providing employment, however light, in field work, both as a means of earning daily food for the family, and also for the advantage of health, in preparation for future usefulness; above all for promoting a character of independence among the sufferers. At first the experiment was tried of employing some fifty men in very simple work on my own ground, called the Talibiyeh, one mile distant from the city gate. Others were also sent to work in the valley of Urtus, beyond Bethlehem, to Mr Meshullam who engaged four. The members who came to us for work increased, and at length... a plot of ground was bought by us for the purpose of such employment and called the Industrial Plantation.[2]

In 1852 the Finns purchased a property on which they employed Jews to clear the land and build workhouses. Within a month of the purchase, there were about a hundred Jewish workers there. Their intention was to illustrate through such an endeavour how Jewish restoration was possible in Palestine. Writing to Lord Clarendon in the Foreign Office in 1857, Finn explained:

> The country is in a considerable degree empty of inhabitants and therefore its greatest need is that of a body of population... Such a people may be found in the Jews: for their affections are centred here and they own no willing subjection to any European crown... I have now the honour to propose for consideration – viz – to persuade Jews

in a large body to settle here as agriculturalists on the soil by a special proclamation from H.M. the Sultan, offering particular advantages to that effect.[3]

To further such plans the Finns founded the Society for the Promotion of Jewish Agricultural Labour in the Holy Land. When they employed a number of Hebrew Christians on their farms the rabbinate was incensed, as was Sir Moses Montefiore. In 1855 Sir Moses arrived in Jerusalem bringing a document from the Sultan authorizing the rebuilding of the Hurva synagogue as well as two letters from the Grand Vizier permitting the Jews of Jerusalem to engage in agricultural pursuits and build a Jewish hospital. Such activity was supported by Finn, who submitted a petition on behalf of Jerusalem's Ashkenazi Jews to the British Ambassador in 1854, requesting permission for them to build a synagogue. Lord Shaftesbury similarly urged the British government to encourage Turkey to allow Jews permission to purchase land.

The existence of the LJS, Christ Church in Jerusalem, and the British consulate and the Protestant bishopric provided a basis for British Christian life in the Holy Land. These institutions served as a framework for all British as well as Protestant activities. Alongside these institutions the publications of the LJS provided information about life in Palestine. With the changed political climate in the Middle East, the Holy Land increasingly came under British control. In 1875 Benjamin Disraeli, the Prime Minister, bought controlling interests in the Suez Canal. Two years later a Russo/Turkish conflict erupted over the Balkans, and Britain gained control of Cyprus from Turkey. This gave rise to expectations that Britain would seek to rebuild the Holy Land.

Travellers and Palestine

During the second half of the nineteenth century, a number of Christian writers and travellers expressed their belief in the feasibility of a Jewish return to the Holy Land. In 1845 the Polish Catholic poet Adam Mickiewicz, for example, delivered a sermon in a Paris synagogue in which he expressed sympathy for Jewish suffering and the deep Jewish yearning for a return to Zion. In 1851 Benedetto Musolino, a Catholic soldier, wrote *Gerusalemme ed il Popolo Ebrea*, in which he analysed the situation of the Jews in the diaspora, and concluded that there should be a Jewish principality in the Holy Land under the Turkish Crown but supported by Britain. The religion of the country, he believed, should be Judaism, and Hebrew should be the language of the land. In Musolino's view, all Jews should be granted the right to become citizens of this principality and allowed to settle there permanently.

Another Catholic supporter of the Jewish return to their ancient homeland was Ernest Laharanne, who belonged to the Secretariat of Napoleon III and composed a treatise about Jewish nationalism, *The New Eastern Question: The Egyptian and Arab Empires: The Reconstitution of the Jewish Nation.* 'We reserved a special place for Palestine,' he wrote, 'in order to bring to the attention of the world the important question, whether ancient Judea can once more acquire its former place in the sun.'[4]

Despite such encouragement, Palestine was desolate and barren, as the American writer, Mark Twain noted in *Innocents Abroad*:

> Of all the lands there are for dismal scenery, I think Palestine must be the prince. The hills are barren, they are dull of colour, they are unpicturesque in shape. The valleys are unsightly deserts fringed with a feeble vegetation that has an expression about it of being sorrowful and despondent. The Dead Sea and the Sea of Galilee sleep in the midst of a vast stretch of hill and plain wherein the eye rests upon no pleasant tint, no striking object, no soft picture dreaming in a purple haze or mottled with the shadows of the clouds. Every outline is harsh, every feature is distinct, there is no perspective – distance works no enchantment here. It is a hopeless, dreary, heartbroken land.[5]

Others, however, viewed the Holy Land more positively. The British Consul in Jerusalem, James Finn, and his wife Elizabeth recorded in their reminiscences that they had seen:

> the four 'holy cities', Jerusalem, Hebron, Tiberias and Safed, and the three places where Abraham had raised his altar and proclaimed the true God to the heathen Canaanites... Shechem, Bethel and Hebron. The word 'called upon' in the Bible describing Abraham's history means 'to proclaim' – he proclaimed the true God to these heathen during his stay among them of one hundred years.[6]

In order to assist the Jewish population, the Finns supported various agricultural projects and experimented with land reclamation including the purchase of a plot of land which they called 'Abraham's Vineyard' near Jerusalem. There they employed a number of Jews and trained them. 'The vineyard was one mile from Jerusalem,' Elizabeth Finn explained, 'and it was something to hear the people returning thence in the evening singing for joy that they had something to do and something to eat.'[7] Building projects were also of central importance, as Mrs Finn noted:

> We wished to teach the Jewish workmen how to build. The Bethlehemites were by this time very good builders, so we sent for one of them and told him that if he would promise to treat the Jews well... we would employ him to teach them how to build. He promised and kept his word, and thus a little house on the vineyard was built, the first cottage outside the walls of Jerusalem... and the first to be built by Jewish hands.[8]

For the Finns this support for Jews was motivated by religious aspirations. It was their hope that the Holy Land would again be peopled by its lawful owners, and would again blossom as the rose. When the Finns' tour of duty in Jerusalem ended, they continued to support the idea of the Jewish return to their ancient homeland. When news of the pogroms in Russia of 1881 reached the Finns in London, Mrs Finn rallied assistance. A special relief committee was formed with Lord Shaftesbury as president. Their first meeting took place in the Jerusalem Chamber in Westminster Abbey and Mrs Finn spoke on behalf of the Jewish nation and entrusted Abraham's Vineyard to the committee.

Sharing similar aspirations, Sir Charles Wilson, a British army officer and topographer, was an early explorer. Between 1864 and 1866 he surveyed Jerusalem and produced a map of the city. Some years later he published a map of the Sinai peninsula. Others commented on the rediscovery of the Holy Land during this period. According to Dean Stanley, Professor of Church History at Oxford:

> Palestine was the scene of the most important events in the history of mankind... Here the Word of God came directly to the Jewish people, and here alone could be studied the surroundings that formed the character of the most remarkable nation which has appeared on earth... Here... the traveller recognizes the wild bloom of the desert as the shrub under which Elijah slept, where he stands on Pisgah and sees the view that Moses saw, where at every hand he finds the local features that have become household imagery of Christendom.[9]

In the light of such interest in Palestine, the Palestine Exploration Fund was established in 1865 and launched by the Finns to sponsor archaeological digs and research on the Bible. After Sir Charles had completed his work, the Palestine Exploration Fund sent out Charles Warren, who surveyed the land and recorded his discoveries in *Land of Promise*. It was his view that the country could be developed with the intention of gradually introducing Jews who could eventually govern the country. It was Wilson's view that the Jewish people were tied to the land as by an umbilical cord, and just as the umbilical cord sustains the foetus, so the Jewish nation's bond to their ancient homeland nourishes them.

Another figure who worked in Palestine was Claude Regnier Conder who arrived in 1872. Together with H.H. Kitchner, he wrote several memoirs and the first three parts of a survey of Western Palestine. Subsequently Conder published a number of books based on his work in Palestine including *The City of Jerusalem*. Conder believed that the country could be revived through the establishment of Jewish agricultural settlements. What was necessary, he emphasized, was the regeneration of the land, swamp drainage, irrigation, the restoration of cisterns and aqueducts, sanitation of populated areas and seeding of grass. In 1892 Conder addressed the London branch of Hovevei Zion, and emphasized the suitability of the Bashan district for agricultural development. According to Conder, a railroad could be constructed through the area east of Jordan which would link Damascus with Haifa. With a railroad, he explained, Jewish villages could flourish and market their products.

When the Palestine Exploration Fund began its work, Palestine was desolate and barren as described earlier by Mark Twain. Yet through the work of Wilson, Warren and Condor a new vision of the Holy Land emerged. In his opening address to the Palestine Exploration Fund, Lord Shaftesbury expressed hope for the future:

> Let us not delay to send out the best agents... to search the length and breadth of Palestine, to survey the land, and if possible to go over every corner of it, drain it, measure it, and, if you will, prepare it for the return of its ancient possessors, for I must believe that the time cannot be far off before the great event will come to pass... I recollect speaking to Lord Aberdeen when he was Prime Minister, on the subject of the Holy Land; and he said to me: 'If the Holy Land should pass out of the hands of the Turks, into whose hands should it fall?' Why, my reply was ready: not into the hands of other powers, but let it return into the hands of the Israelites.[10]

Jews in Palestine

Although Jews had anticipated the return of the Jewish nation to the Promised Land since the destruction of the Temple in 70 CE, only a relatively small number of Jews had lived in the Holy Land. From the seventh century CE, the area had been under Muslim rule almost without interruption; under Ottoman rule since the early sixteenth century, only a limited number of Jews had sought to immigrate. Of 1500 Jews who travelled from Poland, Hungary and Moravia to Palestine in 1700, nearly five hundred died *en route*. Later in 1777 more than three hundred Hasidic families made the journey from Poland to Palestine; in 1812 about four hundred followers of the Vilna Gaon came from Lithuania.

By the middle of the nineteenth century about 10,000 Jews lived in the country, compared with over 500,000 Arabs. Eight thousand Jews resided in Jerusalem; several hundred lived in Safed where several sages were buried, in Peki'in which had a tradition of continuous settlement since Roman times, and in Tiberias on the Sea of Galilee. In the coastal town of Acre there were another 140 Jews and several hundred others lived in Jaffa. Most of these Jews were immigrants from Poland and Lithuania and many of them were supported by Jewish charity. These residents sent letters to their original communities in Europe seeking support and dispatched emissaries to raise funds.

In 1870 a French educator, Charles Netter, with the approval of the Turkish authorities, founded a school for agriculture at Mikveh Israel; located near Jaffa, it served as a settlement to which Jews living in countries where they were subject to various disabilities could come to live and study. In 1878 a number of Jews from Jerusalem established a Jewish village in the countryside. Initially they bought land near Jericho, but the Sultan refused to allow ownership to be transferred to Jews. However, they did manage to purchase land from a Greek landowner in the coastal plain and named their village Petah Tikvah. Yet malaria, poor harvests and disputes among themselves resulted in failure. By 1882 they had abandoned the village.

Also in 1878 religious Jews from Safed who wished to earn their own livelihood founded Rosh Pinah. Owing to their lack of funds and the harassment of local Arabs, they abandoned the project after two years. However, Romanian Jews who had faced persecution and poverty in their own country revived the settlement in 1882, obtaining aid from Baron Edmond de Rothschild. There they grew tobacco and planted mulberry trees for silkworms.

Following the pogroms in Russia in 1881, two movements were founded urging the emigration of Jews to Palestine. The first, Bilu, took its name from the Hebrew initials of the biblical phrase Beth Jacob Lechu Venelcha: 'O House of Jacob, come and let us go.' The second Russian movement was Hibbat Zion ('Love of Zion'). Its first conference took place in 1884 at Kattowitz in Upper Silesia. Its president, Leo Pinsker, encouraged the thirty-six delegates to return to Palestine.

Only a very small number of Russian emigrants went each year to Palestine. Between 1882 and 1903 only 25,000 Jews settled in the country. Known as the First Aliyah, many of them lived by tilling the soil and relied on financial support from the Rothschilds. Many of the Bilu pioneers worked as hired labourers at the Mikveh Israel school. One of these settlers, Vladimir Dubnow, wrote to his brother Simon, describing his motives:

> Do you really think that my sole motivation in coming here is to better myself, with the implication that if all goes well I will have achieved this aim and that if it does not then I ought to be pitied? No. My ultimate aim, like that of many others, is greater, broader, incomprehensible but not unattainable. The final goal is eventually to gain control of Palestine and to restore to the Jewish people the political independence of which it has been deprived for two thousand years.

> Don't laugh; this is no illusion. The means for realizing this goal is at hand; the founding of settlements in the country based on agriculture and crafts, the establishment and gradual expansion of all sorts of factories... in brief – to make an effort so that all the land, all the industry, will be in Jewish hands.

> In addition, it is necessary to instruct young people and the future generation in the use of firearms (in free, wild Turkey anything can be done) and then – here I too am plunging into conjecture – then the glorious day will dawn of which Isaiah prophesied in his burning and poetic utterances. The Jews will proclaim in a loud voice and (if necessary) with arms in their hands that they are masters of their ancient homeland.[11]

In 1882 the town of Zichron Yaakov was established by Jewish immigrants from Romania. The same year Hayyim Amzalak, who had emigrated to Palestine from Gibraltar in 1830, bought the land on which Petah Tikvah had been built and gave it to Bilu pioneers from Russia. Even though the land was plagued by malaria and was under attack from Arab villagers, the pioneers continued their efforts with the support of Baron Edmond de Rothschild. Hayyim Amzalak also helped finance Rishon le-Zion, the first village built by settlers from outside Palestine. When funds were depleted, an emissary from Rishon Le-Zion went to Paris to convince Edmond de Rothschild to provide further funds to dig a deep well. In addition, Baron de Rothschild also sent out experts in agriculture and vine-growing. The first Hebrew-language kindergarten and elementary school in Palestine were opened in Rishon le-Zion.

In honour of the founding of this town, a Romanian Jewish poet, Naphtali Herz Imber, wrote *Hatikvah* ('The Hope') which became the Zionist hymn, and later the State of Israel's national anthem, which was set to music by Samuel Cohen:

> As long as deep in the heart
> The soul of a Jew yearns
> And towards the East
> An eye looks to Zion,
> Our hope is not yet lost,
> The age-old hope:
> To return to the land of our fathers
> To the city where David dwelt.

In 1883 a Jewish immigrant from Russia, Reuben Lehrer, built a house in Wadi Hanin in the coastal plain; later other Jews including Avraham Yalofsky joined him. Lehrer called the village Nes Ziona ('Banner towards Zion'); there he and his friends planted citrus groves, but he was killed by a group of Arabs five years later. Despite such dangers, other Jews continued to come to the country. In 1884 a Russian-born Jew, Yehiel Michael Pines, who represented the Moses Montefiore Testimonial Fund, bought land for Bilu pioneers to found Gederah.

During this period the Russian-born Jew Eliezer Ben-Yehuda and a group of friends including Yehiel Pines crated a society to spread the Hebrew language and speech among all inhabitants of the country. In 1890 they established a committee to set about formulating Hebrew terms for modern words. The purpose of this committee was 'to prepare the Hebrew language for use as a spoken language in all facets of life – in the home, school, public life, business, industry, fine arts, and in the sciences.'[12] The same year a group of Hibbat Zion established a small farming settlement in Upper Galilee on the west bark of the River Jordan: Mishmar Ha-Yarden ('Guard of the Jordan').

During this period the population of Jerusalem grew considerably: Jews had been in the majority in the city since the 1850s; between 1864 and 1889 their number was about 20,000. In 1890 another village was founded in the coastal plain: Rehovot ('Wide Expanses'). The founders sought to create a Jewish village that would not be dependent on the financial support of Edmond de Rothschild. Russian Jews who were members of Hibbat Zion who had left Vilna, Riga and Kovno founded Hadera ('The Green').

Amongst Jews in the diaspora, these early Jewish settlements in Palestine were viewed as a religious community. In fact, however, Jews living in Palestine ranged across the religious spectrum from the strictly Orthodox to the most secular. Yet, despite their differences, they were committed to Jewish existence in the Holy Land. Young Zionists arrived seeking to create a new life in their ancient homeland. Traditionalists, on the other hand, anxiously awaited the return of the Messiah who, they believed, would arrive to bring about the transformation of life on earth and usher in the messianic age.

6

Steps toward
Jewish Statehood

Early Christian Zionists as well as Christian missionaries in the Holy Land were preoccupied with the restoration of the Jews on the basis of their understanding of Scripture. In their view, the return of the Jewish people to their ancient homeland would lead to the fulfilment of God's providential plan. Secular Jews, however, envisaged the return of Jewry to Palestine as a solution to the problem of anti-Semitism. As momentum gathered for the creation of a homeland in Palestine, Theodor Herzl emerged as the leading proponent of this scheme. After meeting with Jewish notables, he composed *The Jewish State* which he published in 1896. With the support of the Christian Zionist William Hechler, he made contact with the Duke of Baden; the next year the First Zionist Congress was convened in Basle. This was followed by a succession of Congresses which formulated plans for the establishment of a Jewish settlement in the Holy Land.

Theodor Herzl and The Jewish State

More than any other figure, Theodor Herzl has become identified with modern secular Zionism. Born on 2 May 1860 in Budapest, Hungary, he was the only son of a rich merchant. After studying at a technical school and high school in Budapest, he went with his family to Vienna, where he enrolled in the law faculty of the university. In 1884 he received a doctorate and worked for a year as a civil servant; subsequently he wrote plays, and in 1892 was appointed to the staff of the *Neue Frei Presse*. As its Paris correspondent, he witnessed the Dreyfus Affair and became convinced that the Jewish problem could only be solved by the creation of a homeland for the Jewish people.

In May 1895 Herzl requested an interview with Baron Maurice de Hirsch to interest him in the establishment of a Jewish state. When the Baron expressed little sympathy for the project, Herzl hoped the Rothschilds would be more receptive and wrote a 65-page proposal outlining his views. This work was an outline of his *The Jewish State*, which appeared in February 1896; this was followed by a utopian study, *Alteneuland* ('Old–New Land') published in 1902.

Herzl's analysis of modern Jewish existence was not original – many of his ideas were preceded in the writings of Moses Hess and Leon Pinsker. Yet what was novel about Herzl's espousal of Zionism was his success as a Jew in stimulating interest and debate about a Jewish state in the highest diplomatic and political circles. This was due both to the force of his personality and the passionate expression of his proposals. Convinced of the importance of his views, Herzl insisted that the building of a Jewish homeland would transform Jewish life. The first entry in his diary of 1895 reflects the intensity of his conviction:

> I have been occupied for some time past with a work which is of immeasurable greatness. I cannot tell today whether I shall bring it to a close. It has the appearance of a gigantic dream... What it will lead to is impossible to surmise as yet. But my experience tells me that it is something marvellous even as a dream, and that I should write it down – if not as a memorial for mankind, then for my own delight or meditation in later years. And perhaps for something between these possibilities: for the enrichment of literature. If the romance does not become a fact, at least the fact can become a romance.[1]

In the preface to *The Jewish State*, Herzl contended that his advocacy of a Jewish homeland was not simply a utopian scheme; on the contrary, his plan was a realistic proposal arising out of the appalling conditions facing Jews living under oppression and persecution. The plan, he argued, would be impractical if only a single individual were to undertake it. But if many Jews were to agree on its importance its implementation would be entirely reasonable. Like Pinsker, Herzl believed that the Jewish question can only be solved if the Jews constitute themselves as one people:

> We have sincerely tried everywhere to merge with the national communities in which we live, seeking only to preserve the faith of our fathers. It is not permitted us. In vain are we loyal patriots; sometimes superloyal; in vain do we make the same sacrifices of life and property as our fellow citizens; in vain do we strive to enhance the fame of our native lands in the arts and sciences, or their wealth by trade and commerce. In our native lands where we have lived for centuries we are still decried as aliens... The majority decide who the 'alien' is; this, and all else in the relations between peoples, is a matter of power.[2]

Old prejudices against Jewry are ingrained in Western society – assimilation therefore will not act as a cure for the ills that beset the Jewish people. There is only one remedy for the malady of anti-Semitism: the creation of a Jewish commonwealth. In *The Jewish State*, Herzl outlined the nature of such a social and political entity. The plan, he argued, should be carried out by two agencies: the Society of Jews and the Jewish Company. The scientific programme and political policies which the Society of Jews will establish should be carried out by the Jewish Company. This body will be the liquidating agent for the business interests of departing Jews, and will organize trade and commerce in the new country. Given such a framework, immigration of Jews will be gradual. Initially the poorest will settle in this new land. Their tasks will be to construct roads, bridges, railways, and telephone installations. In addition, they will regulate rivers and provide themselves with homesteads. Through their labour, trade will be created, and in its wake markets. Such economic activity will attract new settlers, and thus the land will be populated.

Those Jews who agree with the concept of a Jewish state, he continued, should rally round the Society of Jews and encourage its endeavours. In this way they will give it authority in the eyes of governments, and in time ensure that the state is recognized through international law. If other nations are willing to grant Jews sovereignty over a neutral land, then the Society will be able to enter into negotiations for its possession. Where should this new state be located? Herzl proposed two alternatives: Palestine or Argentina. Argentina, Herzl noted, is one of the most fertile countries in the world, extending over a vast area with a sparse population. Palestine, on the other hand, is the Jews' historic homeland. If the sultan were persuaded to allow the Jews to repossess this land, the Jewish community could in return undertake the complete management of the finances of Turkey. In this way, the Jews could form a part of a wall of defence for Europe and Asia, and the holy places of Christendom could be placed under some form of international extraterritoriality. There are therefore advantages for both these options, Herzl asserted, and the Society should take whatever it is given and whatever Jewish opinion favours.

In the conclusion of this tract, Herzl eloquently expressed the longing of the entire nation for the creation of such a refuge from centuries of suffering:

> What glory awaits the selfless fighters for the cause! Therefore I believe that a wondrous breed of Jews will spring up from the earth. The Maccabees will rise again. Let me repeat once more my opening words: The Jews who will it, shall achieve their state. We shall live at last as

free men on our own soil, and in our own homes peacefully die. The world will be liberated by our freedom, enriched by our wealth, magnified by our greatness. And whatever we attempt there for our own benefit will rebound mightily, and beneficially to the good of all mankind.[3]

In his novel *Alteneuland*, Herzl discussed the social and economic structure of such a state in Palestine. The foundation of the economy, he contended, should be co-operative. Here he saw the New Israel as realizing the social vision of nineteenth-century European utopian socialism. In addition, Herzl advocated universal suffrage as well as the full participation of women in the political life of the community. Further, Herzl maintained that schooling should be free and universal from kindergarten to university. At the same time both men and women are to give two years' service to the community in such institutions as hospitals, infirmaries, orphan asylums, vacation camps and homes for the aged. Urban planning is also encouraged in the novel: new towns are to be planned in advance so an electrified system of mass transport and hydroelectric plants would ensure cheap electricity. Herzl moreover suggested that the biblical principle of the jubilee year should be institutionalized into the landowning patterns of society.

These two works – one a passionate call for the creation of a Jewish country, and the other a novelistic proposal for Jewish existence in such a future society in Palestine – strengthened the case for political Zionism. In 1903 the British government offered Herzl a large tract of land in Uganda; in the Zionist Congress of that year, he pressed that the offer be accepted as a temporary haven for oppressed Jewry. Although a resolution was passed to investigate this proposal, the Russian Zionists rebelled. Exhausted by his exertions Herzl died on 3 July 1904. Nearly fifty years later – on 17 August 1949 – his remains were flown in an aeroplane bearing a blue-white flag of the State of Israel to the country he longed to create.

Christian Zionism and a Jewish Commonwealth

At the end of the nineteenth century, Theodor Herzl emerged as the leading proponent of Zionism. One of the most important Christian supporters of Jewish aspirations was William H. Hechler, a British clergyman of German origin. Born in South Africa, he studied theology and became a Protestant pastor. With the recommendation of the British court, he became private tutor to Prince Ludwig, son of Frederick, the Grand Duke of Baden and met the Grand Duke's nephew, the future Kaiser Wilhelm II of Germany. After the Prince's early death, he served in the ministry in England.

Following the pogroms that took place in Russia in 1881, he participated in a meeting of Christian leaders in London which discussed the possibility of settling refugees from Russia, Romania and Palestine. He then visited Russia to help victims of the attack on Jewry, and in 1883 he wrote *The Restoration of the Jews to Palestine*. In this work he argued on the basis of biblical prophecy that the Jews would be restored to the Holy Land between 1897 and 1898. Two years later Herzl published *The Jewish State*, and in March 1896 Herzl and Hechler met. In his diary, he recorded his impressions of Hechler:

> The Reverend William Hechler, Chaplain to the English Embassy here, came to see me. A sympathetic, gentle fellow, with the long grey beard of a prophet. He is enthusiastic about my solution to the Jewish Question. He also considers my movement a 'prophetic turning point' – which he had foretold two years before. From a prophecy in the time of Omar (637 CE) he reckoned that at the end of forty-two prophetic months (total 1260 years) the Jews would get Palestine back. This figure he arrived at was 1897–1898.[4]

The same month Hechler conveyed his pro-Zionist views in a letter to the Duke of Baden in which he included a description of biblical prophecy and a chronological calculation determining the date of Jewish restoration in the Holy Land. 'The return of the Jews,' he wrote, 'would become a great blessing to Europe, and put an end to the anti-Semitic spirit of hatred which is most detrimental to the welfare of all our nations.'[5] In April of the same year, Hechler wrote another letter to the Grand Duke in which he argued that the Jewish State is 'a most serious question as it may be fulfilled in 1897 or 1898, for come it must according to the Prophets and most certainly it will become a great blessing to the whole world. Knowing all this, would it not have been wrong of me to be silent?'[6]

In Hechler's opinion, the matter deserved the support of political leaders. All that this remarkable movement now requires, he wrote, is the public recognition and protection of the Sovereigns of Europe. History repeats itself, he argued, as at the time of the first return of the Jews from Babylon. Millions of believing Jews wish to return to their ancient homeland. The Jewish State will become successful because of biblical teaching, and the Jewish nation will be a blessing to all peoples.[7]

On 23 April 1896 Herzl had an interview with the Grand Duke of Baden. In his diary he wrote: 'I shall be cool, calm, firm, modest, but determined, and speak the same way.[8] After the interview, Herzl recorded his impressions:

> We were led into the first waiting-room. It was the Adjutants' Hall. And this did take my breath away. For here the regimental flags stand in magnificent rank and file. Encased in leather, they rest solemn and silent; they are the flags of 1870–1. On the wall... is a painting of a military review: the Grand Duke parading the troops before Kaiser Wilhelm I. One might say that only now did I realize where I was.[8]

During the meeting the Duke was sympathetic and interested. Yet, his response to Herzl's request for an intercession with the Kaiser did not produce any concrete result. The Duke asked to be kept informed, and Herzl concluded that the interview had been a success. In a letter to Max Nordeau, a leading Zionist, he stated that the greatest strides had been taken towards the realization of his plans.

In March 1897 Herzl recorded a second meeting at Hechler's apartment. Herzl was astonished to discover books from floor to ceiling as well as a military map of Palestine made up of four sheets covering the entire floor of the study:

> He showed me where according to his calculations, our new Temple must be located; in Bethel! Because that is the centre of the country. He also showed me models of the ancient Temple. 'We have prepared the ground for you!' Hechler said triumphantly... I take him for a naive visionary... However, there is something charming about his enthusiasm... He gives me excellent advice, full of unmistakable genuine good will. He is at once clever and mystical, cunning and naive.[9]

Hechler's efforts to persuade the German Emperor to embrace Zionist aspirations did have positive results. In 1898 the Kaiser stated:

> I have been able to notice that the emigration to the land of Palestine of those Jews who are ready for it is being prepared extremely well and is even financially sound in every respect. Therefore I have replied to an inquiry from the Zionists as to whether I am to receive a delegation of them in audience that I would be glad to receive a deputation in Jerusalem on the occasion of our presence there. I am convinced that the settlement of the Holy Land by the financially strong and diligent people of Israel will soon bring undreampt of prosperity and blessing to the land.[10]

For Hechler, the role of the Christian community was to help the Jews to restore their ancient homeland. Unlike earlier Christian Zionists who saw the restoration of the land as a consequence of Jewish conversion to Christianity, he envisaged the return of the Jews as an element of God's providential plan. In a letter to a Christian missionary in Jerusalem written in 1898, he declared:

> Of course, dear colleague, you look for the conversion of the Jews, but the times are changing rapidly, and it is important for us to look further and higher. We are now entering, thanks to the Zionist movement, into Israel's Messianic age. Thus, it is not a matter these days of opening the gates of their homeland, and of sustaining them in their work of clearing the land, and irrigating it and bringing water to it. All of this, dear colleague, is messianic work; all of this the breath of the Holy Spirit announces. But first the dry bones must come to life, and draw together.[11]

Following his meeting with the Duke of Baden, Herzl travelled in the summer of 1896 to meet with the Sultan. *En route* he encountered Sephardic and Ashkenazic Jews at the station in Sofia who hailed him as the 'Heart of Israel'. Joyously they declared '*Leshanah Haba Birushalayim*' (Next year in Jerusalem). Despite such enthusiasm, this mission accomplished little – Herzl failed to see the Sultan and instead met with the Grand Vizier.

Returning to Europe, he spoke to a gathering of poor immigrant Jews in Whitechapel, London. Sitting in their midst, he perceived that the masses saw him as their redeemer, a modern Messiah who would lead them back to the Promised Land. Nonetheless, the leaders of Eastern European Jewry became increasingly agitated about Herzl's appeal. Fearing the consequences of mass hysteria, like that which accompanied Shabbetai Tzevi in the seventeenth century, they were wary of his political activities. In addition, members of Hibbat Zion became suspicious of what they perceived as Herzl's messianic pretensions.

By the autumn of 1896 Herzl was discouraged by these reactions. Yet, he quickly revived and renewed his labours. After conferring with members of Hibbat Zion, Herzl came to the view that a congress of Zionists should be convened in Switzerland. Once invitations to this gathering had been sent, delegates enthusiastically responded. Even the leaders of Hibbat Zion agreed to attend despite their reservations about Herzl's appeal among the Jewish masses. On 29 August 1897, the same year that Hechler viewed as the date of Jewish restoration, the First Zionist Congress opened in the concert hall of Basle Municipal Casino. Over two hundred delegates, including Hechler, attended, representing 24 states and territories.

The Zionist Movement

At the First Zionist Congress in Basle only about half of the participants came from Western Europe; nonetheless, a large proportion of those from Western countries were of Eastern European origin. Half of those from Germany, for example, were originally from Russia. Herzl took special care not to dominate the Congress, and the most moving speech was given by Max Nordeau, who spoke about the dismal conditions of European Jewry at the end of the nineteenth century. Anti-Semitism, he stated, dominated their lives. Not only did the Jews' fellow citizens repel them, but the Jews have no sense of belonging to the countries where they live. Believing that the world hates them, they are unable to find a place where they can feel secure. In his speech to the Congress, Herzl stressed that the creation of a Jewish homeland is an abiding feature of the Jewish tradition.

Paradoxically, however, there was no mention made at the Congress of a Jewish state because mention of such a vision might endanger Jewish settlers in Palestine and future development of the movement. Delegates were well aware that the Sultan had no intention of handing back Palestine to the Jews. Further, even if this had been his intention, he would have feared the Russian response. As Rothschild had explained to Max Nordeau several months previously, the Sultan feared Russia, and Russia would never permit Palestine to fall under Jewish control. This was so because the Russian Orthodox Church would not permit the Jews to become masters of Jerusalem.

In its programme the Congress adopted by acclamation the quest to found a Jewish homeland in Palestine. Yet, after Basle, there were two approaches to Palestine; political Zionism as espoused by Herzl, and practical Zionism, the official policy of Hibbat Zion. Dedicated to settling the land, Hibbat Zion continued with their small-scale settlements in Palestine, committed to the view that the development of a Jewish presence should be a gradual process. Herzl, however, believed that there must be a massive in-gathering into Palestine. Determined to save those Jews who were compelled to live in adverse conditions, Herzl sought to negotiate at the highest levels a grant of land sufficient for Jewish statehood.

In 1898 a Second Zionist Congress was held at Basle with nearly double the number of participants. Since the First Congress, the number of Zionist societies had grown to 913, most of them in Russia and Austria–Hungary. The total membership of these organizations was approximately one hundred thousand. In his address to this body, Herzl emphasized that the emancipation of Jewry did not result in the elimination of anti-Semitism. Rather, Jews have continued to be oppressed and persecuted in the countries in which they reside. As a result the historical intent of emancipation was to create a homeland for modern Jews. This was not possible in earlier times, but it could now become a reality.

Critical of Russian Jews who sought to smuggle settlers into Palestine, Herzl argued that a formal agreement must be reached with the Turkish authorities. In this address, Herzl alluded to the visit of Kaiser Wilhelm II to Constantinople, Jerusalem and Damascus in October and November 1898 – this, he believed, would provide an opportunity to enlist support for the movement, since Imperial Germany was emerging as the patron and protector of the Ottoman Empire. On 18 October 1898 the Kaiser met Herzl in Constantinople at the Yildiz Kiosk, where the Kaiser was staying as the Sultan's guest. During their discussion, Herzl encouraged the Kaiser to ask the Sultan if a chartered company for Jews in Palestine under German protection could be created.

Initially it appeared that the Kaiser viewed this plan favourably, but when he met with a Zionist delegation headed by Herzl in Jerusalem nothing was said about the plan. At the conclusion of his tour in Damascus, the Kaiser declared himself a friend of the Islamic people, and it became an official policy of Germany that no intervention in favour of Herzl's state should be undertaken because of the damage it would inflict on Germany's interests in Turkey. Following the Kaiser's visit, the Sultan announced his decision to award the Deutsche Bank the concession for a railway to Baghdad and the Persian Gulf.

At the Third Congress Herzl stressed that progress had been made toward creating a Jewish state. He had met the Kaiser, and all efforts must now be directed toward obtaining a charter from the Turkish government under the sovereignty of the Sultan. Such an agreement would enable Zionists to undertake widespread settlement in Palestine. In pursuit of this aim, Herzl met with the Sultan on 17 May 1901 at the Yildiz Kiosk, where he had met the Kaiser two years before. Despite Herzl's enthusiasm for this meeting, the interview produced no positive results. Returning to Constantinople, he was conscious that he was up against an insuperable obstacle to his plans.

Not surprisingly the Sultan rejected Herzl's overtures. Herzl and other Zionists believed that they could hide their ultimate objective – the establishment of a Jewish state – by focusing on the formation of a chartered company. Ottoman diplomats, however, were clear about the intentions of the Zionists. Reporting on the Sixth Zionist Congress, which took place in 1903, the Ottoman ambassador to Berlin, Ahmed Tevfik, encouraged his government to draw up special laws to prohibit the purchase of land in Palestine in order to prevent the colonization of the country. This, he declared, was the true aim of Zionists.

Undeterred by such resistance, Herzl concentrated on influencing British opinion. The Fourth Zionist Congress was to be held in London, and Herzl turned his attention to influencing British policy. Giving evidence before the Royal Commission on immigration, he stated that European Jews were subject to increasing anti-Semitism. How were they to escape such persecution, he asked. Emigration would be possible if a Jewish homeland were made available. Joseph Chamberlain, a member of Balfour's Conservative government, was seriously interested in such a project. At a meeting with Herzl in October, 1902 Chamberlain expressed his approval of a Jewish settlement at El Arish in the Sinai peninsula on the border of Palestine. The Foreign Office, however, was opposed to such a solution, as was the *de facto* governor of the area, Lord Cromer.

By this stage Herzl was suffering from heart disease, and pogroms in Russia became increasingly disastrous for the Jewish community. On 6–7 April 1903 the Jews of Kishinev were assaulted by an unruly mob which killed 32 men, six women and three children. In addition, 495 were injured and subsequently eight others died. Herzl's response to this onslaught was to go to St Petersburg to meet with the Tsar's Minister of the Interior, V.K. Plehve. Determined to divert Russian Jews from revolutionary activity and to rid the country of a Jewish presence, Plehve stated that Russia favoured the creation of a Jewish state in Palestine and would intervene in Constantinople to support the establishment of a Jewish settlement. Despite such assurances, little resulted from this meeting.

Returning from St Petersburg on 16 August 1903, Herzl stopped in Vilna, where he was met by crowds of enthusiastic Jews who had thronged to welcome him as their saviour. After encountering those Eastern European Jews, Herzl became even more convinced of the need for a Jewish homeland. Yet, he recognized the difficulties of creating a Jewish state in Palestine. The same month the British Foreign Secretary, Lord Lansdowne, told the Zionists that if a suitable site could be found in East Africa, he would be prepared to entertain favourably proposals for the creation of a Jewish colony or settlement.

At the Sixth Zionist Congress in Basle in August 1903, Herzl encouraged sending a committee to East Africa to investigate. Although this proposal was passed by 295 votes to 178 with 99 abstentions, Russian Zionists were bitterly opposed to such a development. In their view, this was a travesty of Zionist aspirations. The delegates from Kishinev in particular were determined to thwart this scheme;

in November 1903 they met at Kharkov and an ultimatum was sent to Herzl: he was to withdraw the East Africa project, or a new Independent Zionist organization would be formed.

Determined to carry on with negotiations, Herzl met with the King of Italy and Pope Pius X in Rome in January 1904 and explained the importance of creating a Jewish settlement in Palestine. The Pope, however – unlike Protestant Christian Zionists – was insistent that the Jewish people embrace the Christian faith if they were to support the notion of a return to the Holy Land. On 3 July, Herzl died and was buried in Vienna. From throughout Europe thousands of supporters came to his funeral. The next year the Seventh Zionist Congress rejected the East Africa project and declared the movement's commitment to creating a Jewish National Home in Eretz Israel.

7

Jewish Zionism and
Anti-Zionism

At the beginning of the twentieth century, Jewish Zionists were deeply divided. Unlike Christian Zionists who were preoccupied with biblical prophecy, Jewish Zionists were intent on establishing a place of refuge for the Jewish people. Jewish religious Zionists viewed such a settlement as the first stage of messianic redemption; secular Zionists disagreed among themselves about the practical steps to be taken to create a Jewish settlement in *Eretz Israel*. Spiritual Zionists, on the other hand, were preoccupied with the nature of a Jewish state. With the increase of immigration of Jews to Palestine, Jewish thinkers sought to provide a spiritual justification for agricultural activities in the Holy Land. Pre-eminent among such writers, Aharon David Gordon had a profound influence on the philosophy of these early pioneers. Unlike Christian Zionists who viewed the return of the Jewish people to Palestine as the fulfilment of biblical prophecy, Gordon focused on the problem of Jewish regeneration in the modern period. However, within the Jewish community ultra-Orthodox critics of Zionism united in their opposition to what they regarded as a betrayal of traditional Jewish values. Unlike both Jewish and Christian Zionists they believed it was forbidden to accelerate divine redemption through human efforts. Paralleling this critique, liberal Jews assailed Zionism as a misguided utopian scheme.

Jewish Spiritual Zionism

The foremost spiritual Zionist Asher Zvi Ginsberg (later known as Ahad Ha-Am) was concerned with the spiritual redemption of the Jewish people, although his thought was devoid of traditional Jewish ideas of messianic deliverance. Born in Skvira in the Russian Ukraine on 18 August 1856, he initially received a traditional Jewish education. In 1868 his family moved to an estate which his wealthy father leased; there he studied the works of medieval Jewish philosophers and writers of the Enlightenment. At the age of twenty he pursued French and German literature and philosophy, and later unsuccessfully attempted to continue his study in various European capitals. In 1886 he moved to Odessa where he began to publish articles dealing with contemporary Jewish life.

His first essay, 'Wrong Way', which appeared in 1889 set the stage for his role within the Hibbat Zion movement. In this work he advocated the return to Zion, but remained critical of a number of aspects of the movement's platform. In a later essay, 'The Jewish State and the Jewish Problem', written after his return from the First Zionist Congress, he discussed Max Nordeau's opening statement to the Congress. According to Nordeau, the major problem facing Eastern European Jewry was economic misery, whereas Western Jewry was confronted by the failure of the Emancipation to provide a firm base for Jewish identity in modern society. According to Nordeau, these dilemmas pointed to the need for the creation of a Jewish state in Palestine.

For Ahad Ha-Am, however, the matter was more complicated. Assuming that the Zionist movement attains this goal, what will occur when the Jewish state absorbs the first wave of immigrants? Will the Jewish problem be solved? Clearly not all Jews throughout the world (numbering ten million) will be able to settle in Palestine. What will be the result if only a small section of the world Jewish population emigrated? Ahad Ha-Am argued that the economic problems facing Eastern European Jewry would not be solved for those who remained behind. The Jewish state could only contribute to cultural and spiritual regeneration. Thus the central dilemma faced by Zionism was how the spiritual perplexities of Jews in the diaspora could be resolved by the creation of a Jewish homeland.

According to Ahad Ha-Am, Zionism was able to solve the problems of Western Jewry more readily than to ameliorate the condition of Jews in Eastern Europe. The Jew in the West is separated from Jewish culture and simultaneously alienated from the society in which he resides. The existence of a Jewish state would enable him to solve the problem of national identity, compensating him for his lack of integration into the culture of the country in which he lives:

If a Jewish state were re-established [in Palestine], a state arranged and organized exactly after the pattern of other states, then he [the Western Jew] could live a full, complete life among his own people, and find at home all that he now sees outside, dangled before his eyes, but out of reach. Of course, not all the Jews will be able to take wing and go to their state; but the very existence of the Jewish state will raise the prestige of those who remain in exile, and their fellow citizens will no more despise them and keep them at arm's length as though they were ignoble slaves, dependent entirely on the hospitality of others.[1]

It is this ideal which is able to cure the Jew in the West of his social unease, the consciousness of his inferiority in lands where he is an alien.

In Eastern Europe, however, such a solution is inadequate. With the disappearance of ghetto life, Judaism has lost its hold on the Jewish population. In the past, Jews were able to sustain their traditions through common experience. The passing of this closed society led to the disintegration of the Jewish heritage. For Ahad Ha-Am, it is impossible for Eastern European Jews to return to the traditional religious symbolism of the ghetto. What is required is the establishment of a new Jewish social identity in Israel:

> Judaism needs at present but little. It needs not an independent state, but only the creation in its native land of conditions favourable to its development: a good-sized settlement of Jews working without hindrance in every branch of culture, from agriculture and handicrafts to science and literature. This Jewish settlement, which will be a gradual growth, will become in course of time the centre of the nation, wherein its spirit will find pure expression and develop in all its aspects up to the highest degree of perfection of which it is capable. Then from the centre the spirit of Judaism will go forth to the great circumference, to all the communities of the diaspora and will breathe new life into them and preserve their unity; and when our national culture in Palestine has attained that level, we may be confident that it will produce men in the country who will be able, on a favourable opportunity, to establish a state which will be truly a Jewish state, and not merely a state of Jews.[2]

Israel is thus to be a state infused with Jewish values, and not simply a homeland for the Jewish people: it must embody the religious and cultural ideals of the Jewish past. According to Ahad Ha-Am, the strength of Judaism resided in the prophetic emphasis on spiritual values; a Jewish state devoid of such an orientation will lose the support of diaspora Jewry. A secular state is not viable, he argued, because 'a political ideal which does not rest on the national culture is apt to seduce us from our loyalty to spiritual greatness, and to beget in us a tendency to find the path of glory in the attainment of material power and political dominion, thus breaking the thread that unites us with the past, and undermining our historical basis.[3]

After visiting Jewish settlements in Palestine, Ahad Ha-Am wrote an essay, 'Truth from the Land of Israel', filled with his impression of the country. Deploring land speculation, he called on Hibbat Zion to intervene in this odious practice. In addition, he focused on the dilemmas faced by Zionism because of the existence of the sizeable Arab population. This people, he maintained, must be confronted by those wishing to settle in the land. As early as 1891 he recognized that the Arab Palestinians might press for the creation of a national movement. It is a mistake to believe that Palestine is devoid of a native population. He wrote: 'We tend to believe abroad that Palestine is nowadays almost completely deserted, a non-cultivated wilderness, and anyone can come there and buy as much land as his heart desires. But in reality this is not the case. It is difficult to find anywhere in the country Arab land which lies fallow.[4]

What is required is a sense of realism. Jews should not regard themselves as superior to their Arab neighbours. Instead they should perceive that the Arabs are fiercely proud and determined:

> We tend to believe abroad that all Arabs are desert barbarians, an asinine people who do not see or understand what is going on around them. This is a cardinal mistake... The Arabs, and especially the city dwellers, understand very well what we want and what we do in the country; but they behave as if they do not notice it because at present they do not see any danger for themselves or their future in what we are doing and are therefore trying to turn to their benefit these new guests... But when the day will come in which the life of our people in the land of Israel will develop to such a degree that they will push aside the local population by little or much, then it will not easily give up its place.[5]

In order to flourish in the land of their ancestors Ahad Ha-Am stressed that the Jewish people act with love and respect towards those Arabs in their midst. Other Zionists, however, did not share the same concern.

Although Ahad Ha-Am's vision of the return to the Holy Land was not filled with messianic longing, his idealization of the spiritual, religious and cultural dimensions of Judaism and their embodiment in a Jewish state was rooted in Jewish messianism. For Ahad Ha-Am, it would not be a divinely appointed Messiah who will bring about the realization of God's Kingdom on earth. In this respect, he distanced himself from his Orthodox co-religionists, as well as from the messianism of Christian Zionists. Rather, he believed that it would be the task of the Jewish people themselves. Through the creation of a Jewish state, the spiritual values of the faith are to materialize in the Holy Land.

Jewish Pioneers and the Land

In formulating his conception of Jewish life in Palestine, Aharon David Gordon grounded his outlook in a mystical conception of the interaction of human beings and nature. Born in the province of Podolia, Gordon spent his youth in a farming village on an estate which his father managed for the family of Baron Horace Gunzburg. After his marriage, he served as an official from 1880 to 1923 on a large tract of land the Gunzburgs leased for farming. At the age of forty-seven, he emigrated to Palestine where he worked as a labourer in the vineyards and wineries of Petah Tikva. Later he worked in Galilee; his final days were spent in Degania, one of the earliest kibbutzim.

According to Gordon, manual labour is central to both personal and national salvation. In an essay, 'Some Observations', published in 1910, he outlined two alternatives facing the Jewish community in Palestine. The first is 'the practical way of the world wise . . . the continuation of exile life, with all its short-sighted practical wisdom'. For Gordon exile was not simply geographical dislocation; it involved psychological and existential alienation, combining dependence on others and estrangement from creative life. The second alternative called for a renaissance of Jewish life: the way of manual labour. This later option, he believed, would renew the national energies of the Jewish people:

> We have as yet no national assets because our people have not paid the price for them. A people can acquire a land only by its own effort, by realizing the potentialities of its body and soul, by unfolding and revealing its inner self. This is a two-sided transaction, but the people come first – the people comes before the land. But a parasitical people is not a living people. Our people can be brought to life only if each one of us recreates himself through labour and a life close to nature.[6]

Gordon's understanding of Jewish life in the diaspora was related to his theories of anthropology and psychology. To Gordon, a person can become fully human only through contact with nature. Physical labour is thus essential for personal growth and fulfilment. In this light, Jewish existence in the diaspora is a distorted mode of living, not only because the Jewish nation lost its homeland, but also because it lacked the land in which Jews could realize their full human potential through physical work. In Gordon's view, a Jewish national renaissance will not take place simply through migration: it must involve a return to the self through the cultivation of the land. A fundamental distinction must hence be drawn between a transference of exiles to the Holy Land, and a radical reconstruction of Jewish life through agricultural employment.

Such a radical analysis calls for the total transformation of Jewish life. The way of national rebirth, he wrote,

> embraces every detail of our individual lives. Every one of us is required to refashion himself so that the *Galut* (diaspora) Jew within him becomes a truly emancipated Jew; so that the unnatural, defective, splintered person within him may be changed into a natural, wholesome human being who is true to himself; so that his *Galut* life, which has been fashioned by alien and extraneous influences, hampering his natural growth and self-realization, may give way to one that allows him to develop freely, to his fullest stature in all dimensions.[7]

Such a process of rehabilitation must take place if Jewish exile is to cease, even if Palestine becomes populated with Jewish emigrants.

According to Gordon, traditional Jewish life in the diaspora was richer than modern existence in the post-Emancipation world. Prior to the Emancipation, Jews sought to ameliorate their position without abandoning Torah Judaism. Yet today material prosperity has overshadowed all other values. To counteract this corrosive attitude, the 'religion of nature' must become the dominant ideology in Palestine. In an essay entitled 'Labour', Gordon insisted that the Jewish people must be linked to its homeland; if it is divorced from agricultural labour, it becomes disfigured and emasculated. In their advocacy of a Jewish state, modern Zionist writers have overlooked the fundamental requirements for a vibrant national life. He wrote:

> A people that was completely divorced from nature, that during two thousand years was imprisoned within walls, that became inured to all forms of life except to a life of labour, cannot become once again a living, natural, working people without bending all its willpower toward that end. We lack the fundamental element: we lack labour (not labour done because of necessity, but labour to which man is organically and naturally linked), labour by which a people becomes rooted in its soil and its culture.[8]

The absence of physical work is, he believed, an essential defect in the Jewish character. Such a condition was created by the exile, and its perpetuation has contributed to the continuation of exile; paradoxically the denigration of labour enabled Jews to accommodate to a diaspora existence. If, however, the Jewish people had been more concerned with land, they would have sought to return to their former landed existence. Now that the Jews have a country of their own, Gordon was fearful of the resurgence of this contempt for natural work:

> Now let us assume that somewhere we have settled a goodly number of Jews. Will this attitude of ours change there of itself? Will a transformation of our soul take place without a radical cure? Will not our Jewish people at all times prefer trading, speculation, especially business in which others will labour while they will manage the enterprise?[9]

What was required was a cultural revolution. The Holy Land must be cultivated; buildings constructed; and roads built:

> Each piece of work, each deed, each act is an element of culture. Herein is the foundation of culture, the stuff of which it is made. Arrangement, method, shape, the way in which a thing is done – these are forms of culture. What a man does, what he feels, thinks, lives, while he is at work, and while he is not working, the conditions arising from these relations – these mould themselves into a spirit of culture. From these, higher culture draws nourishment – science, art, beliefs and opinions, poetry, ethics, religion.[10]

Authentic Zionism must bring to Palestine the foundations of manual labour from which such a higher culture can emerge. The task of modern Zionism is thus to foster a sense of dedication to ordinary toil: 'We have to work with our very own hands at all things which make up life [in Palestine], to labour with our own hands at all kinds of works, at all kinds of crafts and trades from the most skilled, the cleanest and the easiest to the coarsest, the most despised, the most difficult. We must feel all that the worker feels, think what he thinks, live the life he lives, in ways that are our ways. Then we can consider that we have our own culture, for then we shall have life.'[11]

What is lacking in contemporary Zionism, he argued, is a recognition of the essential link between human beings and nature. This is the cosmic element of national identity. Jews who have been uprooted must learn to know the soil and prepare it for the transplantation of the Jewish nation. It is necessary to study climatic conditions and everything required to grow agricultural produce: 'We who have been torn away from nature, who have lost the savour of natural living – if we desire life, we must establish a new relationship with nature, we must open a new account with it.'[12]

This quest to bring about a radical transformation in Jewish consciousness was motivated by a utopian vision of Jewish life in Palestine, devoid of the messianic expectations of both Jewish and Christian Zionists. Although Gordon's thinking lacked the religious framework of religious Zionists, it nonetheless had quasi-religious connotations reminiscent of previous thinkers who longed for the redemption of the Jewish nation.

Jewish Anti-Zionism

Although some Orthodox Jewish figures endorsed the Zionist movement, Orthodoxy in Germany, Hungary and Eastern European countries protested against this new development in Jewish life. To promote this policy an ultra-Orthodox movement, Agudat Israel, was created in 1912 to unite rabbis and laity against Zionism. Although the Torah maintains that it is the duty of the pious to return to Zion, these Orthodox Jews pointed out that such an ingathering must be preceded by messianic redemption. In the nineteenth century, the spiritual leader of German Jewish Orthodoxy, Samson Raphael Hirsch, decreed before the advent of Zionism that it is forbidden actively to accelerate divine deliverance. In the light of such teaching, Zionism was viewed by the ultra-Orthodox as a satanic conspiracy against God's will and equated with pseudo-messianism. Prominent among Orthodox critics was the nineteenth-century Hasid Zadok of Lublin, who stated that he prayed to the Lord for the day of redemption, but was unwilling to settle in Palestine for fear that such an act would be interpreted as condoning the Zionist movement.

Yet despite such attitudes, Scripture did decree that it was obligatory for Jews to return to the Holy Land, and this prescription called for an Orthodox response. Accordingly, ultra-Orthodox figures differentiated between the obligation to return to the Holy Land and the duty of residing there. Orthodox Jews, they argued, were exempt from actually settling in the land for such reasons as physical danger, economic difficulties, inability to educate the young, etc. In addition, these critics maintained that Zionism was not simply a movement to rebuild Palestine, it was a heretical attempt to usurp the privilege of the Messiah to establish a Jewish kingdom. Further, ultra-Orthodox spokesmen declared that Zionism sought to leave religion out of the national life – as a result the Jewish state would betray the ideals of the Jewish heritage. Throughout its history, the nation had been animated by spiritual principles, and refused to perish because of its adherence to traditional precepts. If Israel endured through thousands of years of persecution, it would be folly to abandon the religious values which kept alive the hope for Jewish survival. Hence, ideologists of the ultra-right such as Isaac Breuer insisted that

Zionism was depriving the Jewish people of its religious commitment in a misguided pursuit of modern notions of nationhood. This, he believed, was the most pernicious form of assimilation.

Paralleling the Orthodox critique, liberal Jews attacked Zionism for its utopian character. According to these critics, it was simply impossible to bring about the emigration of millions of Jews to a country which was already populated. In addition, in Western countries nationalism was being supplanted by a vision of a global community – it was thus reactionary to promote the creation of a Jewish homeland. In Eastern Europe, on the other hand, there was still a Jewish national consciousness. Yet Zionism was unable to solve the problem facing Jewry. Multitudes of Jews in Eastern Europe were enduring hardship; only a small minority of these individuals would be able to settle in Palestine. Hence these liberal propagandists maintained that assimilation alone could serve as a remedy for the Jewish problem.

In response Zionists protested that assimilation was undesirable and inevitably impossible – such a stance was influenced by racial theories published during the first two decades before the First World War. According to these writings, distinctive qualities were inherited regardless of social, cultural or economic factors. For the Zionists, the Jewish people constituted an identifiable ethnic group whose identity could not be manipulated through social integration. Anti-Semitism, they argued, could not be eradicated. It was an inevitable response to the Jewish populace no matter what efforts were made to assimilate Jews into foreign cultures. Further, since Jews were predominantly involved in trade and the professions – rather than agriculture and industry – they were bound to be the first targets during times of crisis. Pointing to Jewish history, the Zionists emphasized that in the past there were rich and powerful Jews, but without warning they lost their positions and were reduced to poverty. There was thus no security for Jews in societies where they were in the minority. Zionism was the only solution.

Liberals viewed this interpretation of Jewish history as a distortion of the past. Previously, Jewish emancipation depended on the goodwill of rulers, but in contemporary society, they stated, it would result from global socio-economic factors. The Zionists disagreed. The lessons of Jewish history, they believed, must guide current Jewish thought and action. Judaeophobia is an inherent aspect of modern society, and those who championed liberal ideologies such as socialism would be disappointed. In the words of Max Nordeau, the Zionist literary figure and leader, 'Socialism will bring the same disappointments as did the Reformation, the Enlightenment, the movement for political freedom. If we should live to see Socialist theory become practice, you'll be surprised to meet again in the new order that old acquaintance, anti-Semitism.'[13]

In Nordeau's opinion, the Jews have become rootless, and in his address to the First Zionist Congress he discussed the social exclusion of Jews in Western lands. Although Jews were emancipated and enfranchised, he stated, they were unable to join Gentile clubs and organizations. Everywhere Jews encountered the sign: 'No Jews admitted'. Despite the fact that modern Jewry had been assimilated into foreign cultures, they were not fully accepted. Having dissociated themselves from their coreligionsists, they were rejected by their Christian neighbours. In spite of fleeing from the ghetto, they were not at home in their adopted countries. These new marranos were thus strangers alienated from themselves and their tradition.

This depiction of the Jew as a wanderer between two worlds with no home became a dominant theme among Zionist writers. In Germany, Moritz Goldstein published an article in 1913 which provoked a storm of controversy. According to Goldstein, the Jews held sway over German culture, yet were rejected by it. Almost all directors of Berlin theatres were Jews; German music was dominated by Jewish artists; literary study was in the hands of Jewish scholars – nonetheless Jews were viewed as outsiders. What the Jews lacked was a native homeland which would provide the soil from which their true greatness could flower. Not surprisingly, Goldstein's opinions were bitterly criticized by the liberal establishment. For Ernst Lissauer, any attempt to establish a Jewish ghetto on German soil was misguided. Rather, he argued that assimilation must be promoted – this would eradicate any residual anti-Semitic attitudes among the German people.

During this period other voices were also raised against Zionism throughout the Western world. After Herzl issued his summons to the First Zionist Congress, the executive of the German rabbis issued a declaration stating that the desire to create a Jewish state contradicted the messianic longings in Scripture. The Jewish faith, they believed, obligated the community to serve the countries where they lived. In France, Joseph Reinarch declared that Zionism was a trap set by anti-Semites for the naive. English liberals declared that Judaism is a religion; for this reason British Jews could fully identify with the society in which they resided. Thus Claude Montefiore, the leader of Liberal Judaism in Britain wrote: 'Liberal Jews do not wish or pray for the restoration of Jews to Palestine.'[14] Similarly in the United States, liberals denounced zionist ideology as misreading the modern situation.

8

Christian Missionaries and Jewish Settlers

During the later decades of the nineteenth century, Jewish immigrants to Palestine were helped by Christian Zionists who viewed their return as the fulfilment of biblical prophecy. Despite the establishment of St George's Cathedral, of the LJS and the CMS, Christian evangelists continued with their missionary activities among the Jewish community in Palestine. Within the Jewish community, Jewish settlers founded a variety of settlements and institutions in the Holy Land.

First Aliyah and Christian Zionists

Following the Russian pogroms of 1881, a meeting was held at Mansion House in London to call for assistance for Russian Jewry. As President of the LJS, Lord Shaftesbury opened the meeting; subsequently William Hechler and Laurence Oliphant were involved. The Mansion House Fund for Relieving the Persecuted and Homeless Jews of Russia was opened and raised £100,000 to help Jewish refugees leave for safer conditions. In July 1882 the Syrian Colonisation Fund was formed with Lord Shaftesbury as President. Hechler and others supported its aim to create a Jewish colony somewhere in greater Syria. Property was acquired outside Beirut and at the end of August forty-five Russian families left London for their new home.

Determined to help Eastern European Jews, the LJS issued an official statement concerning Jewish refugees:

> The Committee of the London Society for Promoting Christianity amongst the Jews, in view of the grave crisis through which the Jews are passing in different parts of Europe, and especially in the Russian Empire, desire publicly to express their deep sympathy with them in

the indignities and sufferings they are undergoing at the hands of a relentless and enraged population... In these trials the Committee, in common with very many friends of Israel, think they see the beginning of a fulfilment of the prophetic Scriptures foretelling the return of the Jews to their own land. Such an upheaving of the people may, they think, be a preparatory movement towards their complete uprooting in the lands of their adoption, leading them to turn their eyes to the land promised to their fathers for an everlasting inheritance.[1]

During this period a group of Russian Jews met together and formulated a plan to settle in Palestine. Referring to themselves as Bilu (from the Hebrew 'House of Jacob let us go'), they were encouraged by an assurance of financial and political support from Jews living in Jaffa. Jewish newspapers stated that a committee of Jews there were ready to provide these settlers with land. Concerned about the welfare of these emigrants, the Revd H. Friedlander, an LJS missionary, met about fifty Russian refugees and explained that there were Jews in Palestine who believed in Christ and had sympathy for their aspiration to create a Jewish homeland.

When Jewish agencies failed to provide financial help for these refugees, over thirty camped in the garden of the mission house in Jaffa. Provoked by the LJS's interest in these settlers, the Jewish community complained of the dangers facing their coreligionists. As the *Jewish Chronicle*'s Jerusalem correspondent wrote on 28 July 1882:

> It is to be hoped that the friends of education, of religion, and of Jerusalem will assist... We should then no longer have the pain of seeing those who seek in the ancestral land a refuge from intolerance and persecution fall into the snares of the Protestant missionaries.[2]

Given the extra workload entailed by helping these refugees, two new missionaries were sent to Palestine by the LJS: Leo Oczeret and Ben Zion Friedman. Oczeret later commented on the activities of these immigrants:

> Some 70 to 75 Jews are daily employed on the large plot of ground belonging to our Society... To watch some of these refugees, who are bowed down by age, suffering and infirmities, digging, planting and watering in the land once given to their fathers, would cheer the heart of many a Christian well-wisher of Israel. Those who lift up holy hands, praying for the peace of Jerusalem, and the restoration of the Jews to the promised land, would be encouraged to pray more fervently, seeing that God's own time to favour Zion is fast approaching.[3]

These refugees placed enormous burdens on the funds of the LJS mission in Jerusalem; this led to the creation of a special Jewish Refugees Fund in England to help the situation. Responding to these missionary activities, the Jewish communities in Israel and the diaspora offered help to their coreligionists. In August, 1882 Charles Netter, the founder of Mikveh Israel, arrived in the Holy Land to assess the situation. He had just returned from Brody where he had met with Laurence Oliphant and a Polish rabbi who wished to colonize Palestine. On 13 August one of the founders of Rishon L'Zion left for Europe with Netter's support, where he hoped to raise funds for agricultural colonies. On the day that he met with Baron Rothschild, Netter died of a fever at Jaffa. Although Rothschild was opposed to the nationalist motives of Hibbat Zion, he was sympathetic to the plight of Jews living in Palestine and concerned about the increasing influence of Christian missionaries.

During the early months of 1883, the LJS was entering a new phase. Following the 1883 AGM, the Society published a statement resolving that the Committee had no power to make direct grants from the General Fund towards the support of destitute Jews. As a consequence of this declaration, it was agreed that LJS employees should not engage in colonization schemes. Nonetheless it was agreed that a separate organization for the purpose of purchasing land in *Eretz Israel* on which to settle Russian Jews who desired to remain in contact with the LJS could be established. This society was named the Jewish Refugees Aid Society; the London committee consisted of three members of the LJS general committee; the Jerusalem committee comprised the British consul. The first report of this body stated:

> It may be that it is not solely the simple desire to relieve the temporal wants of the Jews, and to bring them individually under the influence of the Gospel, which has drawn out this sympathy; but also the joy which is kindled in the hearts of our friends when they consider whether this movement of the Jews towards Palestine may not be an indication that God has not forgotten his promise to his people of their national restoration, and to His Church of the Second Coming of the Lord.[4]

In 1883 over £3,000 was collected; this enabled the JRAS to purchase a 1,250-acre property. Committed to aiding these new settlers, the JRAS stated:

> This Committee will certainly do nothing to induce any Jews to come to the Holy Land, as that is not their work; but if Jews will come, and are willing to place themselves under their direction, and under the

influence of the Gospel, they will be quite ready to enlarge their operations if the necessary funds are placed at their disposal... On such a settlement as Artouf they may seek Jesus, no man making them afraid, and may confess Him and yet remain in Palestine, as witnesses to the power of the Gospel on the hearts of the Jews.[5]

Deeply concerned with the spiritual welfare of these settlers, the JRAS declared:

What their friends may be permitted to see on Artouf and elsewhere, may be the means of quickening them to pray for the hastening of that day when the restored Jews, touched by the Spirit, shall be led to look on Him whom they pierced; and the restored nation acknowledging Messiah as their King and Saviour shall 'sit every man under his vine, and under his fig tree.'[6]

Eventually a small church and mission school were established which LJS missionaries from Jerusalem or Jaffa visited. As a frequent visitor reported:

Many of the refugees, though thoroughly imbued with a sceptical spirit, have nevertheless felt an attraction for the Gospel, simply because they had been strongly impressed with the national misery of the Jews all over the world. On hearing that the New Testament throws light upon the national fate of the Jews, in that it shows that the national restoration must be connected with national conversion to Christ, they could not help admitting that this gives a reasonable explanation of the unfortunate history of the Jews... How important it is not to lose sight, whilst working and praying for the conversion of individual hearts, of the glorious national promises given to Israel.[6]

Zionist Anglicans

In 1841 Germany had proposed the bishopric scheme in Jerusalem; by 1881 conditions had changed and Chancellor Otto von Bismark re-evaluated Germany's international policies and treaties including the Anglo-Prussian bishopric in Jerusalem. The next year the German Emperor had instructed his ambassador to Britain to cancel the 1841 agreement. The same year William Hechler was instructed by the LJS to compile a book containing all the original papers pertaining to the bishopric. Hechler visited Berlin, Russia and Constantinople concerning Jewish refugees leaving Russia. The next year his compilation *The Jerusalem Bishopric* was published. Hechler himself was a candidate for this position, but his nomination was rejected by the

Archbishop. Despite the desires of evangelicals led by the LJS and CMS, the Anglo-German agreement was annulled.

Despite this development, the Archbishop of Canterbury believed that the bishopric should continue despite the opposition by the high church party. Supported by the Greek Orthodox Church, he turned to the LJS and the CMS for financial assistance. When the LJS agreed to help on the condition that they and the CMS would be included in the nomination of a new bishop, the Archbishop refused. Despite this decision, in February 1887, the LJS and the CMS agreed to donate £300 each towards the bishop's stipend. The Archbishop then embarked on a search for a suitable candidate.

When George Francis Popham Blyth was appointed, a number of supporters of the LJS and CMS were disappointed because they found him too ritualistic. Nonetheless Bishop Blyth arrived in Palestine in May, 1887, seeing his role as representative of the Church as a whole. Unhappy with the independence of the CMS and the LJS, he attempted to assert his authority over these bodies. In a letter to Sir John Kennaway, the LJS president, he proposed to enlarge Christ Church to become the collegiate church with a dean, two canons and two honorary canons. In a letter to Kennaway, the chairman of the LJS, W.N. West wrote:

How alien to our spiritual work among Jews, is all this array of outward dignity and circumstance! What, I reflect, does our Society want with a Dean, Archdeacons, Canons and all the concomitants of an ornate Cathedral system? . . . of one thing I feel certain, and that is, the alarming effect it would inevitably have upon our evangelical supporters . . . In acceding to the Bishop's wishes should we not lose all control over our Church, the funds for these extensive alterations being of his own providing?[8]

Some days later Kennaway wrote to Blyth, indicating that the time was not right for such changes, and on 10 February 1888 the Society passed a resolution against these proposals. Despite such opposition, Blyth had received funds for his plans and he created his own centre. In addition, he was given permission by the Greek Orthodox Patriarch to hold services in the Chapel of Abraham in the Church of the Holy Sepulchre. As time passed, Blyth and the CMS continued to disagree about the direction of the church and in 1892 Blyth began a building project, to establish a Church of England institution independent of the LJS and the CMS. Once St. George's Cathedral was established, it was consecrated by the Bishop of Salisbury, representing the Archbishop of Canterbury.

Additional opposition to the LJS stemmed from both the religious and secular Jewish communities. Nearly every week the Hebrew paper contained attacks on the Society's work. The LJS's schools were of particular concern since over 100 children were exposed to Christian teaching. B'nai Brith opened a branch in Jerusalem in 1888 and waged war on the Anglican mission. In 1894 the Hebrew newspapers threatened to publish the names of those attending LJS schools. However, despite such criticism, the LJS continued its work. In 1889 a medical mission began and plans were made to found a new hospital. On 13 April 1897 the LJS Mission Hospital was opened, evoking Jewish concern.

Opposition to the activities of Christian missionaries in Palestine was reported by the *Jewish Chronicle* in July 1897. The *cherem* issued by the rabbis against the LJS stated:

> From the Great and Mighty Rabbis of the Jewish *Bet Din* It is well known that more than fifty years ago... It was unanimously prohibited by the Sephardim and Ashkenazim Rabbis of that time that any son of Israel should enter within the threshold of the hospital of the enticers; and now that the enticers have built a new hospital without the city, and no one can watch those who enter therein, every man doing what is right in his own sight, thus transgressing the aforesaid great and grave prohibition, which prohibition still stands... Therefore we... have unanimously decided to order and decree according to our writ, that it is unlawful for any *Shochet* to kill either beast or fowl for the use of the aforesaid hospital. Likewise it is unlawful for any Israelite to sell, provide or permit to be sold, any kosher meat to the aforesaid hospital.[9]

Determined to deter the LJS, several Jewish demonstrations against the opening of the LJS Mission Hospital took place. Placards were set up signed by the rabbis who denounced the activities of the Society, and patients were assaulted. Unmoved by such hostility, the LJS Report stated:

> If the Mission Hospital had to be closed we should still know that a great work had been done, since the Jews themselves have been stirred up to look after their sick, and to provide hospitals and doctors for them.[10]

As conflict intensified, the British Prime Minister and the Foreign Secretary, Lord Salisbury, requested the Anglo-Jewish Association to intervene. The Association wrote to Salisbury and to the Chief Rabbi in Jerusalem, noting that the Jews of Jerusalem had been warned of the consequences of attending the hospital and expressing their disapproval of any act of violence.

Despite the warnings of the Jewish establishment, by the late 1890s over 400 Jewish men attended the House of Industry; 41 were baptized prior to entry; 142 during their apprenticeship; and seven after leaving. Over forty continued in full-time mission work. Work among Jewish women also continued: there were visits to the hospital, instruction in the Enquirers' Home, reading at the Jewesses' Institution and a weekly mothers' meeting. Similarly, school work continued, and a service was held for boys and girls in Christ Church. The curriculum included Hebrew studies, the reading of the Psalms and hymns, and grammar and composition. In 1892 a Girls' Boarding School was opened. In Safed, schools were also established, a book depot was opened, and missionaries visited continually. In Jaffa, regular Sunday services took place in the mission house, and in 1894 a chapel was opened. In 1896 a temporary hospital was founded. Responding to such activities, a Jewish group, the 'Holy Watch', was organized to counter the LJS.

When the Zionist Congress met in Basle in 1897, the LJS devoted seven pages to this gathering in an edition of *Jewish Missionary Intelligence*. It stated:

> The Zionist Congress – whose ulterior object is the acquisition of Palestine, and its conversion into a Jewish State and which met at Basle on August 29–31, appears to have kindled a considerable amount of enthusiasm in Jewish circles, and has been watched with sympathetic interest by Christians who have the welfare of the Jews at heart.[11]

Following this meeting, Herzl cultivated important figures in Turkey, Austria, Germany and Russia to further his plans. In 1902 a British Royal Commission on Alien Immigration was appointed with Lord Rothschild as one of its members. On 7 July 1902 Herzl appeared before the Commission, declaring that further Jewish immigration to Britain should be accepted but that the ultimate solution to the refugee problem was the recognition of the Jews as a people and the finding by them of a legally recognized home.

This appearance brought Herzl into contact with the Colonial Secretary, Joseph Chamberlain, who subsequently suggested to Herzl that a Jewish homeland could be established in Uganda. Fearful of the plight of Russian Jewry, Herzl was prepared to accept the proposal. As a result, Lord Lansdowne, the Foreign Secretary, wrote in a letter:

> If a site can be found which the [Jewish Colonial] Trust and His Majesty's Commission consider suitable and which commends itself to HM Government, Lord Lansdowne will be prepared to entertain favourable proposals for the establishment of a Jewish colony of settlement, on conditions which will enable the members to observe their national customs.[12]

After Herzl read Lansdowne's letter to the Sixth Zionist Congress, a number of Russian delegates who viewed the Uganda Plan as a betrayal of Zionism walked out. At the next Congress, Uganda was formally rejected as a place for a national homeland. Meanwhile in Palestine various opposing factions struggled against one another: Zionists, Orthodox Jews, settlers sponsored by Rothschild, and proponents of Hebrew as the national language. In addition, the LJS came under increased attack for its missionary work.

Jewish Settlement in Palestine

In 1903 Menachem Ussishkin travelled from Russia to Palestine to convene a conference at Zichron Yaakov, where he encouraged delegates to remain faithful to the Zionist vision. Before returning to Russia, he founded the Hebrew Teachers' Federation in Palestine. From 1904 until the First World War a further wave of immigration – the Second Aliyah – took place. In 1906 the first Hebrew high school was founded in Jaffa. Two years later, Arthur Ruppin became head of the Palestine Office of the Zionist Executive and encouraged the creation of Jewish farming settlements. In addition, he arranged for the purchase of land and set up an agricultural training farm at Kinneret. The money for this acquisition came from the Jewish National Fund, as did funds that were used to buy farming land at Hulda in the Judaean Hills. In 1910 Aaron Aaronsohn set up the Jewish Agriculture Experiment Station at Athlit.

During this period Tel Aviv was founded just north of Jaffa on land purchased from local landowners. The Jewish National Fund provided funds needed to build the first sixty houses, and foundations were laid for the creation of a Hebrew language high school, the Herzliya Gymnasium. In 1911 the first Jewish hospital was opened in the Arab port of Haifa by Elias Auerbach, a German-speaking doctor who had emigrated to Palestine. The following year the Hadassah Women's Zionist Organization of America sent two members to establish a clinic in Jerusalem. In the same year a girls' agricultural farm was created at Kinneret.

In 1914 supporters of the establishment of the Hebrew University sought to persuade Sir John Gray Hill to sell them his house on Mount Scopus. Much of the money for this project was raised by Hibbat Zion at the instigation of Menachem Ussishkin. On 9 March 1914 Arthur Ruppin recorded in his diary that he had been successful in acquiring an option to purchase Sir John Gray Hill's property. Four years later this option was acted upon. Other early institutions founded in Palestine included the Bezalel Art School, which was founded by Otto Warburg and a group of German Zionists. An American Jew, Nathan Strauss, provided funds to establish a Jewish hospital in Jerusalem.

Simultaneously, Jewish settlements continued to be created in Palestine. In 1914 a group of Hibbat Zion from Russia founded Nahalat Yehuda north of Rishon le-Zion. By this stage there were approximately 90,000 Jews living in the Holy Land, of whom 75,000 were immigrants. In the years following the creation of the Jewish National Fund at the beginning of the century, 43 settlements had been created with a population of 120,000. The majority of those who had emigrated to Palestine were from Russia and Romania – they either worked on the land as farmers or agricultural labourers or were employed as shopkeepers, artisans and labourers. By contrast, the number of Arabs in Palestine was about half a million.

Anxious about the influx of Jewish settlers, the Arab population began to engage in political activity. Two Jerusalem Arabs were elected to the Ottoman Parliament in Constantinople as anti-Zionists. In the summer of 1914 the Turkish government imposed strict measures to curtail Jewish immigration. Later, when Turkey entered the First World War on the side of the Central Powers, France and Russia became Turkey's enemies. As a result, the Jews of Palestine suffered great hardships as food supplies dwindled and the Turkish government came to regard the Jewish population with hostility since large numbers of Jewish immigrants were Russian in origin.

The Turkish military commander, Jemal Pasha, sought to quell both Jewish and Arab national sentiments. In Beirut and Jerusalem several Arab leaders were hanged, and 18,000 Jews were expelled or fled from Palestine to Alexandria. In addition, Jews known to have been active in Zionist circles were expelled from the country. In response to these developments, the Jaffa Group, consisting of a number of Jewish fighters, was established to defend Jewish settlements in Palestine. With the outbreak of war, a number of Zionists were anxious to establish a Jewish legion to fight alongside the Allies against the Turks. It was the aim of this group to participate in the liberation of Palestine from Turkish control and to convince the Allies of the need for a Jewish homeland. Pre-eminent among these Zionists, Vladimir Jabotinsky, a Russian correspondent of a Moscow newspaper who was based in Egypt, encouraged Zionists there to join in political and military alliance with the British, French, and Russians against the Germans and Turks.

Another major Jewish figure in this campaign was Joseph Trumpledor, a veteran of the Russo-Japanese war of 1904–5. Strongly in favour of a Jewish military force, he joined with Jabotinsky in an effort to persuade the British government to create a Jewish defence force, the Zion Mule Corps, to serve on the Gallipoli Peninsula, where an Anglo-French force had landed. Although the Allied offensive at Gallipoli was unsuccessful, the efforts of the Zion Mule Corps were appreciated by the British, an outcome that encouraged the Allies to include Jewish troops in the conquest of Palestine. Yet, as the war intensified, Turkish troops were successful in keeping the British out of the country.

Throughout the war, the defence of outlying settlements in the north became a priority. In 1916 kibbutz Kfar Giladi was established by members of Ha-Shomer to guard the northern settlements against Arab attack. In Tel Aviv a committee headed by Meir Dizengoff, head of the local Israel council, was created to help those suffering in the war. Like other Jews, he was expelled by the Turks and sent to Damascus, where he remained until liberated in 1918 by the British. During this period, a spy ring working behind Turkish lines, known as Nili (from the initial letters of the Hebrew verse 'Nezah Yisrael Lo Yeshakker' ('The strength of Israel will not die'), had been set up in Palestine to support the British. One participant in this action, Aaron Aaronsohn, was instrumental in the quest to persuade the British government to allow Jews to create a national home in Palestine.

After more than a year of negotiations between the Zionists and the British government, the Balfour Declaration was issued. Such a solution to the Jewish problem was in line with the British aspiration of defeating Turkey and becoming the major power in the Middle East. In a letter from the British Foreign Secretary, Arthur Balfour, to Lord Rothschild, dated 2 November 1917, the British government resolved to create a National Home for the Jewish people in Palestine:

> Her Majesty's Government view with favour the establishment in Palestine of a national home for the Jewish people, and will use their best endeavours to facilitate the achievement of this object, it being clearly understood that nothing shall be done which may prejudice the civil and religious rights of existing non-Jewish communities in Palestine, or the rights and political status enjoyed by Jews in any other country.[13]

Such a resolution was a cause for rejoicing throughout the Jewish world. In Odessa 250,000 Jews followed Ussishkin and his colleagues in a motor-car in a massive procession. However, in the United States, David Ben-Gurion, the future Prime Minister of Israel, was more reserved. Britain, he declared, had not given back Palestine to the

Jewish people. The British had made a magnanimous gesture in recognizing the right of the Jewish population to their own country. But it was only the Jewish people, he emphasized, who could transform such a decree into a historical reality.

Within a month of the Balfour Declaration, the British had driven the Turkish forces from Jerusalem. Only the northern half of Palestine remained in Turkish hands. Following this victory, it became possible for Zionists to work with the British in establishing a Jewish National Home as promised in the Balfour Declaration. As a result of the war the entire population of Palestine, including Jews, Muslims and Christians, had suffered considerably. The total population had fallen from 800,000 in 1914 to about 640,000 consisting of about 512,00 Muslims, 66,000 Jews, and 61,000 Christians.

In order to ensure that a Jewish National Home would be created in Palestine, a Jewish delegation headed by Chaim Weizmann addressed the Paris Peace Conference in February 1919. After listening to impassioned speeches by the delegates, the Paris Peace Conference agreed to grant the Palestine Mandate to Great Britain, and accepted the need to establish a Jewish homeland in Palestine as outlined by the Balfour Declaration.

9

The Balfour Declaration and American Christian Zionism

The Balfour Declaration marked a turning point in the history of the Zionist movement. Although there were those in British government circles who opposed the declaration, it had wide support. With formal recognition of the plan to establish a Jewish commonwealth in Palestine, the Zionist aspiration of creating a homeland had become a reality. While Zionists in Europe were engaged in agitating for the creation of a Jewish homeland in Palestine, Christian supporters of a Jewish return to the Holy Land in the United States actively promoted their vision of God's providential plan for the Jewish people. During this period one of the most influential dispensationalists was Cyrus Ingerson Scofield whose Reference Bible had an important impact on Christian fundamentalism in the United States.

Christian Zionism and the Balfour Declaration

During the latter half of the nineteenth century Christian proponents of the Jewish return to Zion prefigured the efforts of Herzl and others. One outstanding figure of this period was the Swiss Calvinist Jean Henry Dunant. Awarded the Nobel Peace Prize in 1901, he was deeply concerned about Jewish suffering in Eastern Europe. In the 1860s he sought to interest Napoleon III and other heads of state in the resettlement of Jews in their ancestral home and founded the Association for the Resettlement of Palestine. 'Palestine is a rich and fertile country,' he explained, 'although now little populated . . . A great economical revulsion in the old world is preparing, and the coast of Palestine will again become as in days of old, in common with that of Lower Egypt, the centre of all exchange between the old continents.'[1] In 1875 Dunant founded the Palestine Colonization

Society in London; two decades later he was one of the first Christian guests at the First Zionist Congress.

Another Christian participant at the First Zionist Congress was a German Lutheran pastor, Johannes Lepsius. At the Congress, he presented a paper: 'Armenians and Jews in Exile, or the Future of the East with Reference to the Armenian Question and the Zionist Movement.' 'When the time comes,' he asked, 'will anyone be able to prevent them? Even if the Zionist Movement has an exclusively national character, there is yet a strong religious undercurrent. We believe that the Jewish nation has a future before it, and that this future will be a glorious one.'

Another proponent of Zionist settlement was the British economist and industrialist Edward Cazalet. In 1879 he wrote a pamphlet: 'England's Policy in the East: Our relations with Russia and the future of Syria' in which he argued for the Jewish contribution to the development of the Holy Land:

> There is another influence which would greatly assist the colonization of the country. It has long been a cherished project with the Jews to establish a college in the Holy land, which would serve as a centre of Jewish philosophy and science. Such an institution would readily meet with support, and incalculably quicken the pulses of their national life... The land of Palestine... is capable of supporting ten times its present population... they still consider this to be their fatherland. But, if they are denied the actual possession of it, they still bear it in their hearts. Three times a day every Jew offers up a prayer for the restoration of his people to the Land and the Temple, from which he has been exiled for eighteen centuries. It is a remarkable fact that this scattered and downtrodden people possess within themselves all the elements which go to form a united nation.[2]

Later Christian Zionists continued to press for Jewish settlement of Palestine. In August 1917, just three months before the Balfour Declaration, Lieutenant Colonel John Henry Patterson, a Protestant Irishman and associate of Vladimir Jabotinsky, became the commander of the Jewish Legion. In his *With the Judaeans in the Palestine Campaign*, he stated that:

> the formation of a battalion of Jews for service in the British army is an event without precedent in our annals, and the part played by such a unique unit is assured of a niche in history owing to the fact that it fought in Palestine, not only for the British cause, but also for the restoration of the Jewish people to the Promised Land.[3]

When the Balfour Declaration was issued, Patterson remarked:

By pious Jews it was regarded as little short of the voice of God, bringing their long-cherished aspirations within sight of fulfilment... All down the centuries from the time of the dispersion it has been the dream of the Jew that one day he would be restored to his ancestral home. In his exile the age-long cry of his stricken soul has ever been 'next year in Jerusalem.'[4]

Such a reaction was grounded in his belief in biblical prophecy:

Christians, too, have always believed in the fulfilment of prophecy, and the restoration of the Jewish people is of no little interest to them, so it can be imagined with what feelings of joy and gratitude the masses of the Jewish people looked upon this promise of England, holding out as it did the prospect of the realization of their dearest hope. Nothing like it has been known since the days of King Cyrus.[5]

Balfour himself was of Scottish descent and deeply influenced by Scripture. Yet, unlike others who viewed Jewish settlement in their ancient homeland as an essential feature of millenarian eschatology, he viewed the Holy Land as an inherent ingredient of the Jewish faith. When the Uganda plan was rejected by the Zionist movement, he met with Chaim Weizmann who explained to him the significance of the Holy Land for world Jewry. This meeting reinforced his belief that religion, race, and land were inseparably interconnected. Similarly, David Lloyd George, the Prime Minister, was committed to creating a Jewish homeland in Palestine. Lloyd George's first encounter with Zionism took place in 1903 when his law firm prepared a draft for the East Africa temporary asylum plan. When it was rejected, he accepted the Zionist argument. Concerning the Balfour Declaration, he remarked that the upbringing of his colleagues had influenced their attitude toward Zionism:

It was undoubtedly inspired by natural sympathy, admiration and also by the fact that, as you must remember, we had been trained even more in Hebrew history than in the history of our own country. I could tell you all the kings of Israel. But I doubt whether I could have named half a dozen of the kings of England!... So the case was put before us, and when the War Cabinet began to consider the case for the Declaration, it was quite unanimously in favour.[6]

Years later, Lloyd George commented on this decision:

As to the meaning of the words, 'National Home' to which the Zionists attach so much importance, he (Balfour) understood it to mean some form of British, American or other protectorate, under which full facilities would be given to the Jews to work out their own salvation and to build up, by means of education, agriculture and industry, a real centre of national culture and focus of national life.[7]

Reflecting on the Balfour Declaration, Patterson paid homage to the British statesmen who paved the way to creating a Jewish commonwealth in the Holy Land:

> Britain's share towards the fulfilment of prophecy must... not be forgotten and the names of Mr Lloyd George and Sir Arthur Balfour, two men who were raised up to deal justly with Israel, will, I feel sure, live for all time in the hearts and affections of the Jewish people. It is owing to the stimulus given by the Balfour Declaration to the soul of Jewry throughout the world that we are now looking upon the wonderful spectacle unfolding itself before our eyes, of the people of Israel returning to the Land promised to Abraham and his seed forever. In the ages to come it will always rebound to the glory of England that it was through her instrumentality that the Jewish people were enabled to return and establish their National Home in the Promised Land.[8]

Another supporter of Zionist aspirations during this period was Charles Prestwich Scott, the editor of the *Manchester Guardian*, who had met Chaim Weizmann in September 1914. In his view, the creation of a Jewish homeland in Palestine would enable Jewry to rise in the estimation of the world. Other British advocates of a return to Zion included Lord Milner who advocated the Balfour Declaration, and Lord Robert Cecil, who similarly endorsed Britain's support of a Jewish commonwealth in the Middle East. For the Jewish people, such support for this historic Declaration was understood as paving the way for the realization of Herzl's vision less than 20 years after his death.

Christian Zionism in America

Owing to Darby's tours of the United States, his conception of premillennial dispensation gained a wide audience among evangelicals. Those mostly influenced by Darby included James Brookes, Arno Gaebelein, D. L. Moody, and William Blackstone. Brookes served as minister of Walnut Street Presbyterian Church in St. Louis, Missouri, and has been described as the father of American Dispensationalism. From 1864 to 1865, Darby made five visits to St. Louis; Darby and Brookes met again in 1872–7 when Darby preached in Brookes' church. Later Brookes was instrumental in bringing Moody to St Louis and introducing C.I. Scofield and possibly Darby to Moody. Amongst Darby's followers, Brookes became the most important lobbyist for dispensationalism. Through his Bible classes, he nurtured a number of Christian leaders, including Cyrus Scofield, who became his friend and disciple.

In 1878 Brookes organized the New York Prophecy Conference and served as president of the annual Niagara Bible Conference until his death in 1897. In his magazine, *The Truth*, he espoused the restorationist views of Revd A.C. Tris, who discussed the question whether Israel was a nation or sect. In Tris' opinion, the Jewish community was a scattered nation whose future was of central importance. Following Darby's dispensational distinction between Israel and the Church, Brookes wrote *Israel and the Church* in which he rejected the notion that God's purpose was for Jews to be converted and drawn into the Church. Instead, he maintained, the biblical promises concerning Israel should not be spiritualized, nor should they be understood as fulfilled in the Church. In *Till He Come*, Brookes depicted a premillennial scheme in which the Jews will be restored to the ancient land. In *The Truth*, he argued that Christians should express love and compassion toward the Jewish people and support the Zionist quest.

Another evangelist who was influenced by Darby was D.L. Moody who similarly shared a passion for the Jewish people. In a sermon preached in 1877, he explained the meaning of God's promise to Abraham:

> Now let me ask you, hasn't that prophecy been fulfilled? Hasn't God made that a great and mighty nation? Where is there any nation that has ever produced such men as have come from the seed of Abraham? There is no nation that has or can produce such men... That promise was made 4000 years ago, and even now you can see that the Jews are a separate and distinct nation, in their language, in their habits and in every respect. You can bring almost every nation here and in fifty years they will become extinct, merged into another, but bring a Jew here, and in fifty years, a hundred years, or a thousand years, he is still a Jew. When I meet a Jew I can't help having a profound respect for them, for they are God's people.[9]

For Moody, the Jews remained God's chosen people who would be converted at the return of Christ, a nation separate from the Church. Moody's greatest service to Darby, however, was through the establishment of the Bible Institute for Home and Foreign Missions of the Chicago Evangelization Society Founded in 1886. This organization, later referred to as the Moody Bible Institute, trained numerous future leaders and became a model for other institutions including the Bible Institute of Los Angeles, and the Northwestern Bible Training School of Minneapolis.

Another disciple of Darby was William E. Blackstone who settled in Chicago after the Civil War. In 1887 he wrote *Jesus is Coming* which adopted a premillennial dispensationalist stance, stressing that the Jews have a biblical right to Palestine and would be restored there. Like William Hechler, he agitated for the Zionist movement which he viewed as a sign of the imminent return of Christ. 'The Zionists,' he wrote:

> have seized the reins and eschewing the help of Abraham's God they have accepted agnostics as leaders and are plunging madly into this scheme for the erection of a godless state. But the Bible student will surely say, this godless national gathering of Israel is not the fulfilment of all the glorious restoration, so glowingly described by the prophets. No indeed.[10]

Nonetheless, Blackstone argued, the Bible predicted that Israel would be gathered together in the Holy Land prior to Jesus' coming.

In 1887 he founded the Chicago Hebrew Mission which later became the American Messianic Fellowship. The next year he travelled to London for the General Missionary Conference, and then went on to Europe, Palestine and Egypt. Returning in 1890, he organized the first conference of prominent Christian leaders and Reform rabbis, entitled: The Past, Present, and Future of Israel. To his dismay, he discovered that these Reform rabbis were not supportive of Zionist aspirations. Later he lobbied the US President, Benjamin Harrison and his Secretary of State with a petition signed by 413 Jewish and Christian leaders, calling for an international conference concerning the Jewish return to Palestine. Known as the Blackstone Memorial, the petition asked:

> Why not give Palestine back to them [the Jews] again? According to God's distribution of nations it is their home, an inalienable possession from which they were expelled by force. Under their cultivation, it was a remarkably fruitful land, sustaining millions of Israelites, who industriously tilled its hillsides and valleys. They were agriculturalists and producers as well as a nation of great commercial importance – the centre of civilization and religion. Why shall not the powers which under the treaty of Berlin, in 1878, gave Bulgaria to the Bulgarians and Servia to the Servians now give Palestine back to the Jews?[11]

Together with Justice Louis Brandeis, Blackstone sought to convince successive presidents of the validity of the Zionist claims to Palestine. During this period Blackstone contributed large sums of money to the Zionist cause. In 1917 Blackstone was enthused by the defeat of the Turks and the entry of the Allies into Jerusalem. The next year he spoke at a large Jewish gathering in Los Angeles and stressed that he had been committed to Zionism for 30 years. As he explained: this was because he believed that true Zionism is founded on the plan and purpose of God as prophetically recorded in the Bible. In his view there were only three options open to the Jew. The first was to accept Christ. Few Jews, he believed, would adopt this option. The second was to become a true Zionist and hold fast to the ancient hopes of the fathers and the assured deliverance of Israel through the coming of the Messiah and the national restoration in Palestine. The third option was embrace assimilation.

Speaking to his audience, he said:

> Oh, my Jewish friends, which of these paths shall be yours? We are living in tragic times. The most momentous events of all human history are impending. God says you are dear unto Him and that 'He that toucheth you toucheth the apple of his eye' (Zech 2:8). He has put an over-whelming love in my heart for you all, and therefore I have spoken plainly... study this wonderful Word of God... and see how plainly God Himself has revealed Israel's pathway unto the perfect day.[12]

The Scofield Bible and Christian Zionism

Cyrus Ingerson Scofield was influenced by both James Brookes and J.N. Darby. Initially he served as Brooke's assistant, and popu-larized Darby's dispensationalist views. In 1888 he published *Rightly Dividing the Word of Truth* in which he presented the principles of dispensationalism he had been teaching in his Bible classes; Scofield's views later became the religious presuppositions behind the notes of his *Scofield Reference Bible*. This work began with a quota-tion from Paul's second letter to Timothy: 'Do your best to present yourself to God as one approved, a workman who does not need to be ashamed and who correctly handles the word of truth' (2 Timothy 2:15).

The first section offers a novel interpretation of the verse: 'Give no offence, neither to the Jews, nor the Gentiles, nor to the church of God' (1 Corinthians 10:32). Scofield attempted to justify the division of the world into Jews, Gentiles and the Church, and went on to explain that biblical history should be divided into seven dispensa-tions. According to Scofield, if one does not accept dispensational eschatology, he does not believe in the Lord's return and is not submitting to the authority of Scripture. Subsequently, Scofield was determined to compose a commentary on Scripture, as one of his colleagues, Arno C. Gaebelein, explained:

> One night, about the middle of that week, Dr. Scofield suggested, after the evening service, that we take a stroll along the shore. It was a beautiful night. Our walk along the shore of the sound lasted until midnight. For the first time he mentioned the plan of producing a reference Bible, and outlined the method he had in mind. He said that he had thought of it for many years and had spoken to others about it, but had not received much encouragement. The scheme came to him in the early days of his ministry in Dallas, and later, during the balmy days of the Niagara Conference he had submitted his desire to a number of brethren, who all approved of it, but nothing came of it. He expressed the hope that the new beginning and this new testimony in Sea Cliff might open the way to bring about the publication of such a Bible with references and copious footnotes.[13]

In 1909 the Scofield Bible was published, containing illustrative notes and cross references. In the introduction to this work, Scofield claimed that over the previous 50 years there had been a growing interest in Bible study; his work was based on such investigation. In his presentation, he noted:

> all the greater truths of divine revelation are so traced through the entire Bible, from the place of first mention to the last, that the reader may himself follow the gradual unfolding of these, by many inspired writers through many ages, to their culmination in Jesus Christ and the New Testament Scriptures. This method imparts to Bible study an interest and vital reality which are wholly lacking in fragmented and disconnected study.[14]

Explaining the nature of premillennial dispensations, he argued that dispensations should be understood as periods of time during which human beings are tested in relation to their obedience to a specific revelation of the will of God. These dispensations exhibit the progressive order of God's dealings with humanity from the beginning of the life of humanity to the end of time. Historically Christianity viewed national Israel as a precursor of the Church. Scofield, however, attempted to demonstrate that such a perception is mistaken. Rather, he insisted that the Church has not replaced or succeeded Israel as God's people. Influenced by Darby, he argued that the Church age will end in failure and apostasy and be replaced by a revived national Israel who will experience the blessings of the final kingdom dispensation.

Following Darby, Scofield maintained that God has a separate plan for Israel and another for the Church: Israel's destiny is on earth while the Church's is in heaven. During the great Tribulation on earth a remnant of Israel will turn to Jesus as the Messiah and become his witnesses after the removal of the Church. For Scofield, Israel is the earthly wife of God whereas the Church is the heavenly bride of Christ. Referring to Hosea 2:2, he wrote:

> That Israel is the wife of Jehovah now disowned but yet to be restored, is the clear teaching of the passages. This relationship is not to be confounded with that of the Church to Christ... in the mystery of the Divine tri-unity both are true. The N.T. speaks of the Church as a virgin espoused to one husband (2 Cor.11:1,2), which could never be said of an adulterous wife, restored in grace. Israel is, then to be the restored and forgiven wife of Jehovah, the Church the virgin wife of the Lamb... Israel Jehovah's earthly wife (Hos. 2:23); the Church the Lamb's heavenly bride.[15]

Like Darby, Scofield taught that it was God's intention to bring the Jewish nation back to Palestine, reconstitute the priesthood, and rebuild the ancient Temple. There would thus be a glorious future for Israel. Concerning these future events, he wrote:

> This final restoration is shown to be accomplished after a period of unexampled tribulation (Jer. 30:3–10), and in connection with the manifestation of David's righteous Branch (v.5), who is also Jehovah-*tsidkenu* (v.6). The restoration here foretold is not to be confounded with the return of a feeble remnant of Judah under Ezra, Nehemiah, and Zerubbabel at the end of the 70 years (Jer. 29:10). At His first advent Christ, David's righteous Branch (Luke 1:31–33), did not 'execute justice and judgment in the earth' but was crowned with thorns and crucified. Neither was Israel the nation restored, nor did the Jewish people say, 'The Lord our righteousness' cf. Rom. 10:3. The prophecy is yet to be fulfilled (Acts 15:14–17).[16]

At the Niagara Prophetic Conference of 1897, Scofield depicted the notion of the failing Church and imminent rapture of the saints:

> The signs and portents of the end-time are now so many and so ominous than men of vision everywhere, and in every walk of life, are taking note of them; and this quite apart from the interpretation of them which prophecy gives. Men like Gladstone and Bismark have said that the catastrophe of present day civilization is near and cannot be averted; that the destructive agencies are more and mightier than the forces of conservatism, and that no man may predict what form the reconstructed social order will assume after the inevitable cataclysm.[17]

In his *Reference Bible*, Scofield reiterated that these terrible events would take place:

> Armageddon [the ancient hill and valley of Megiddo, west of Jordan in the plain of Jezreel] is the appointed place for the beginning of the great battle in which the Lord, at his coming in glory, will deliver the Jewish remnant besieged by the Gentile world-powers under the Beast and False Prophet.[18]

For Scofield there are three classes of peoples: Jews, Gentiles and the visible Church. Hence, he regarded the return of Jesus Christ as having a threefold relation to the Church, to Israel, and to the nations. In his view, after the judgement there will be forgiveness and blessing for both Jews and Gentiles as long as the Church has been raised to heaven:

> (a) To the Church the descent of the Lord into the air to raise the sleeping and change the living saints is set forth as a constant expectation and hope...
> (b) To Israel, the return of the Lord is predicted to accomplish the yet unfulfilled prophecies of her national regathering, conversion and establishment in peace and power under the Davidic Covenant...
> (c) To the Gentile nations the return of Christ is predicted to bring the destruction of the present political world-system... the judgement of Mt. 25:31–46, followed by world-wide Gentile conversion and participation in the blessings of the kingdom...[19]

Scofield's Reference Bible had a profound impact in the years following its publication. By 1945 more than two million copies of the *Scofield Reference Bible* had been published in the United States, and between 1967–1979 a further one million copes of the *New Scofield Reference Bible* appeared, and in 1984 a new edition was published. By the 1950s half of all conservative evangelical student groups were using the *Scofield Reference Bible* and it became the single document of all fundamentalism. In many Bible schools, institutes and seminaries, its theology had confessional status. In time it came to influence hundreds of thousands of committed Christians, who came to view Israel as of fundamental importance in God's providential plan for the world.

10

Political Agitation and
the Jewish Homeland

While Christian Zionists in the United States were propounding pre-millennial dispensationalism, Jews in Palestine were actively involved in creating a Jewish homeland. Within a month of the Balfour Declaration, the British had driven the Turkish forces from Jerusalem. Only the northern half of the country remained in Turkish hands. Following this victory, it became possible for Zionists to work with the British in establishing a Jewish National Home. Just as Christian Zionists supported the Balfour Declaration, they were enthusiastic about the possibilities of the creation of a Jewish homeland under the Mandate.

Zionism and Realpolitik

Born in 1880 in Odessa, Vladimir Jabotinsky went abroad in his last year of high school as a foreign correspondent. After studying for three years at the university in Rome, he joined the staff of another Odessa daily, and in 1901 was recalled to join its editorial staff. In 1903 he helped organize a Jewish self-defence corps in Odessa, and subsequently became a Zionist propagandist. In the following years he travelled throughout Russia and Europe.

After the outbreak of the First World War, he worked in northern and western Europe as a correspondent for a liberal Moscow daily. Once Turkey joined on the side of Germany, he became convinced that the future of Jewish interests in Palestine rested with the allies. Opposed to the Zionist leadership who advocated neutrality, Jabotinsky persuaded the British to form three Jewish battalions. Yet, after the war Jabotinsky became sceptical of British support for Jewish interests, and during the violent Arab protests of 1920 he organized a self-defence corps in Jerusalem.

Imprisoned by the British military administration and sentenced to fifteen years' imprisonment for illegally possessing arms, he was eventually pardoned. In 1921 Jabotinsky was elected to the Zionist Executive, but quarrelled with Chaim Weizmann. In 1925 he organized the Revisionist Party; several years later this group left the Zionist movement and established the New Zionist Organization. Under his leadership illegal immigration to Palestine took place and the Irgun, an underground military organization founded by members of Betar and the Revisionists, engaged in a struggle with the British.

In his autobiography, Jabotinsky noted that he first encountered Zionism as a young man in Berne when he attended a lecture by Nachman Syrkin. At that gathering, he wrote, 'I spoke Russian, in the following vein: I do not know if I am a socialist, since I have not yet acquainted myself with this doctrine; but I have no doubt that I am a Zionist, because the Jewish people is a very nasty people, and its neighbours hate it, and they are right; its end in the diaspora will be a general Bartholomew Night, and the only rescue is general immigration to Palestine.'[1] Later in Italy, he was influenced by the national movement and became persuaded that liberalism is irrelevant in the modern world. In an essay written in 1910, 'Man is a Wolf to Man', he emphasized that it is a mistake to rely on liberal ideas to bring about political reform:

> It is a wise philosopher who said, 'Man is a wolf to man'; worse than the wolf is man to man, and this will not change for many days to come. Stupid is the person who believes in his neighbour, good and loving as the neighbour may be; stupid is the person who relies on justice. Justice exists only for those whose fists and stubbornness makes it possible for them to realize it... Do not believe anyone, be always on guard, carry your stick always with you – this is the only way of surviving in this wolfish battle of all against all.[2]

Such ideas were central to his insistence on Jewish self-defence and self-determination. Jabotinsky's advocacy of Jewish nationalism was expressed in a wide range of articles dealing with national unity and discipline. For Jabotinsky the essential element of the nation consists in its racial component. It is not territory, religion or a common language that comprises the substance of nationhood; rather its essential character is determined by its racial composition. In *On Race* Jabotinsky argued that 'a nation's substance, the alpha and omega of the uniqueness of its character – this is embodied in its specific physical quality, in the component of its racial composition.'[3] In this context Jabotinsky asserted that the Jews are a superior race. In a dialogue between an imaginary Russian and a Jew in 'An Exchange of Compliments' published in response to an anti-Semitic tract, the Jewish disputant states: 'But if we are going to make comparisons, everything depends on the criteria to be used, and then, you should know, I will insist on my own criterion: he who is steadfast in spirit – he is superior . . . He who will never give up his internal independence, even when under a foreign yoke – he is superior . . . We are a race that will never be harnessed.'[4]

In Jabotinsky's view the Jewish people as an emerging nation needs founders and builders who are able to animate its latent potential. 'We need', he wrote, 'a generation ready for all kinds of adventures and experiences, a generation that can find its way in the most dense forest. We need young people who can ride horses and climb trees and swim in the water and use their fists and shoot a gun; we need a people with a healthy imagination and a strong will, striving to express themselves in the struggle for life.'[5]

Regarding the Arab population, Jabotinsky emphasized that the Jewish people in returning to its ancestral homeland is not returning to oriental culture. In 'The Arabesque Fashion', he maintained that the Jews are a European people:

> We the Jews... have no connection with that 'Orient'; perhaps even less than other European people... The spiritual atmosphere of Europe is ours, we have the same rights in it just like the Germans and the English and the Italians and the French... And in Palestine this creativity will continue. As Nordau has put it so well, we come to the Land of Israel in order to push the moral frontiers of Europe up to the Euphrates.[6]

According to Jabotinksy the Muslims are a backward people, and the Western powers have nothing to fear from the Arab nations if they support Zionist policies. In 1937 Jabotinsky gave evidence before the Peel Commission (the Royal Commission on Palestine), arguing for the establishment of a Jewish state covering all of the original Palestine Mandate, including Transjordan. Aware that this would turn the Arabs in such a state into a minority, he contended this would not be detrimental to the Arab populace:

> I have also shown to you already that, in our submission, there is no question of ousting the Arabs. On the contrary, the idea is that Palestine on both sides of the Jordan should hold the Arabs, their progeny, and many millions of Jews. What I do not deny is that in that process the Arabs of Palestine will necessarily become a minority in the country of Palestine. What I do deny is that it is a hardship. It is

not a hardship on any race, any nation, possessing so many national states now and so many more national states in the future. One fraction, one branch of that race, and not a big one, will have to live in someone else's state. Well, that is the case with all the mightiest nations of the world.[7]

Arguably Jabotinsky's legacy to modern Zionism was his recognition of the importance of power in determining the fate of the Jewish nation. For Jabotinsky it is not morality but power that is of supreme importance in political affairs. In the subsequent history of Israel, this principle became a central feature of the Jewish state's defence policy. Yet Jabotinsky's inability to recognize the national aspirations of the Arab population was a failure of insight. For a subdued populace the denial of national rights led to frustration and anger. The bloody history of Arab–Jewish relations in the years following Jabotinsky's death illustrates his lack of perception about Arab aspirations in the Holy Land.

Christian Zionists in Palestine and the Balfour Declaration

With the onset of the First World War, Christian Zionists were anxious to assist those Jews who were harshly treated by the Turkish government. When the British government endorsed the idea of a Jewish homeland in Palestine in 1917, Jewish missionaries rejoiced. This, they believed, was the first stage in the unfolding of God's providential plan. Yet, they realized that the creation of a Jewish state would inevitably curtail their missionary activities amongst the Jewish population.

At the beginning of the twentieth century, Hebrew Christians and Arab Anglicans living in Palestine created associations independent from the LJS and the CMS. At this time there were about 83 Hebrew Christians living in Jerusalem. During this period the LJS expanded its activities, and an extension of the chancel of Christ Church was completed. The largest building project was the new Girls' Day School. In addition, education work was a high priority: many young Jewish men attended a night school where English was taught. In 1905 seven Jewish boys were baptized, and a considerable number of Jewish children were exposed to the gospels. The LJS Bookshop and the House of Industry were also active as was the LJS Hospital. Not surprisingly such outreach caused considerable agitation within the local community.

During the First World War, the Turkish government ordered the expulsion of 6000 foreign Jews in the Holy Land. As the *Evening Standard* recorded:

> The unfortunate captives were literally thrown into the boats, while on the way the Arab boatmen brandished knives and robbed them of what little they possessed. Moans, tears, hysterical shouts filled the air. Then, without any warning, the steamer weighed anchor and left. It was late in the evening and you could imagine the horror of the situation.[8]

Within months of this expulsion about 7000 Jews left *Eretz Israel*. The LJS endeavoured to assist these refugees by sending financial and other support. As war became imminent, the LJS withdrew English missionaries, and their work continued under local Hebrew Christians; however, the Turkish government seized the LJS's hospitals and girls' day schools as well as missionary houses. St George's was closed, and a number of the buildings associated with the Cathedral were seized. During 1915 the Jewish ladies offered their help to the Red Crescent and the hospital became an isolation hospital for infectious diseases. In August 1916 the Boys' and Girls' Boarding Schools were closed and many children were removed to orphanages. In the Spring of 1917 the Boys' Schools were taken over by the Turks.

When children were taken from the LJS schools, a number went back to their parents. However, the remainder were forced to attend Turkish schools. The mission in Safed was also subject to harsh control. The LJS Hospital, its school and two houses were eventually taken over by the Turkish authorities. Aware of the distress facing Europe, the LJS began making plans for relief and began a compassion fund. The plight of Russian Jewry was also a major concern, and the LJS established a 'Distress Fund'. As the war continued, military moves commenced which would lead to the liberation of Palestine from the Turks. In 1915 the president of the LJS observed:

> That great things are happening today... there can be no doubt... all pointing to the conclusion that the reign of the Turks in Jerusalem is speedily drawing to an end... Finally, there is this terrible war – greater in area and scale than any since the world began, and of which we cannot understand the reason or foresee the end. We can only rest in the thought that God is working His purpose out, and that purpose we know is to bring repentance to Israel.[9]

After Lloyd George became Prime Minister in 1916 and Arthur Balfour the Foreign Minister, Sir Mark Sykes met with Chaim Weizmann on 7 February 1917 and suggested a future arrangement between the British government and the Zionists. On 17 June the Zionist leadership was encouraged to formulate a declaration of Jewish national hopes in Palestine which Balfour could submit to the cabinet. This proposal was submitted to the cabinet by Balfour on 3 September and agreed upon by the pro-Zionists led by Lloyd George and Balfour. On 2 November the cabinet decision became public when it was presented in a letter from Balfour to Lord Rothschild.

In an article in its publication, *Jewish Missionary Intelligence*, the LJS expressed its approval:

> The following announcement in *The Times* on Friday, November 9, 1917, is truly inspiring to the Bible-loving Christian who has been watching the Jews and the Zionist movement since 1897... With one step the Jewish cause has made a great bound forward. For centuries the Jew has been downtrodden, depressed, hated and unloved by all the nations. For 2000 years now the Jew has suffered as no other nation on the earth's surface in his restless wanderings. Wherever he has gone he has been ill-treated, but now there is at least a prospect of his settling down once again in his own country, and of becoming in the eyes of men a nation amongst the nations, in place of being a wanderer in every clime. He is now to have a home for himself in his God-given land. The day of his exile is to be ended. What does this mean for us Christians? In the light of prophetic Scripture we recognise that such an action on the part of our government and on the part of the Allied Powers, in being united in their resolve to reinstate the Jew in his own land is full of significance. Our Lord, when asked the question, 'What shall be the signs of thy coming and of the end of the age', gave one of the signs, in St Luke 21:24, to be that 'Jerusalem shall be trodden down of the Gentiles [nations] until the times of the Gentiles [nations] be fulfilled.' Ever since AD 70 Jerusalem and Palestine have been under Gentile domination, and now we seem to be on the very verge of a literal fulfillment of the last prediction, and it is certainly a distinct warning to us that the Lord 'is near, even at the very doors' (St Matt. 24:32).[10]

Yet, paradoxically, the LJS recognized that missionary work amongst the Jews would become increasingly difficult if a Jewish state were created. In May 1918 an editorial in *Jewish Missionary Intelligence* outlined this problem:

> The present phase which the Society is now passing through is unique in its history. Hitherto, the Jews have been a people 'scattered and peeled, robbed and spoiled', wandering on the face of the earth without common leaders, without a country and without national cohesion.

Today, this state of affairs seems to be coming to an end. The Jewish race is organizing itself in such a way that we believe that we are actually seeing that come to pass which was prophesied by Ezekiel (ch. 37), viz., a movement amongst the 'dry bones' of Israel, bone is uniting to bone, i.e., there is cohesion. The uniting element being the possibility in the very near future of their being allowed to organize a Jewish State in their own God-given country of Palestine.

This national movement amongst the Jews is destined to make missionary work amongst them more difficult. It stands to reason that, if a people is organized, they are better able to cope with those forces that work amongst them, which they do not like. There is no need for us to hide the fact: the Jew, from the national standpoint, does not love the missionary. For he ignorantly imagines that one of the results of missionary propaganda is the denationalizing of individual Jews. We are most anxious, therefore, to be in such a position in Jerusalem and Palestine to prove to the Jew that the converted Jew need not necessarily be denationalized. To do this effectively, the LJS ought to have well-equipped mission stations dotted about Palestine, surrounded by whole-hearted Jewish converts who at the same time could prove themselves to be Jewish patriots.[11]

Aftermath of the Balfour Declaration

In order to ensure that a Jewish homeland be created, Chaim Weizmann addressed the Paris Peace Conference on 27 February 1919. After listening to impassioned speeches by the delegates, the Conference agreed to grant the Palestine Mandate to Great Britain, and accepted the need to establish a Jewish homeland in Palestine as outlined by the Balfour Declaration.

In the meantime Jewish settlements in Upper Galilee were caught in the conflict between local Arabs and French authorities who controlled the area following the war. Subsequently the territory was transferred to Britain, yet Arabs continued to attack the Jewish population. In response, Joseph Trumpeldor, who had returned to Palestine, led the defence of these northern settlements. On 1 January 1920 he began to fortify Tel Hai; two months later this settlement was attacked by armed Bedouin. Wounded in this conflict, Trumpeldor died along with five other Jewish settlers.

In the years following the First World War, a further wave of immigration – the Third Aliyah – took place; approximately 35,000 settlers entered the country, including Jews who were inspired by socialist values. In order to unify the various Labour Zionist Groups that had developed since the First World War, the General Federation of Jewish Labour, or Histadrut, was founded in December 1920. These steps towards the creation of a Jewish homeland were met by increasing hostility on the part of the Arab population, which erupted in the 1920 riots. After attempting to protect the Jewish population from attack, Vladimir Jabotinsky was arrested by the British and put into prison. At the Histadrut conference in December 1920, it was agreed that a defence organization was now needed. In March 1921 the Haganah was established as a secret body, acting without the consent of the British authorities.

During this period of instability an English Jew, Sir Herbert Samuel, arrived on 30 June 1920 in Palestine as High Commissioner and Commander in Chief. Although Samuel was an ardent Zionist, he believed that Jews would be able to live harmoniously with the Arab population. In August 1920 Samuel authorized a Land Transfer Ordinance that made it possible for Zionists to acquire land; in September an Immigration Ordinance opened Palestine to legal immigration from those who obtained visas from the Zionist Organization.

When Palestine was transferred from the Foreign Office to the Colonial Office under Winston Churchill, a conference of senior British officials in the Middle East took place in Cairo in order to reach a settlement with the leaders of Arab nationalism. A focus of Arab resentment was the increasing number of Jews who had entered Palestine; by April 1921 nearly 10,000 Jews had come into the country under Samuel's Immigration Ordinance. Added to Arab fears about Zionist aspirations was the dispute about the election of the Grand Mufti of Jerusalem, the supreme representative of Muslim Arabs.

Once the post of Grand Mufti became vacant, it was to be filled according to Ottoman procedures. An election took place. Hajj Amin, the principal instigator of the anti-Jewish riots of Easter, 1920 and his followers declared that the elections had been rigged by the Jews. Although Samuel's main advisor on Arab affairs encouraged him to invalidate the elections, Samuel made no decision. When this matter remained unresolved, further anti-Jewish protests took place on 1 May. In the next few days, rioting spread to other coastal centres.

In order to calm Arab feeling, Samuel introduced a temporary suspension of immigration and agreed to Richmond's recommendation about the election of the Grand Mufti. One of the three Arabs who had been elected was encouraged to stand down, and Hajj Amin became Grand Mufti of Jerusalem. The Jewish community was incensed. In the same year the military sought to subvert the Balfour Declaration.

During the years 1920–1 there were grave doubts about the possibility of establishing a Jewish national home in Palestine. Although Samuel sought to create representative institutions in Palestine, the Jewish population was fearful of representative institutions, since Jews constituted only 11 per cent of Palestine's population. In addition, the Arab birth rate was higher than that among Jews. In such conditions, it seemed certain that the Arabs would constitute the majority in any institution that would be established. Samuel and Churchill, however, envisaged the creation of a Middle East Federation, of which the Jewish national home would be a part. Although there was some support for this notion in Jewish circles, the Yishuv was bitterly opposed.

Despite such resistance, Samuel initially established a nominated Advisory Council in October 1920 with a majority of Arab notables. After the May 1921 protests, he proposed that the Advisory Council be elected as a step towards self-government. At the same time Samuel declared that the Balfour Declaration did not imply that a Jewish government would be formed to rule over the Muslim and Christian majority. Rather, he insisted that the British government would never impose a policy that would be contrary to the religious, political and economic interests of those living in Palestine. In August 1921 an Arab delegation went to London to meet with British officials; because the Arabs were not able to secure an assembly with legislative and executive powers to control immigration and to receive a repudiation of the Balfour Declaration, they rejected the offer of an elected assembly.

Once the League of Nations Council meeting in London on 24 July 1922 passed the Mandate for Palestine, the British government proposed a Palestinian Constitution which established a Legislative Council. Although such a body would have had an Arab majority, the Palestinian Constitution was accepted by the Jewish population. The Arabs adamantly rejected such a plan at a Palestinian Arab Congress in Nablus. Undeterred by the Arab reaction, the British proceeded with elections. The Palestinian Arab Executive decided on a boycott which effectively undermined the Legislative Council. Samuel then sought to reconstitute an Advisory Council and establish an Arab agency. Both of these bodies were similarly rejected by the Arab representatives.

With the fall of the Lloyd George government, the Arabs hoped to influence the new British leadership. However, neither the government of Bonar Law nor any future government had any intention of repudiating the Mandate. As far as the Zionists were concerned, Arab non-cooperation suited their purposes. They had accepted the

Palestine Constitution, and thereby proved to be co-operative partners in the quest to find a solution to the problems of the Middle East. The Arabs, on the other hand, were intractable in their opposition to the creation of a Jewish homeland as envisaged by the Balfour Declaration and the Mandate.

In the last year of Samuel's administration, there was a massive increase in Jewish immigration to Palestine. From 1920 to 1923 approximately 8000 Jews a year had settled in the Holy Land. In 1924 the rate increased to about 13,000. In 1925 it was over 33,000. This increase was due to the political and economic crisis in Poland, the relaxation of Soviet emigration controls, and restrictions on immigration to America. Such an influx of Jewish settlers – referred to as the Fourth Aliyah – resulted in a significant increase of Jews residing in Jerusalem, Haifa and Tel Aviv. Surprisingly, this did not give rise to public demonstrations as had occurred only a few years previously.

With the retirement of Samuel in June 1925 and the appointment of Baron Plumer of Messines as High Commissioner, the British were anxious to ensure that the Mandate was upheld. Among Jews in the diaspora, Plumer's period in office marked a positive step towards settlement; it appeared that the Arab population had accepted the implications of the Balfour Declaration. Within Palestine, however, the Jewish population continued to be aware of Arab hostility towards Jewish settlement. In the Yishuv two opposing approaches to the Arab situation emerged during this period. On the one hand, some Jews believed that some type of reconciliation might be possible. The second approach was of a pragmatic character: with the Yishuv a number of influential Zionists maintained that Arab hostility was inevitable and would eventually lead to armed conflict. The main proponent of such a view was Vladimir Jabotinsky.

Following the massive immigration from Poland and Russia in 1925, relatively few Jews arrived in Palestine. By the end of the decade, there was a change in Whitehall in London: the Conservative government fell and was replaced by a Labour government under Ramsay MacDonald. Britain was now governed by those who had no past links with the Balfour Declaration; in addition the new Colonial Secretary was unsympathetic to the notion of a Jewish national home in Palestine. In June 1929 an agreement was reached that the proposed legislative council would consist of ten Muslims, three Jews and two Christians. The Grand Mufti, however, had other plans. In his view the Holy Places in Palestine were under threat from the Jewish population and he initiated a campaign against the Jews in the mosques and the press. In August, an incident inflamed both Jewish and Arab hatred.

A boy kicked a ball into an Arab garden; in the ensuing fight he was stabbed and killed. After the boy's funeral, a Zionist demonstration took place at the Wall. This was followed by a sermon from the Mufti in the Mosque of Al-Aqsa. Then on 22 and 23 August, large crowds of Arabs made their way to Jerusalem armed with clubs and knives. The Chief of Police in Jerusalem did not have enough men to disarm this mob, and the Jewish community was severely attacked in Jerusalem and later in other Jewish centres.

11

Palestine in the Post-Balfour Era

Just as Christian Zionists supported the Balfour Declaration, they were enthusiastic about the possibilities of the creation of a Jewish homeland in Palestine under the Mandate. Following the massive immigration from Poland and Russia in 1925, relatively few Jews arrived in Palestine. Between 1926 and 1931, the Jewish population increased from 149,640 to 174,606. At the same time, the Arab population increased from 675,000 to 759,000. Yet during these years, Christian Zionists continued to agitate for the restoration of the Jewish people to the land of their ancestors.

Christian Zionists and the Mandate

The Balfour Declaration had been signed by a Christian with deep spiritual commitments to the restoration of the Jews in Palestine. Subsequently the League of Nations, which was composed largely of countries with Christian heritages, endorsed this document. The Mandate itself was designed to wrest the Holy Land from Muslim domination and transfer power to a European Christian power. Previously this transformation had not been accomplished through the Crusades; in modern times, it had been achieved through an international treaty. Like the Balfour Declaration, the Mandate stated that recognition had been given to the motives for reconstituting the Jewish home in Palestine, and it stipulated that Britain was selected as the controlling power.

In a memo to the Paris Peace Conference, Balfour explained that he had no desire to consult the Arab population in achieving this end:

> In Palestine we do not propose even to go through the form of consulting the present inhabitants. Zionism is of far greater import than

the desire and prejudices of the 700,000 Arabs who now inhabit that ancient land. I do not think Zionism will hurt the Arabs, but they will never say they want it.[1]

When Balfour appeared before the House of Lords to state his support for the Zionist cause, he focused on the problems confronting Jews in the modern world:

Zionism is a partial solution to the great and abiding Jewish problem. It deals with the Jewish tragedy, the tyranny and persecution which they have suffered for centuries. They have rowed all their weight in the boat of scientific, intellectual and artistic progress. Christendom must give them the chance of showing whether they can organize a culture in a home where they would be secure from oppression, some local habitation where they can develop the traditions which are peculiarly their own. The Mandate will send a message to every land where the Jewish race has been scattered, a message which will tell them that Christendom is not oblivious of their faith, and that we desire, to the best of our ability, to give them the opportunity of developing in peace and quietness, under British rule, those great gifts which hitherto they have been compelled to bring into fruition in countries which know not their language and belong not to their race.[2]

Balfour's niece, Blanche Dugdale, echoed her uncle's view. Dedicated to Zionist ideals, she attempted to influence British politicians and addressed public meetings. During a crisis in the British administration's dealing with the Zionists, she wrote:

The Zionists have made of Palestine a spiritual home of the Jewish nation, and the country so economically developed that the control of it brings political and strategic rewards as well as obligations to the Mandatory Power, far greater than could be foreseen when the Balfour Declaration gave the Jews the right to restore their ancient land. The Jewish question was one among many which called for action after the last war. When the present war [the Second World War] ends, it will stand foremost among the problems that call for solution. In 1917 certain British statesmen perceived that this must be sought in Palestine. Today it is clear that there alone can it be found. Palestine can provide work and a future for hundreds of thousands, even millions of Jews, who have neither... Even in 1917 the need of the Jews for a homeland was in sharp contrast to the lot of the Arab people, liberated from the Turk, with vast empty territories open for unchallenged expansion.[3]

Even though the United States did not join the League of Nations, it too was committed to the Zionist cause. A Joint Resolution of the

Congress of the United States adopted on 30 June 1922 which was signed by President Harding was prefaced by the following preamble:

> Whereas the Jewish people have for many centuries believed in and yearned for the rebuilding of their ancient homeland; and Whereas owing to the outcome of the World War and their part therein the Jewish people are to be enabled to recreate and reorganize a national home in the land of their fathers, which will give to the House of Israel its long-denied opportunity to re-establish a fruitful Jewish life and culture in the ancient homeland.[4]

Although the British government subsequently had grave reservations about the implementation of the Balfour Declaration, a number of British officers enthusiastically supported the Zionists. Sir Wyndham Deeds, who served as Chief Secretary under the High Commissioner Sir Herbert Samuels, was a Christian who was sympathetic to the plight of the Jews. In his diary, he recorded his reflections about the Zionist cause:

> This question, Zionism, can, I think, almost be called one of the big world questions... Those who do not wish as yet to consider the question of a Jewish government rely on the creation in Palestine of a 'cultural home' for Jews throughout the world. One tangible form which this idea will take will be the creation of a university, but their idea is that Jews throughout the world should look towards Palestine as their spiritual centre and the cradle of their race, thereby making a bond of union between them, and emphasizing the fact that they are a nation and not only a sect.[5]

Another Zionist supporter during this period was Colonel Richard Meinertzhagen, who served as chief political officer in the British post-war administration. Commenting on Zionist aspirations, he wrote:

> I believed in the Old Testament prophecy. I believed that Christianity itself depended on a Jewish Palestine. I believed that a people whose history and tradition went back four thousand unbroken years, a people who gave us the Old Testament, our monotheist religion and Jesus of Nazareth, a people who have contributed so much to art and science – that such people should continue to suffer and be homeless when we [the British] could alleviate that suffering and grant that home, was to me a disgrace to civilization. I am convinced that the fundamental basis of Zionism lies deep-seated in religion. Such an aspect is not so manifest as the political and economic factors which are more apparent than the religious factor.[6]

Meinertzhagen also played an important role in the formulation of the historic message, sent by Emir Feisal the head of the Hedjaz (Hashemite) Delegation to Felix Frankfurter, a senior member of the Zionist delegation at the Paris Peace Conference:

> Dear Mr. Frankfurter,
>
> I want to take this opportunity of my first contact with American Zionists to tell you what I have often been able to say to Dr. Weizmann in the past.
>
> We feel that the Arabs and Jews are cousins in race, have suffered similar oppressions at the hands of powers stronger than themselves, and by a happy coincidence have been able to take the first step towards the attainment of their national ideals together.
>
> People less informed and less responsible than our leaders and yours, ignoring the need for co-operation of the Arabs and Zionists, have been trying to exploit the local difficulties that must necessarily arise in Palestine in the early stages of our movements. Some of them have, I am afraid, misrepresented your aims to the Arab peasantry and our aims to the Jewish peasantry, with the result that interested parties have been able to make capital out of what they call our difference.
>
> I wish to give you my firm conviction that these differences are not on a question of principle but on matters of detail such as must inevitably occur in every contact of neighbouring peoples, and are as easily adjusted by mutual goodwill...
>
> We Arabs, especially the educated among us, look with the deepest sympathy on the Zionist movement. Our deputation here in Paris is fully acquainted with the proposals submitted yesterday by the Zionist Organisation to the Peace Conference, and we regard them as moderate and proper...
>
> I look forward and my people with me look forward to a future in which we will help you and you will help us, so that the countries in which we are mutually interested may once again take their place in the community of civilised peoples of the world.[7]

Another British figure of this period was Josiah Clement Wedgwood who had met the Zion Mule Corps and their commander Joseph Trumpeldor in 1915. Following the British Mandate, he proposed a scheme for the creation of the Jewish national home. At the founding of the Hebrew University, he declared:

> You are going to do something even greater than lay the foundations of a Hebrew University. You are to lay a foundation-stone to convert a race into a nation – more than a nation, an inter-nation. You Jews

come from all corners of the globe. In Palestine you are to set up your own house. See that it is a home where the evils of the old nations be forgotten.[8]

Jews and the Arab Uprising

During this period it looked unlikely that there could ever be a Jewish majority in the land. Added to this difficulty, the Yishuv faced severe economic difficulties in the late 1920s. At the end of the decade an agreement was reached that a proposed legislative council would be established with ten Muslims, three Jews and two Christians.

The Grand Mufti, however, had other plans. In his view the holy places in Palestine were under threat from the Jewish population and he initiated a campaign against the Jews in mosques and the press. Following an incident in which an Arab boy was killed, large crowds of Arab peasants attacked Jews in Jerusalem and other Jewish centres. This hostility between Jews and Arabs led to a reorganization of the Haganah. Supporters of military force emphasized that the Haganah had saved the Jewish communities of Jerusalem, Tel Aviv and Haifa; others were critical of its efforts. As a result, a major restructuring took place. Yet this did not avert a split in its ranks: the political leadership of those who succeeded was furnished by Betar, an activist movement founded in 1923 in Riga, Latvia under the influence of Vladimir Jabotinsky.

In 1931 a group of Haganah members left the organization in protest against its policies and joined forces with Betar in order to create a more militant armed underground organization, the Irgun. The first Betar congress took place in 1931 in Danzig, where Jabotinsky was elected head of the movement. Rejecting the Histadrut and Haganah policy of self-restraint, Betar adopted retaliation as its strategy in dealing with the Arabs. In the Arab world, the events of 1929 led to increased support for the Mufti. In Palestine and elsewhere the Grand Mufti was perceived as the leading figure in the struggle against the Zionist threat.

In August 1929 the first Royal Commission determined that the attacks on the Jewish population were not premeditated. Although it criticized the Grand Mufti for not doing more to deter the mobs, it did not conclude that he was responsible for the atrocities that took place. A second Royal Commission applied the criterion of absorptive capacity of the country to restrict immigration. Palestine, it was believed, was not able to absorb more than 50,000 more Jewish immigrants. In a report to the Permanent Mandates Commission of the League of Nations, the British government argued that the lack of any self-government in Palestine did not result from a lack of goodwill on the part of the Mandatory power. Subsequently the conclusions of these reports were incorporated into a White Paper published on 21 October 1930 which proposed the creation of a legislative council.

Concerned about the implications of governmental policy, Weizmann resigned as president of the Zionist Organization; this decision highlighted his view that the Balfour Declaration had been betrayed by the British. Even though the British Prime Minister subsequently wrote to Weizmann emphasizing that the Mandate had an obligation to facilitate Jewish immigration to Palestine, many Zionists were not satisfied. From 1933 the Zionists and the Nazis co-operated in the emigration of Jews from Nazi Germany. In Palestine, Jabotinsky and his colleagues denounced such arrangements, and at the Eighteenth Zionist Congress held in Prague in the summer of 1933 Jabotinsky called for a worldwide boycott of Germany.

During this period the immigration policy of the Mandatory power was relatively liberal, but the number of those without capital who were allowed to immigrate was severely restricted. Nonetheless, between 1933 and 1939 a significant amount of Jewish capital was imported into the country. As a result of this influx of new immigrants, the Arab population became increasingly agitated. Not only were the Jews viewed as enemies of the Arab cause, but the British also came under attack. In October 1933 anti-British disturbances broke out in Jaffa, Nablus, Haifa and Jerusalem. During this period the Jews, too, rebelled against British rule. The Nineteenth Zionist Congress in Lucerne in 1935 rejected the notion of a legislative council in Palestine.

In Palestine itself, the conflict between Jews and Arabs intensified. In a terrorist operation, Sheikh Izz al-Din al-Qassam and his band were surrounded and killed. As a martyr of the Arab cause, al-Qassam's death put pressure on Hajj Amin to launch a Muslim revolt. On 15 April a group of armed Arabs took two Jews off a bus in the Nablus mountains and killed them. Several days later members of the nationalist Haganah murdered two Arabs in retaliation. Following these events, Arab demonstrations took place in Jaffa, Nablus and elsewhere.

The shift from an anti-Jewish to an anti-British stance was not a simple option for Hajj Amin. If he complied with this policy, he risked losing his power as head of the supreme Muslim Council, which was appointed by the British. However, if he failed to comply, he might forfeit his prestige as leader of Muslim nationalism. As a consequence, he acceded to the demands of the young militants by becoming head of the Higher Arab Committee. Because this was a lawful body, such a position was reconcilable with his leadership of the Supreme Muslim Council.

Throughout June the Supreme Muslim Council encouraged Muslims to join in this rebellion. The Jews, they stated, aimed at reconstructing a Jewish Temple in the place of the Mosque of al-Aqsa. Having refused Muslim demands, Britain was perceived as supporting the Jewish people in this quest. Throughout the summer the revolt spread, and attacks took place along the roads and against the Haifa-Lyddah railway line. The first conflict between British troops and Arab forces occurred near Tulkarm. During the next two months, clashes continued and were accompanied by a general strike. Although British forces defended themselves, there was no concerted attempt to suppress the revolt. Any political solution to this conflict required concessions to Arab demands. During this period three Arab princes, Abdul Aziz Ibn Saud, King of Saudi Arabia, Ghazi, King of Iraq, and Abdullah of Transjordan became involved in the Mandatory government. All three detested Zionism and saw that personal political gains could be made from their participation in the affairs of Palestine.

During this period the British created the Peel Commission, which was empowered to look into the roots of the Palestinian question. In 1936 this Commission arrived in Palestine and held 66 meetings, which were largely dominated by Jewish evidence, since the Arabs boycotted most of the proceedings. In July 1937 the Commission published its report in which it declared that the Palestinian problem was insoluble. It arose within the narrow bounds of a small country in which approximately one million Arabs were in conflict with 40,000 Jews. Since in its view neither group could justify rule over all of Palestine, the Commission concluded that the country should be partitioned.

In this light the Commission recommended that the Mandate for Palestine should be terminated and replaced by a Treaty System, and a new Mandate for the holy places be established. Further, it suggested that a Treaty of Alliance should be negotiated between the government and Transjordan, and that the Zionist organization should be responsible for a Jewish state. The Commission assigned to the Jewish state a coastal strip from the south of Jaffa to the north of Gaza along with Galilee from the sea to the Syrian border. Jerusalem, with a corridor to the sea, was to be placed under the new Mandate. The remainder of the country was to be the new Arab state.

Even though this scheme was endorsed by the British government, it was strongly opposed by the Palestinian Arabs. On the Jewish side, Weizmann and Ben-Gurion favoured the principle of partition because it would have created a Jewish homeland. Under their influence, the Twentieth Zionist Congress held in Zurich in August 1937 approved the plan, and the Zionist Executive was authorized to negotiate with the Mandatory power for the purpose of ascertaining the British terms for the proposed establishment of a Jewish national home.

In the summer of 1937 the Arab revolt, which had been suspended during the deliberations of the Peel Commission, was renewed following meetings of nationalists in Syria. Eventually a full-scale Arab uprising occurred which was severely repressed by the British government. At this time steps were taken towards abandoning the partition plan. In December 1937, the Prime Minister, Neville Chamberlain, supported the Foreign Office, which opposed partition as well as the creation of a Jewish state. Despite such a shift in policy, the British sought the support of the Yishuv in repressing the Arab uprising.

In Palestine a section of Jewish youth joined the National Military Organization, Irgun Tzevai Leumi, which was opposed to the Haganah policy of self-restraint. In June 1938 the British hanged a young Revisionist for attacking an Arab bus; in response, the Irgun exploded land mines in Haifa. This act was condemned by both Zionist and Haganah leaders. On 17 September 1938 partition was reaffirmed by the League of Nations, and the British appeared to be committed to the Jewish state because of their repression of the Arab revolt. Nonetheless, in November the British government officially confirmed its intention to abandon the policy of partition and invited the governments of Iraq and Egypt to prepare for a London conference on the future of Palestine.

This gathering was held in St James' Palace and was attended by representatives of five Arab countries as well as a Palestinian delegation, the Zionist Executive and the British. On 17 March 1939 the conference ended without any agreement between the various parties. In May 1939 a further White Paper was published which ruled out partition and the creation of a Jewish state. However, the White Paper decreed that a Palestine state be established within ten years, and that after five years Jewish immigration would not be allowed unless approved by the Palestinian Arabs. Despite this anti-Jewish bias, the White Paper allowed for 75,000 more Jews to be allowed to settle in Palestine within a five-year period, and maintained that the independence of a Palestinian state depended on adequate safeguards for the Jewish community.

In effect, the White Paper endorsed a double veto. The Arabs were empowered to block the growth of the Jewish national home, whereas the Jews could prevent the Arabs from having an independent state. Anxious to avert this change in policy, the Jews contested the legality of the White Paper. In its report to the Council of the League, the Permanent Mandates Commission stated that the White Paper was not in accord with the interpretation that the Commission had placed upon the Palestine Mandate. Such a change of policy was profoundly disturbing to the Yishuv. The Zionists perceived that Britain had abandoned the Balfour Declaration. For many Zionists, it had become clear that force was now required to oppose the White Paper.

Christian Zionists in the Post-Balfour Era

Following the Balfour Declaration, the LJS Committee sent its secretary, Mr Gill, to oversee the reconstruction of the LJS work in Palestine. During this period, there was considerable instability in the country. Nonetheless, the LJS was confident about the future. At the LJS annual meeting in 1919 the Bishop of Armagh stated:

> No reader of prophecy, I think, can fail to see that God is working out in our time the fulfilment of the latter-day promises regarding the Jews...
>
> I believe that, in the work of God we are doing for the London Jews Society, we are preparing for the great future that God has for the Jews, when from Jerusalem shall go forth the word of the Lord, when the Jews shall be great ministers to win those who are still left upon the earth, when they will be God's great missionaries.[9]

When Britain was awarded a Mandate for Palestine in 1920, the LJS (which was then called the Church's Mission to the Jews, CMJ) was enthusiastic:

> As citizens of the Empire we are concerned with the political responsibilities entrusted to Great Britain in Palestine and Mesopotamia, and are thankful beyond measure that, in the Providence of God, our nation has been chosen for preparing the Holy Land for the great future that lies before it...
>
> We regard the incorporation of the Balfour Declaration of 1917 in the Peace Treaty with Turkey... as one of the most wonderful instances on record of the working out of God's promises to that nation that He loves with an everlasting love.[10]

Following the appointment of Sir Herbert Samuel as High Commissioner, the Zionists pressed on with plans for further immigration. According to the CMJ:

Other young Jews who had received a fair secular education in Poland and other European countries have been induced by Zionist acquaintances to come to Palestine. Full of enthusiasm and 'nationalist' ideas, they hoped to find their fortunes here, but on arrival most of them were set to work at road building or swamp drainage, work for which they were physically unfit. In consequence of this many succumbed to the effects of the climate, hard work, poor food and other discomforts, and when the Zionist funds became low and their pay decreased, they wanted to be sent home. Being refused their return fare, and also being unable to obtain permits from the authorities for leaving the country, a great many applied to the Mission for help to get permits and for the means of travelling, promising, of their own principle of free-will, to place themselves under Christian instruction with a view to baptism – if this help were granted.[11]

With thousands of Jews arriving in Palestine during the Third Aliyah, the Jewish community in Palestine became increasingly agitated about missionary activity. A more serious threat, however, was the attitude of the Arab population in Palestine. With the appointment of Hajj Amin al-Husseini as Grand Mufti, the Arab community was determined that drastic measures be taken against the Jews. Alarmed by this prospect, the CMJ declared:

The real source of the trouble must be sought in the attitude of unbending and implacable hostility towards the realization of the aspirations of Zionism, adopted by the Third Arab Palestine Congress held at Haifa a couple of months ago. The remarkable memorandum, presented to Mr Winston Churchill by a deputation of that Congress, and drawn up by a skilful hand, breathes defiance in every line, and protests against the handing over of Palestine to the Jews on legal, moral, historical, economic and political grounds.[12]

Undeterred by Arab resistance, the CMJ commented:

The 'Return' of the Jews to Palestine will... have to proceed at a somewhat slower tempo, but this can only prove a blessing in disguise, for the tragic occurrences of the last few months have encouraged the enemies of Zionism to come out into the open, and they are more numerous than the Jews may have been aware of.[13]

Concerned about these events, the Society reaffirmed its belief in the restoration of the Jews despite the attitude of a number of leading Christians in the country including Bishop MacInnes, who was sympathetic to the Arab cause.

Although the activities of the CMJ continued during this period, the opposition of the Grand Mufti caused considerable consternation. These events evoked a theological interpretation among evangelical Christians. According to Rev. Maxwell:

Years ago some of us were taught and brought up to believe that Ezekiel, chapters 36, 37 and 38 were an outline of the history of what might be called 'modern Zionism', and were led to believe that the Jewish people would be brought back in their thousands to Palestine, where they would acquire not only land but a semblance of power also. 'The king of the north' – whatever interpretation might be put upon that phrase – would then resent this power in the hands of the Jews and say, 'I will go up to the land of unwalled villages, I will go to them that are at rest, that dwell safely [confidently], all of them dwelling without walls, and having neither bars nor gates, to take a spoil, to turn [mine] hand upon the desolate places that are now inhabited, and upon the people that are gathered out of the nations...'

Thus would begin the 'time of Jacob's trouble', which would usher in the battle of Armageddon. In their distress the people would then turn unto the Lord once more, and call upon Him for help in their extremity. And the result would be a national conversion for which the missionary work of the past century had been preparing, by sowing the seeds of truth, and by gathering out the 'remnant' which was to be saved during that period.

Whether this interpretation is correct or not, there is no denying the fact that many of the features portrayed in Ezekiel 38 bear a very striking resemblance to conditions in Palestine today.[14]

Following the publication of a White Paper in 1930 which restricted Jewish immigration, the CMJ expressed its deep disfavour of British policy:

It is impossible to follow political reasoning and therefore it is incomprehensible to us why the official interpretation of Jewish national home should not have been made clear a long time ago... In the midst of the turmoil, all those of us who hold clear the objects of our Society, can take comfort in the knowledge that the return of the Jews to the Holy Land is assured as in the purposes of Almighty God for the World. Time has no meaning to Him, the hindrances and obstacles of men are always utterly powerless against those purposes.[15]

Supportive of the Jewish cause, the CMJ stressed that Arab opposition to the creation of a Jewish homeland was misguided:

> It may well be... that this 'Arab' cry is simply a convenient slogan with which to rally a Pan-Islamic crusade. A Jewish state in Palestine is the only obstacle to an Arab state stretching from Persia to the Red Sea and the Mediterranean. Great Britain has helped to build and secure three Arab kingdoms, covering many thousands of square miles. It can hardly be regarded as an injustice if she seeks to secure for a homeless race equal rights with the Arab in a little land no bigger than Yorkshire. It is altogether ignored by British sympathizers with Arab claims that Palestine is the property of the Jew by the title deeds bestowed by the highest authority the Christian recognises (Genesis 13:15; 18:18; 17:8). The Jew, moreover, has been domiciled in the land and exercised paramount authority over it for a longer period than any other people.[16]

When the Peel Commission arrived in Palestine in November, 1936, Bishop Brown, representing St. George's, issued a statement negating any biblical connection with Palestine – such a view was rejected by CMJ, which continued its commitment to the creation of a Jewish homeland. Despite the Peel Commission's recommendations that a Jewish state be created in Palestine, the British government issued a White Paper in 1939 which demanded a cessation of Jewish land purchase and restricted Jewish immigration. Such legislation constituted the most serious threat to the aspirations of Christian Zionists in the Holy Land.

12

Christian and Jewish
Support for a Jewish State

During this period of unrest, a number of Christian supporters of the
Jewish return to Palestine were anxious to aid the Jewish community.
Despite British opposition, Jews in Palestine were determined to press
forward with their Zionist plans. Even though the Yishuv was deeply
divided, the aspiration to create a Jewish state remained a primary
goal. In the United States, both American politicians and Christian
Zionists continued to agitate for the return of the Jewish people to
the Holy Land.

Christian Zionists and the Arab Revolt

Pre-eminent among these figures was Captain Charles Orde Wingate,
who arrived in Palestine in 1936. Assigned to Jerusalem as an intelligence officer, he witnessed a new wave of Arab terror. Sympathetic to
the Zionist cause, he told a prominent Jew in Haifa, David Hacohen,
that he would do everything in his power to help the Jews:

> This is the cause of your survival. I count it as my privilege to help
> you fight your battle. To that purpose I want to devote my life. I believe
> that the very existence of mankind is justified when it is based on the
> moral foundation of the Bible. Whoever dares lift a hand against you
> and your enterprise here should be fought against. Whether it is
> jealousy, ignorance or perverted doctrine such as have made your
> neighbours rise against you, or 'politics' which make some of my
> countrymen support them, I shall fight with you against any of these
> influences.[1]

After visiting various Jewish villages, Wingate saw that their methods
of defence were inadequate. He maintained that instead of simply
defending their property from attack, the Jews should go out on

offensive forays. Initially the Jewish commanders rejected his recommendations, but as Arab attacks increased, they accepted the need for proactive assault. Wingate then set about training special units known as the Special Night Squads. In 1939 Wingate left Palestine and several parties were held in his honour. At one he said in Hebrew:

> I am sent away from you and the country I love. I suppose you know why. I am transferred because we are too great friends. They want to hurt me and you. I promise you that I will come back, and if I cannot do it the regular way, I shall return as a refugee.[2]

Another figure of this period was Colonel Clement Wedgewood. While serving on the Gallipoli front, he met fighters from the Zion Mule Corps including Joseph Trumpeldor. Later he produced a plan for the creation of the Jewish national home, which was to join other dominions of the British Empire. He initially took part in the political efforts which resulted in the Balfour Declaration and later was among those who influenced US President Wilson's delegate at the Versailles Peace Conference to adopt a position favourable to Zionism. Later he travelled on Zionist missions. Throughout the period of the Mandate, he was an active supporter of Zionist ideals. When the Hebrew University was established, he declared:

> You are going to do something even greater than lay the foundation of a Hebrew University. You are to lay a foundation-stone to convert a race into a nation – more than a nation, an inter-nation. You Jews come from all corners of the globe. In Palestine you are to set up your own house. See that it is a home where the evils of all the old nations will be forgotten; where centuries of intolerance will be ended in centuries of tolerance.[2]

Following the publication of the White Paper of 1939, he advocated a policy of civil disobedience: Jews in Palestine, he believed, should refuse to recognize the jurisdiction of British courts in Palestine, refuse to pay taxes, and demonstrate against illegal immigration.

Other British figures of this period who supported the Zionist cause included Leopold Amery, who voted against the White Paper of 1939, Major Ormsby-Gore, who helped draft the Balfour Declaration and later prepared a report for the partition of Palestine after the 1936 Arab riots, and Sir Stafford Cripps who joined those who supported the partition plan. Cripps' proposal was that there be two autonomous states in Palestine, established within a joint Palestine Federation. The grandson of Edward Cazalet, who had espoused the idea of Jewish settlements along a railroad to be built through Syria and Iraq in 1879, was Victor Alexander Cazalet, a Conservative member of Parliament who served as the chairman of the Pro-Palestine Committee. A friend of Chaim Weizmann, he later persuaded Lord Halifax to relax his policy towards refugees who were escaping from Nazi Germany.

Winston Churchill also favoured the return of Jews to Palestine. As early as 1920 he declared that no thoughtful person can doubt the fact that the Jews are the most remarkable race on earth. Sympathetic to Zionism, he issued the White Paper of 1922 that separated Trans-Jordan from Palestine and created the desert Emirate of the Hashemites; this was the first partition of the Holy Land. In 1939 he opposed the White Paper restrictions. In the House of Lords, the Archbishop of Canterbury similarly expressed deep misgivings:

> I venture to think that it was precisely from this permanent minority status that they [the Jews] had hoped to escape. They had hoped that in one place on this earth this people of something like sixteen and a half million ought to have a sphere of their own, where they could show what was in them, and where they could be masters of their own destiny and affairs, and where there could be a centre of Jewish life, culture and influence throughout the world. If they have, for obvious reasons, thrown very special emphasis on numbers, I believe that in their hearts what Zionists have desired more than anything is that they should get their freedom from this minority status. Now, I have to repeat, they are given the prospect that the minority status will be permanent, and whatever a National Home may have meant... it surely cannot have meant that. It surely must have meant that somewhere in Palestine there would be a place where the Jews would be able to fulfil their aspirations in some territory in which they had some autonomous control.[4]

In the United States, leading figures also expressed sympathy for the Zionist cause. During British rule in Palestine, President Woodrow Wilson declared:

> I welcome an opportunity to express... satisfaction... in progress... since the Declaration of Mr. Balfour on... the establishment in Palestine of a National Home for the Jewish people, and his promise that the British Government would use its best endeavours to facilitate the achievement of that object.[5]

In 1921 President Warren Harding stated: 'It is impossible for one who has studied the services of the Hebrew people, to avoid the fact that they will one day be restored to their historic national home and there enter on a new and yet greater phase of their contribution to the advance of humanity'[6] Again, in 1924 President Coolidge expressed support for the creation of a Jewish homeland:

> I have... many times reiterated my interest in this great movement... but I am nevertheless glad... to express again my sympathy with the deep and intense longing which finds such fine expression in the Jewish National Homeland in Palestine.[7]

When Palestine was conquered from the Turks and the National Home became a possibility, President Herbert Hoover stated:

> I have watched with genuine admiration the steady and unmistakable progress made in the rehabilitation of Palestine which, desolate for centuries, is now renewing its youth and vitality through the enthusiasm, hard work, and self-sacrifice of the Jewish pioneers who toil there in a spirit of peace and social-justice... this cause... merits the sympathy and moral encouragement of everyone.[8]

In the same year that Hitler rose to power in Germany, President Franklin Delano Roosevelt declared:

> It is hardly necessary for me to reiterate the interest with which I have followed the work... toward assisting in the establishment in Palestine of a National Home for the Jewish People... the Jews in the United States may well feel proud of the part they have played in the rebirth and upbuilding of the Holy Land.[9]

The Jewish State

The 1930s witnessed various divisions within the Zionist ranks. In 1931 Weizmann was forced to give up the presidency of the World Zionist Congress owing to pressure from the Mizrahi. In the same year elections to the Zionist Assembly resulted in a split between Mapai (the Labour Party), the Revisionists, and Mizrahi (the Religious Party). In the military sphere the Revisionists, Mizrahi and other Zionists split from the Haganah to form Irgun. At this time the Revisionists were condemned by Mapai as fascists. On 16 June 1933 the head of the Political Department of the Jewish Agency, Chaim Arlosoroff, was murdered; two extreme Revisionists were arrested, charged with murder, but later acquitted. Yet despite such internal divisions, after the outbreak of war in 1939 the establishment of a Jewish state became the central concern of all Zionists.

Although the Jews supported the allies, Jewry was committed to overturning British policy as enshrined in the 1939 White Paper. During this period the British attempted to prevent illegal immigrants from landing in Palestine: if their ships got through they were captured and deported. In November 1940 the *Patria*, which was about to set sail for Mauritius carrying 1700 deportees, was sabotaged by the Haganah; it sank in Haifa Bay with the loss of 250 refugees. Two years later the *Struma*, a refugee ship from Romania, was refused landing permission, turned back by the Turks, and sunk in the Black Sea with the death of 770 passengers. Such events, however, did not alter Britain's determination to prevent the entry of illegal immigrants.

In 1943 Menahem Begin, formerly chief of Betar, took control of the Revisionist military arm, the Irgun. With 600 agents under his control, he blew up various British buildings. On 6 November 1944 the ultra-extreme group, the Stern Gang, which had broken away from the Irgun, murdered the British Minister for Middle Eastern Affairs. Outraged by this act, the Haganah launched a campaign against both the Sternists and the Irgun. While he was fighting the British and other Jews, Begin organized a powerful underground force in the belief that the Haganah would eventually join him in attacking the British. In 1945 a united Jewish Resistance movement was created which embraced the various Jewish military forces, and on 31 October it began blowing up railways. In retaliation the British made a raid on the Jewish Agency on 29 June 1946, arresting 2718 Jews. Begin, however, persuaded the Haganah to blow up the King David Hotel where a segment of the British administration was located. When Weizmann heard of this plan he was incensed, and the Haganah was ordered to desist. Begin refused, and on 22 July 1946 the explosion took place, killing 27 British, 41 Arabs, 17 Jews and 5 others. In consequence the Haganah commander Moshe Sneh resigned, and the resistance movement divided. The British then proposed a tripartite plan of partition which was rejected by both Jews and Arabs. Exasperated by this conflict, the British Foreign Secretary, Ernest Bevin, declared he was handing over this dispute to the United Nations.

Despite this decision, Begin continued with his campaign of terror, insisting on the right of the Irgun to retaliate against the British. In April 1947 after three members of the Irgun were convicted and hanged for destroying the Acre prison fortress, Begin ordered that two British sergeants be hanged. Such an act of revenge provoked worldwide condemnation, and anti-Jewish riots took place throughout Britain. These incidents encouraged the British to leave Palestine as soon as possible, and also coincided with the succession of Harry S. Truman as President of the United States. Sympathetic to the Jewish cause and anxious for the support of American Jewry in the

1948 election, Truman pressed for the creation of a Jewish state. In May 1947 the Palestinian question came before the United Nations, and a special committee was authorized to formulate a plan for the future of the country. The minority recommended a binational state, but the majority suggested that there be both an Arab and a Jewish state as well as an international zone in Jerusalem. On 29 November this recommendation was endorsed by the General Assembly.

After this decision was taken, the Arabs began to attack Jewish settlements. Although the Jewish commanders were determined to repel this assault, their resources were not considerable compared with the Arab side. The Haganah had 17,600 rifles, 2700 sten guns, about 1000 machine guns, and between 20,000–43,000 men in various stages of training. The Arabs on the other hand had a sizeable liberation army as well as the regular forces of the Arab states including 10,000 Egyptians, 7000 Syrians, 3000 Iraqis and 3000 Lebanese as well as 4500 soldiers from the Arab Legion of Transjordan. By March 1948 over 1200 Jews were killed; in April, Ben Gurion ordered the Haganah to link the Jewish enclaves and consolidate as much territory as possible under the United Nations plan. Jewish forces then occupied Haifa, opened up the route to Tiberias and eastern Galilee, and captured Safed, Jaffa, and Acre. On 14 May Ben Gurion read out the Scroll of Independence in the Tel Aviv Museum:

> The Land of Israel was the birthplace of the Jewish people. Here their spiritual, religious and national identity was formed. Here they have achieved independence and created a culture of national and universal significance. Here they wrote and gave the Bible to the world.
>
> Exiled from Palestine, the Jewish people remained faithful to it in all the countries of their dispersion, never ceasing to pray and hope for their return and the restoration of their national freedom.
>
> Impelled by this historic association, Jews strove throughout the centuries to go back to the land of their fathers and regain their Statehood. In recent decades they returned in their masses. They reclaimed the wilderness, revived their language, built cities and villages and established a vigorous and ever-growing community, with its own economic and cultural life. They sought peace yet were prepared to defend themselves. They brought the blessings of progress to all inhabitants of the country.
>
> In the year 1897 the First Zionist Congress, inspired by Theodor Herzl's vision of the Jewish State, proclaimed the right of the Jewish people to national revival in their own country. This right was acknowledged by the Balfour Declaration of 2 November 1917, and reaffirmed by the Mandate of the League of Nations, which gave

explicit international recognition to the historic connection of the Jewish people with Palestine and their right to reconstitute their national home.

The Nazi holocaust, which engulfed millions of Jews in Europe, proved anew the urgency of the re-establisment of the Jewish State, which would solve the problem of Jewish homelessness by opening the gates to all Jews and lifting the Jewish people to equality in the family of nations...

On 29 November 1947 the General Assembly of the United Nations adopted a Resolution for the establishment of an independent Jewish State in Palestine, and called upon inhabitants of the country to take such steps as may be necessary on their part to put the plan into effect.

This recognition by the United Nations of the right of the Jewish people to establish their independent state may not be revoked. It is, moreover, the self-evident right of the Jewish people to be a nation, like all other nations, in its own sovereign state.

Accordingly, we the members of the National Council, representing the Jewish people in Palestine and the Zionist movement of the world, met together in a solemn assembly today, the day of the termination of the British Mandate for Palestine and by virtue of the national and historic right of the Jewish people and of the resolution of the General Assembly of the United Nations, hereby proclaim the establishment of the Jewish State in Palestine, to be called Israel.[10]

American Christian Zionists and the United Nations

Alongside politicians who supported Zionism, a number of American Christians had shown their support of a National Home in Palestine. Following the Arab riots of 1929, a pro-Palestine Federation was established which published the *Pro-Palestine Herald*. Explaining its aims, this organization stated:

As a result of the Arab riots in Palestine in 1929, and the subsequent assault upon the rights of the Jewish people contained in the Mandate, through the Passfield White Paper, leading Christian Americans, Ministers of the Gospel, College Professors, professional men and eminent public figures formed the Pro-Palestine Federation of America. This organization, embodying the finest Christian principles, is dedicated to the task of encouraging closer co-operation between Jew and Gentile, and also to the defence of the Jewish National Home as defined in the Mandate for Palestine.[11]

Subsequently a larger group, the American Palestine Committee was launched in January 1932 which included a number of senators and members of the House of Representatives as well as senior officials in the Administration. Meanwhile the Pro-Palestine Federation continued its activities, and later in May 1936 it sent a message to the British Prime Minister in the name of concerned American Christians requesting that Jews from Nazi Germany be allowed to settle in Palestine. This document expressed unwavering support for the creation of a Jewish National Home and stressed that the restoration of Jews in the Holy Land was a central goal in the struggle for a better world and humanity.

During the same year the Pro-Palestine Federation convened an American Christian Conference in New York which was sponsored by State governors, university presidents, senators and clergy. This Pro-Palestine body continued its support of Jewish settlement throughout the 1930s and 1940s and held a number of meetings during the last years of the Mandate which endorsed Zionist demands for Jewish immigration to Palestine. In 1940 the American Palestine Committee was renewed. Within two years its membership included over two-thirds of the US Senate as well as numerous members of the House of Representatives. This body defined itself as a vehicle for the expression of the sympathy and goodwill of Christian America for the movement to re-establish the Jewish National Home in Palestine.

With the entry of the United States into the Second World War, the Zionists' movement began to consider ways of safeguarding Zionists aims. It was believed that Britain's involvement in the Middle East would be subject to increasing American influence. It was imperative, therefore, to ensure that the voice of the Zionist movement would be heard in the United States. In pursuit of this aim, a Zionist Conference was held at the Biltmore Hotel in New York to rally gentile support in the United States. On the 25th anniversary of the Balfour Declaration, the American Palestine Committee issued a declaration signed by 68 Senators and 193 Representatives:

> Twenty-five years ago the British Government issued the Balfour Declaration pledging itself to facilitate the establishment of a National Home for the Jewish people in Palestine. The Declaration was published to the world with the approval of the other powers allied with Great Britain in the World War, and with the encouragement and support of the Government of the United States. It was written into the Peace Treaty with the aid and approval of President Wilson who publicly expressed his confidence that the purposes of the Declaration would be fulfilled... The Balfour Declaration was justly hailed

throughout the world as an act of historic reparation, and as a charter of freedom for the Jewish people. It was designed to open the gates of Palestine, to homeless and harassed multitudes and to pave the way for the establishment of a Jewish Commonwealth.

The reasons which, twenty-five years ago, led the American people and the Government of the United States to favour the cause of the Jewish National Home restoration in Palestine are still valid today... We, therefore, take this occasion... to record our continued interest in and support of the purposes and principles which it embodies. We wish to send a message of hope and cheer to those in Palestine who are confronting the common enemy with courage and fortitude... Faced as we are by the fact that the Nazi government in its Jewish policy is intending to exterminate a whole people, we declare that, when the war is over, it shall be the common purpose of civilized mankind to right this cruel wrong insofar as may lie in our power.[12]

During this period the Christian Council on Palestine was formed, composed of Christian clergy. Their aim was to enlist the aid of ministers so that the lay constituency of the Churches would be urged to action on the problems affecting Palestine. According to Reinhold Niebuhr of the Union Theological Seminary, who was a member of the Council, Jewish claims should be satisfied by compensating the Arabs in a total settlement of the Middle East situation. At the first meeting of the Council, the Methodist Bishop of New York, Francis J. McConnell, called for continued Jewish immigration to Palestine. In March 1944 a Christian National Conference was called in Washington which adopted a number of resolutions, including the need for the reconstitution of Palestine by the Jewish people. The following year an International Christian Conference for Palestine took place in Washington which urged Jewish immigration to Palestine, the repeal of British land purchase laws, and the establishment of a Jewish state. After the war an Anglo-American Committee of Inquiry was created to examine the matter of Jewish refugees in Europe. In his testimony to the Committee Dr Daniel A. Poling, representing the Christian Council on Palestine, stated:

> Christians believe overwhelmingly – 882,000,000 as of the latest reports – that Palestine was divinely selected as the site of the Jewish Nation and that the continuance of that site of Jewish culture, philosophy and idealism under the protection of national status would meet with divine blessing and approval.[13]

In 1946 the American Palestine Committee and the Christian Council on Palestine merged, forming the American Christian Palestine Committee. From 1946 to 1948 it combated the White Paper policy of 1939 and agitated for the admission of holocaust survivors to Palestine and the need to mobilize Christian opinion in support of Jewish settlement in the Holy Land.

When on 29 November 1947 the United Nations voted in favour of a partition plan for Palestine, and the State of Israel was proclaimed on 14 May 1948, this was followed by Israel's request to become a member of the United Nations, and a number of delegates from Christian countries expressed their support. Colombia's Urdaneta Arbelaez, for example, declared in the Security Council:

> Until the question of the existence of the State of Israel is cleared up, the struggle will be fiercer every day and mediation will be more difficult. ... I firmly believe that once the question of the existence of the State of Israel is removed and Israel is accepted as a legal entity by the Arab countries, a solution will be enormously facilitated and we shall open the way to a friendly settlement between both peoples.[14]

Representing France in the United Nations, Mr Chauvel expressed his support for this proposal:

> A solemn hour is about to strike, an hour which will crown a long wait, a long patience, a great courage and a high hope. At this time it is impossible not to think of all those who, in the course of the terrible years of war, and even before the war, suffered the most terrible persecutions at the hands of the totalitarian regimes, and France, for its part, cannot forget the ancient and strong links which connect France with the countries of the Middle East.[15]

Speaking on behalf of Poland, Mr Drohojowski stated:

> Poland had actively assisted the Jews in their aspirations for a national home but also for full statehood. The Poles and the Jews had been associated for a thousand years; they owed much to each other, they had suffered together, and many Jews had suffered from racial hatred... Poland supported the cause of Israel without mental reservations because it believed that the new state had all the possibilities of becoming a useful member of the family of nations.[16]

Israel was admitted to the United Nations on 11 May 1949, and once he took his seat in the Assembly, Moshe Sharret, representing Israel, mounted the rostrum and declared:

This is, indeed, a great moment for the State of Israel. It is a great moment for the Jewish people throughout the world. One is awed by the responsibility it entails. One is uplifted by the vision it reveals for the future. The admission of Israel to this Assembly is the consummation of a people's transition from political anonymity to clear identity; from inferior to equal status; from mere passive protest to active responsibility; from exclusion to membership of the family of nations.[17]

13
Arabs, Jews and
Christian Zionists

Despite the opposition of Arab Christians to the creation of a Jewish homeland, Christian Zionists in Palestine pressed for the restoration of the Jewish people in their ancestral land. While Christian Zionists pursued their aims in Palestine, American Christian figures continued to be preoccupied with theological speculation. Although the United Nations had authorized partition of Palestine, the Arab world refused to accept that a Jewish homeland should be established in the Holy Land.

Christian Missionaries

When Prime Minister Clement Attlee became Prime Minister after the elections of July 1945, Britain gave serious attention to the situation in Palestine. Anxious not to alienate the Arabs, the government continued to oppose Jewish immigration to Palestine. In retaliation, the Irgun and the Stern Gang joined the Haganah in opposition to British rule in the Holy Land. To deal with the situation, Attlee proposed the formation of a joint Anglo-American Commission to investigate the situation in Palestine.

In Palestine itself, some Arab Christians were sympathetic to individual Hebrew Christians, but there was universal opposition to the creation of a Jewish National Home. In his statement to the Commission, however, the Anglican Bishop of Jerusalem adopted a middle line. Although he was sympathetic to Jewish suffering, he refused to accept any connection between Jewish restoration and the fulfilment of biblical prophecy:

> There is a not uncommon tendency today, both in England and in America, to base large Zionist claims on the Old Testament history

and prophecies, and thereby to win support from many Christians whose respect for the Bible is perhaps greater than their understanding of it... The Christian doctrine of the New Testament is that the new spiritual Israel of the Christian Church, with its descent by the spiritual birth of baptism, is the sole heir to the promises themselves also spiritualized, which had been forfeited by the old Israel after the flesh, with its descent by human generations.[1]

As violence erupted in Palestine, the CMJ was enmeshed in the conflict. In August 1946 the British police took over Immanuel House, which was located near Arab Jaffa and Jewish Tel Aviv, and the CMJ had to move to the former German consulate. In Jerusalem the Society's property was also located in a strategic position, and the former Boys' School which had become the Jerusalem Hospital was the scene of an attack by Jewish forces on 30 November 1946. In January 1947 the British authorities decided to evacuate all British families and non-essential personnel; some CMJ staff decided to leave, but a number remained. During this period a number of Hebrew Christians were kidnapped and interrogated. One of those kidnapped, Peter Immanuel, gave an account of this ordeal: he was taken to a house, questioned for several hours and accused of being an agent of the British. In response he explained that the Society was not a political agency but was engaged in missionary work.

When the United Nations voted for partition on 29 November 1947, members of the CMJ were overjoyed. Hannah Hurnard, a worker at CMJ, for example, noted:

> Advent Sunday, November 30 1947, was a memorable day in the history of Jerusalem. We were wakened in the middle of the night by sounds of revelry. The whole of the Jewish Quarter of Jerusalem seemed to have turned out into the streets by 1:30 am shouting and cheering... Was not this very scene of rejoicing a sign and promise that His Advent must be near? First a restored Israel, and then the Coming of their King.[2]

Once Jews were under siege from their Arab neighbours, it became increasingly difficult for CMJ missionaries and their flock. Joseph Hirschfeld, a Hebrew Christian, for example, was abducted near Jaffa Gate by an Arab mob. When he protested that he was a Christian, the Arabs were furious and began to beat him. Eventually they stood him against a wall and shot him. One bullet grazed his head, another his thigh and a third his leg. He fell to the ground and suddenly jumped up and headed for Christ Church. The Arabs were astonished at this show of strength and were completely dumbfounded when he managed to escape into the Hotel compound pursued by Arabs. Rescued by a fellow Hebrew Christian and an Arab gate-keeper, he was taken to hospital.

When Jerusalem was besieged, the Jews fought back. Sometimes Jewish fighters drove into crowded Arab towns and threw grenades or destroyed buildings believed to have housed Arab fighters. This fighting posed serious problems for members of CMJ. Suspected by the Haganah and the Stern Gang, they were subjected to severe harassment. Evacuation seemed inevitable, and thus began 'Operation Mercy'. By mid-1948 it became impossible to continue to run the Hospital and it was turned over to Jewish authorities.

When the British Mandate ended, there was considerable rejoicing amongst the evangelical community about Jewish restoration in the Holy Land. Commenting on these events, Hannah Hurnard wrote:

> Surely 1948 has been one of the most momentous years in the history of the world, perhaps the most momentous since that amazing time when God Himself appeared upon the earth in the form of a man... in this amazing year of 1948, another God-planned and prophet-fore-told wonder has just taken place – the rebirth of the unchanging, undying, unassimilated Jewish nation... On May 15th as the new State of Israel was proclaimed, the British Mandate ended, and as Israel again became a nation in the land of Israel, the thirtieth chapter of Ezekiel was read in Hebrew over the radio – the glorious prophecy of the scattered dry bones which were suddenly joined together with flesh and sinews, and then received the life of God. ... It was an astonishing and awe-inspiring event... On May 15th 1948, with the termination of a Gentile Mandatory Government, this amazing return culminated in the formation of the first Jewish State in the Land of Israel...
>
> I must confess, humbly and honestly, that the successful establishment of the Jewish State in Israel came as a completely unexpected, and at first, incomprehensible surprise. Perhaps to other Christians, especially in Palestine, the same problem has presented itself. Many of us who believed in the Bible prophecies concerning the final restoration of Israel to the Promised Land, and the ultimate fulfilment of all God's purposes of blessing for them, and through them, to the whole world, found it almost impossible to believe that Modern Zionism, which is a political and largely non-religious power, could achieve possession of the land of Israel by its own strength...[3]

When the State of Israel was declared, a struggle took place for the Old City of Jerusalem. The fall of the city marked the end of a Jewish community situated there as well as the fate of CMJ. Christ Church was cut off from the Jewish people, and it was proposed that St Paul's on the Jewish side become the basis for missionary activity. Such a move, however, was opposed by Hugh Jones, the leader of CMJ:

> I cannot see that there is any case for any transfer of Christ Church at present. I feel we need to aim and pray that Christ Church as in the past may once again become the meeting place for worship for Christians of all nationalities... If feel bound to say that I feel that the spirit that prevailed in the former St Paul's congregation would not augur well for Christ Church and all that Christ Church stands for which has been built up by the prayers and labours of Christian well-wishers of Israel over the past hundred years and is dear to the hearts of thousands of CMJ supporters all over the world.[4]

Jones' fear was that the spirit of Arab nationalism which became a feature of Anglican life in Palestine from 1948 on would overshadow the missionary activities of the past: in the view of Christian Zionists, the Anglican Church was betraying the message of the Gospel.

American Dispensationalists

Pre-eminent among these dispensationalists was Arno C. Gaebelein who was the source of the prophetic notes in *Scofield's Reference Bible*. A regular speaker at the Niagara Prophecy Conferences, he lectured at the Evangelical Theological College in Dallas, which subsequently became Dallas Theological Seminary. In 1893 he commenced publishing a Yiddish periodical, *Tiqweth Israel* – 'The Hope of Israel Monthly'. Later he edited an English version called *Our Hope*. The purpose of this journal was to inform Christians about the Zionist movement and the imminent return of Christ. Scofield himself wrote a foreword to Gaebelein's *The Harmony of the Prophetic World*.

Despite his support of Jewish restoration in the Holy Land, Gaebelein has been criticized for his apparent anti-Semitic attitudes. According to Gaebelein, the *Protocols of the Elders of Zion* – a tract which contains allegedly secret plans of a worldwide Jewish conspiracy – is authentic. According to Gaebelein. it was the work of a Jew, and he believed that:

> they certainly laid out a path for the revolutionary Jews that has been strictly and literally followed. That the Jew has been a prominent factor in the revolutionary movements of the day, wherever they may have occurred, cannot truthfully be denied, any more that it was a Jew who

assassinated, with all his family, the former Autocrat of all the Russians; or than that a very large majority (said to be over 80%) of the present Bolshevist government in Moscow, are Jews; while along other lines, in the assembly of the League of Nations, the Jew's voice is heard, and it is by no means a plaintive, timid, or uninfluential one – the Jew is the coming man.[5]

Later he discussed the problem of Jewish leadership in Russia, claiming that 44 out of 50 of the Bolshevik leaders were of Jewish descent. These individuals were not devout Jews, but rather those who had cast off the faith of their fathers. In a further article, 'Aspects of Jewish Power in the United States', he claimed:

> The new volume issued by the 'Dearborn Independent' contains a great deal of truth concerning the Jews, especially that part of Jewry which rejects the law and testimony of their fathers... there is nothing so vile on earth as an apostate Jew, who denies God and His word. It is predicted in the Word of God that a large part of the Jews will become apostate, along with the Gentile masses. But not all Jews are liquor fiends, apostates and immoral. There is another side to this question![6]

Although Gaebelein was persuaded that the return of the Jews to their ancient homeland was part of God's providential plan, he was critical of secular Zionism. 'Zionism', he wrote,[6] 'is not the divinely promised restoration of Israel . . . [and] is not the fulfilment of the large number of predictions found in the Old Testament Scriptures, which relate to Israel's return to the land. Indeed, Zionism has very little use for arguments from the Word of God. It is rather a political and philanthropic undertaking. Instead of coming together before God, calling upon His name, trusting Him, that He is able to perform what He has often promised; they speak of their riches, their influence, their Colonial Bank, and court the favour of the Sultan. The great movement is one of unbelief and confidence in themselves instead of God's eternal purposes.'[7]

Yet, despite such critical remarks about Jewry, Gaebelein was enthusiastic about the return of Jews to the Holy Land. It was, he believed, the starting point of the signs of our times. In *Our Hope* he emphasized how prophecy was being fulfilled in Palestine. Following the writings of other dispensationalists, he distinguished between God's purposes for the Jewish people and the Church. Although he supported the Jewish restoration to Israel, he viewed this event as a preparation for the Battle of Armageddon in which most would be killed.

As fundamentalism became more prevalent in American life, other theological matters became more pressing. Between 1910 and 1915 a series of booklets, *The Fundamentals*, were published in which a range of authors defended a conservative, evangelical approach. Initially these conservatives were suspicious of premillennial doctrines; in time, however, they welcomed the support of dispensationalists such as Gaebelein. Such a rapprochment helped to spread the dissemination of premillennialist ideas. During the first half of the twentieth century, a number of dispensationalists were committed to a biblical basis for the realization of a Jewish restoration to Palestine. Among these figures were Harry Ironside, M.R. DeHann, and Reuben A. Torrey. Others viewed the rise of Japanese imperialism and Chinese communism as signs of the coming battle of Armageddon.

When the State of Israel was founded in 1948, dispensationalists such as DeHann interpreted this event in the light of the Abrahamic covenant. In DeHann's view, it was a mistake for Balfour not to set aside the whole of Palestine for the Jewish people. For DeHann, the British reluctance to create a Jewish state and clear the land of its unlawful population was a grave error. 'Now the land of Palestine', he wrote, 'is the Holy Land because in His eternal purposes and programme, God has set it aside for the one purpose of occupation by his peculiar people, the descendants of Jacob, and because it is God's Holy Land, anyone who tampers with it and seeks to separate its people from their possession comes under the judgement of God.'[8]

Later, following the Six Day War, Nelson Bell, editor of *Christianity Today*, stated that for the first time in more than 2000 years Jerusalem is now completely in the hands of the Jews; this, he believed, gives a student of the Bible a thrill and a renewed faith in the accuracy and validity of the Bible.'[9]

Later President Lyndon B. Johnson similarly stressed the Biblical background to his support for a Jewish state:

> Most, if not all of you, have very deep ties with the land and with the people of Israel, as I do; for my Christian faith sprang from yours. The Bible stories are woven into my childhood memories as the gallant struggle of modern Jews to be free of persecution is also woven into our souls.[10]

Similarly, President Jimmy Carter acknowledged his pro-Zionist beliefs, as did Ronald Reagan. By 1981, he had read Hal Lindsey's *The Late Great Planet Earth* and other books about Armageddon. As governor of California, he discussed these convictions with a colleague, James Mills. Based on Ezekiel 38, he insisted that Israel would soon come under attack from ungodly nations:

Do you understand the significance of that? Libya has now gone communist, and that's a sign that the day of Armageddon isn't far off... It's necessary to fulfill the prophecy that Ethiopia will be one of the ungodly nations that go against Israel... For the first time ever, everything is in place for the battle of Armageddon and the Second Coming of Christ... Ezekiel tells us that Gog, the nation that will lead all the other powers of darkness against Israel, will come out of the north. Biblical scholars have been saying for generations that Gog must be Russia... now that Russia has become communist and atheistic, now that Russia has set itself against God.[11]

In another conversation, Reagan described how he was persuaded that God was bringing the Jews back to their homeland. On numerous occasions Reagan stated that we could be the generation that experiences Armageddon. With the election of Reagan as president, several Christian Zionists were given leading governmental posts, including such individuals as Attorney General Ed Meese, Secretary of Defence Caspar Weinberger, and Secretary of the Interior, James Watt. In addition, White House seminars included Jerry Falwell, Mike Evans and Hal Lindsey. In a personal conversation reported in the *Washington Post*, Reagan outlined his own personal convictions concerning the Middle East:

You know, I turn back to the ancient prophets in the Old Testament and the signs foretelling Armageddon, and I find myself wondering if – if we're the generation that is going to see that come about. I don't know if you've noted any of these prophecies lately, but believe me they certainly describe the times we're going through.[12]

Conflict and War

Once the Jewish state was established, Arab nations attacked Israel. After fierce fighting, a truce was concluded on 11 June 1948. In the next month conflict broke out and the Israelis seized Lydda, Ramleh and Nazareth as well as large areas beyond the partition frontiers. Within ten days the Arabs agreed to another truce, but outbreaks of hostility continued. In mid-October the Israelis attempted to open the road to the Negev settlements and took Bersheba. On 12 January 1949 armistice talks took place in Rhodes and an armistice was later signed by Egypt, Lebanon, Transjordan and Syria. These events served as the background to the ongoing Arab–Palestinian problem: 656,000 Arab inhabitants fled from Israeli-held territories: 280,000 to the West Bank; 70,000 to Transjordan; 100,000 to Lebanon; 4000 to Iraq; 75,000 to Syria; 7000 to Egypt; and 190,000 to the Gaza Strip.

On the basis of the 1949 armistice, the Israelis sought agreement on the boundaries of the Jewish state. The Arabs, however, refused to consider this proposal – instead they insisted that Israel return to the 1947 partition lines without giving any formal recognition of the new state. Further, despite the concluding of the armistice, fedayeen bands continued to attack Israeli citizens, and boycotts and blockades sought to injure Israel's economy. After King Abdullah was assassinated on 20 June 1951, a military junta ousted the Egyptian monarch. On 25 February 1954 President Gemal Abdul Nasser gained control of the country. From September 1955 the Soviet bloc supplied weapons to the Arabs, and this encouraged Nasser to take steps against the Jewish state. From 1956 he denied Israeli ships access to the Gulf of Aqaba (they had already been prevented from using the Suez Canal). In April 1956 he signed a pact with Saudi Arabia and Yemen, and in July he seized the Suez Canal. Fearing Arab intentions, Israel launched a pre-emptive strike on 29 October, and in the war that followed Israel captured all of Sinai as well as Gaza, and opened a sea route to Aqaba.

At the end of the Sinai War Israel undertook to withdraw from a protective *cordon sanitaire*. This arrangement endured for ten years, but attacks still continued during this period. In 1967 Nasser launched another offensive, and on 15 May he moved 100,000 men and armour into Sinai and expelled the UN army. On 22 May he blockaded Aqaba; several days later King Hussein of Jordan took up positions in Jordan. In the face of this Arab threat, Israel launched a strike on 5 June, destroying the Egyptian air force on the ground. On 7 June the Israeli army took the Old City, thereby making Jerusalem its capital. On the next day the Israeli forces occupied the entire Left Bank, and during the next few days captured the Golan Heights and reoccupied Sinai.

Despite such a crushing defeat, the Six Day War did not bring security to the Jewish state. Nasser's successor President Anwar Sadat expelled Egypt's Soviet military advisers in July 1972, cancelled the country's political and military alliance with other Arab states, and together with Syria attacked Israel on Yom Kippur, 6 October 1973. At the outbreak of war the Egyptians and the Syrians broke through Israeli defences, but by 9 October the Syrian advance had been repelled. On 10 October the American President Richard Nixon began an airlift of advanced weapons to Israel; two days later the Israelis engaged in a counter-attack on Egypt and moved towards victory. On 24 October a cease-fire came into operation.

Later after the Labour coalition lost the May 1977 election and handed over power to the Likud headed by Menahem Begin, Sadat offered to negotiate peace terms with Israel. On 5 September 1978 at the American presidential home Camp David, the process of reaching such an agreement began and was completed thirteen days later (although another six months were required before a detailed treaty was formulated). The treaty specified that Egypt would recognize Israel's right to exist and provide secure guarantees for her southern border. In return Israel would hand over Sinai. In addition, she would undertake to negotiate away much of the West Bank and make concessions over Jerusalem as long as a complementary treaty was agreed with the Palestinians and other Arab countries. This latter step, however, was never taken. This meant that Israel was left with the responsibility for overseeing Arab Occupied Territories.

In the years that followed, Arab influence grew immeasurably, due to the Arabs' control of oil in the Middle East. As the price of oil increased, Arab revenue provided huge sums for the purchase of armaments. At the UN the Arab world exerted its power, and in 1975 the General Assembly passed a resolution equating Zionism with racism. Further, Yasser Arafat, the leader of the Palestine Liberation Organization, was accorded head of government status by the UN. Fearing the growing threat of Palestinian influence and terrorism, Israel launched an advance into southern Lebanon in June 1982, destroying PLO bases. This Israeli onslaught and the subsequent occupation served as the background to the killing of Muslim refugees by Christian Falangists in the Sabra and Shatilla camps on 16 September 1982. Throughout the world this atrocity was portrayed as Israel's fault. In response to this criticism, the Israeli government ordered an independent judicial inquiry, which placed some blame on the Israeli Minister of Defence, Ariel Sharon, for not having prevented this massacre.

After the Israeli conquest during the Yom Kippur War, the State of Israel took control of the Occupied Territories. In the following years, the Palestinians staged demonstrations, strikes and riots against Israeli rule. By 1987 the Palestinians in the West Bank and Gaza were largely young educated people who had benefited from formal education. Yet despite such educational advances, they suffered from limited job expectations and this situation led to political radicalism. Such frustration came to a head on 9 December 1987 in Jabaliya, the most militant of the refugee camps. An Israeli patrol was trapped there during a protest about the death of four Jabaliya residents who were killed in a road accident the previous day. The soldiers shot their way out, killing one youth and wounding ten others. This event provoked riots throughout the Occupied Territories. By January 1989 the Israeli Defence Forces declared that 352 Palestinians had died, more than 4300 were wounded, and 25,600 had been arrested. In addition, 200 Arab homes had been sealed or demolished. As hostilities increased, the intifada (shaking off) demonstrated that occupying the West Bank and the Gaza Strip would be a perpetual problem.

The Jewish state was unprepared for such a situation, and the army was forced to improvise. As time passed, the intifada became more resilient and its tactics changed to ambushes, small-scale conflicts and selective strikes. In addition the technology of modern communications was used to apply pressure against the Israelis. Yet, despite having such an impact, the intifada created tensions within the Palestinian community. As the resistance developed, Islamic revivalism spread from the Gaza Strip to the West Bank and Jerusalem and posed a serious threat to secular Palestinian nationalism. Such a division was aggravated when the PLO endorsed a two-state solution to the Palestinian problem. Such a policy was bitterly condemned by fundamentalists. Hamas, the Islamic Resistance movement, insisted on a Muslim Palestine from the Mediterranean to the Jordan. Yasser Arafat, however, adopted a more pragmatic approach and abandoned any maximalist formulation of the Palestinian position in favour of a policy that took into account the reality of Israel's existence.

From the Israeli side, the Israeli Defence Forces viewed the intifada in the context of Israel's relationship with its Palestinian neighbours and the world in general. Despite such a stance, the intifada was generally regarded as more than a local skirmish, and throughout the world Israelis were viewed as guilty of brutality. As a result there was a growing feeling that Israel should abandon the Occupied Territories. Hence after several years of Palestinian revolt in the Occupied Territories, the Israeli population become more prepared to settle its dispute with its Arab neighbours, as was evidenced by the peace talks beginning in 1992 between Israel and the Palestinians.

14
American Premillennial Dispensationalism

As Israel struggled during this period against the Arab world, Christian Zionists speculated about the end of history. Pre-eminent among
premillennial dispensationalists, Hal Lindsey deeply influenced
millions of Christian readers with his vision of the coming of
Armageddon. Along with Hal Lindsey, Tim LaHaye is one of the
most significant popularizers of dispensationalism. Together with
evangelical Christians, many Messianic Jews similarly adopt a pre-
tribulationist stance. In their view, all believers in Yeshua (Jesus) will
be raptured at the beginning of the Great Tribulation – this will be a
time of intense anti-Jewish hostility that will encompass the entire
earth in the last days. These popular American and Messianic views
have significantly influenced Zionism in the last decade or so.

Hal Lindsey and Christian Zionism

Hal Lindsey is one of the most significant Christian dispensationalists of the twentieth century. The author of over 20 books, he has propounded a dispensational view of the future drawing on previous
premillennialist theology. Lindsey's most famous work, The *Late,
Great Planet Earth* was a best seller, and has profoundly influenced
the direction of premillennialist thought. Since its publication in
1970, its sales have continued and his views remain popular amongst
a wide circle of readers. Like J.N. Darby and C.I. Scofield, he claimed
that on the basis of the Bible, he is able to determine future events,
and like Darby, he believed that his interpretations were revealed by
God. In the 1980s with the election of Ronald Reagan, Lindsey along
with leading evangelists such as Jerry Falwell and the Christian tele-
vangelist Mike Evans were included in White House Seminars.

Like other dispensationalists, Lindsey adopts a literalist approach to Scripture. Like Darby and Scofield he interpreted references to the Hebrew Bible as applying to contemporary events. Throughout his writings, Lindsey asserts that the earth is in danger of destruction:

> We are the generation the prophets were talking about. We have witnessed biblical prophecies come true. The birth of Israel. the decline in American power and morality. The rise of Russian and Chinese might. The threat of war in the Middle East. The increase in earthquakes, volcanoes, famine and drought. The Bible foretells the signs that precede Armageddon... We are the generation that will see the end times... and the return of Jesus.[1]

According to Lindsey, the battle of Armageddon is unavoidable: only by believing in Jesus, he argues, can the faithful be raptured and avoid the global holocaust which is coming. Today, he contends, there is no hope or purpose other than escaping the period of Tribulation:

> You won't find another book quite like this one. We will examine why and how the world is hurtling toward disaster... My background as a student of prophecy allows me to place all this information in perspective in a way that is sure to lead many people to the ultimate truth about the coming global holocaust – and, if they are open, to a wonderful way of escaping it.[2]

In presenting his predictions, he is sympathetic to Israel. Like other dispensationalists, he argues that the promises, blessings, and protection made to Abraham are eternal: today, he maintains, the State of Israel is the beneficiary:

> There has been much infidelity in Jewish history, and their present worldwide dispersion and persecution have been their divine discipline. However, God made unconditional promises of eternal blessings to the Jewish patriarchs and will someday restore the Jews to a position of special favour with Himself. God has promised never to abandon his chosen people, no matter how despicably they treat him. (Romans 11:1,2.) The divine hand of protection of the Jews during their recent Six Day War was just a token of that protective care.[3]

For Lindsey, God will not forsake the Israelis, nor let them be destroyed. All other nations will receive blessings through Israel. Such biblical prophecies demand a national restoration of the Jewish people. Nonetheless, Lindsey believes that many Israelis will suffer and die in the nuclear war of Armageddon. Yet, Lindsey argues in line with other dispensationalists that the Church will be replaced by Israel as the people of God on earth:

> At some point in history – very soon I believe – God's special focus and blessing is going to shift back to the Jews. At that moment, the Jews will once again be responsible, as God's representatives, to take His message to the whole world. This mission – incomplete and seemingly impossible for the last 2000 years – will be accomplished by the 144,000 Jewish Billy Graham's in seven years.[5]

Within this framework, Lindsey insists that the settlement and integration of the Occupied Territories in Israel is essential to maintain the promise made to Abraham. Further, the occupation of Jerusalem is of fundamental significance – it signifies the return of the Messiah. Eventually, he argues, Jerusalem will become the spiritual centre of the entire world: all peoples will come there to worship Jesus who will rule from Jerusalem. In this connection, he insists that the Jewish Temple must also be rebuilt. Many prophecies demand the rebuilding of the ancient Temple, he believes, indicating that the event is a significant prophetic sign.

In this context, Lindsey is deeply antagonistic to Muslim states that seek to destroy Israel. America, however, is perceived as Israel's strongest ally. Yet, despite this role, Lindsey, like other Christian Zionists, is convinced that a holocaust is inevitable:

> And look what's happening in the Middle East – Ground Zero in the endtimes events... This phoney peace deal in the Middle East thus only ensures that eventually there will be a thermonuclear holocaust in the Middle East... This seems to parallel predictions in Revelation and elsewhere.[6]

In *The Late, Great Planet Earth*, Lindsey described what the war will be like:

> The armies of all nations will be gathered in the area of Israel, especially around Jerusalem. Think of it: at least 200 million soldiers from the Orient, with millions more from the forces of the West... Messiah Jesus will first strike those who have ravaged His city, Jerusalem. Then he will strike the armies amassed in the Valley of Meggido. No wonder blood will stand to the horses' bridles from a distance of two hundred miles from Jerusalem! (Revelation 14: 20). It's grizzly to think about such carnage, but just to check all this out I measured from the point where the Valley of Armaggedon sloped down to the Jordan Valley. From this point southward down the Valley through the Dead Sea to the port of Elath on the Gulf of Aqabah measures approximately two

hundred miles. Apparently this whole valley will be filled with war materials, animals, bodies of men, and blood![6]

Based on this vision, he believes that full-scale nuclear disaster will affect the entire earth:

> While this great battle is raging, every city in the world is going to be levelled. This will take place by what is called an 'earthquake', but that's not the only meaning. The word by itself simply means 'a great shaking of the earth'. The earth could be shaken either by a literal earthquake or by a full-scale nuclear conflict; I believe that when these powers lock forces here, there will be a full-scale exchange of nuclear weapons, and it is at this time that 'the cities of the nations fall'. Just think of the great cities of the world – London, Rome, Paris, Berlin, New York, San Francisco, Los Angeles, Mexico City, and Tokyo – all these great cities are going to be judged at that time.[7]

Despite such disaster, Christians who embrace a dispensational theology will be raptured to heaven just before Tribulation begins. Believers will in this way escape the coming holocaust and witness these terrible events from the heavenly heights. In Lindsey's view, God will supernaturally deliver 144,000 Jews to serve as his evangelists:

> The fact that God redeems 144,000 literal Jews and ordains them His evangelists not only makes good sense but fits in with the counsel of God. So I say loud and clear: the 144,000 described here are not Jehovah Witnesses, or Mormon elders, or some symbol of the Church; they are Jews, Jews, Jews.[8]

Tim LaHaye and the End of the World

In 1979 LaHaye joined Jerry Falwell in establishing the Moral Majority, determined that conservative Christians could reorient American life. Along with co-author Jerry B. Jenkins, he has written the *Left Behind* series of novels about the End Times which have sold over 50 million copies. Drawing on dispensational theology as propounded by Darby, Scofield, Lindsey and others, LaHaye's writings promote an eschatology of disengagement and the politics of fear.

Implicit in his works is a fatalistic view of the future. As a consequence, many of his readers believe that the Bible teaches that everything is destined to get worse; as a result, there is no reason to work for social change. The best we can do is to persuade others to accept Christ in anticipation of the final Tribulation. LaHaye's mission is to galvanize support for the political agenda of the religious right. The *Left Behind* series reinforces the fictional fear that there is a sinister group actively at work creating a one-world socialist gulag for those who are left behind.

According to LaHaye, these novels are true to the literal interpretation of Biblical prophecy. The Left Behind books chronicle the seven years of Tribulation, beginning with *Left Behind*, a novel of the earth's last days. In this novel, passengers aboard a Boeing 747 *en route* to Europe disappear instantly. Nothing remains except their rumpled piles of clothes, jewellery, fillings and surgical pins. Vehicles, suddenly unmanned, career out of control. People are terror-stricken as loved ones vanish before their eyes. Some blame space aliens; others claim it is a freak of nature; still others argue that a military attack by a world conqueror has taken place. However, airline captain Rayford Steele's wife had warned him of this event. If Irene Steel was right, both she and their son have disappeared although there are doubts about his sceptical daughter, Chloe. In the midst of this crisis, Rayford must search for his family as well as for answers. As devastating as the disappearances have been, the darkest days may lie ahead.

The second novel, *Tribulation Force*, continues this saga with an account of those left behind who are desperate to determine what has happened including Pan-Continental airline pilot Rayford Steele, *Global Weekly* senior writer Cameron (Buck) Williams, New Hope Village Church minister Bruce Barnes, and Stanford University student Chloe Steele. This end-time force band together to witness for truth and to battle the enemies of God and discover that the disappearances have ushered in a seven-year period called the Tribulation during which the earth will suffer from the most catastrophic calamities. Those left behind face war, famine, plagues and natural disasters so devastating that only one in four people will survive.

The next novel, *Nicolae*, describes the rise of the Antichrist. Rayford Steele, his new wife Amanda, and Buck and Chloe who are now married, make it their mission to win as many people to Christ as possible. The seven-year Tribulation is nearing the end of the first quarter, and the Tribulation Force faces conflict at every turn in their holy war against Nicolae Carpathia, the ruler of the new Global community. Rayford and Buck work directly for Carpathia, who knows of Rayford's true allegiance, but not of Buck's. Here Rayford becomes one of the Tribulation Saints at the highest levels of the Carpathia regime. Meanwhile, Buck attempts a dramatic rescue run from Israel through the Sinai.

In the fourth novel, *Soul Harvest*, Rayford Steele and Buck Williams fear they are alone. Each has survived the wrath of the Lamb, a global earthquake in the twenty-first month of the Tribulation. Neither knows whether the other is alive, and each is searching for his wife. Their mentor, Tsion Ben-Judah, is trapped beneath the rubble of their church, and no-one knows what has happened to their friend, Hattie Durham. As the world hurtles toward the Trumpet Judgements and the great soul harvest prophesied in Scripture, Rayford and Buck begin searching for their loved ones. With the fulfilment of more judgement prophecies, hardly any sceptics remain. Even the enemies of God now know whom they are fighting.

The next novel, *Apollyon*, describes the unleashing of the Destroyer. While the world is assaulted by God's judgements, the faithful band of believers are forced underground as they are declared international fugitives by Global Community Potentate Nicolae Carpathia. The world watches as the Tribulation Force risks their lives to attend the great Meeting of the Witnesses that will result in a showdown between the Force and the Global Community regime. Tens of thousands of the 144,000 witnesses prophesied in Scripture meet at Teddy Kollek Stadium to sit under the teaching of their pastor-teacher, Tsion Ben-Judah. Rayford Steele and Buck Williams have become international fugitives and they must flee before the conference begins. The Tribulation calendar moves ever closer to the halfway point. Meanwhile the fourth Trumpet Judgement strikes the solar system, crippling life on earth. The Fifth Trumpet Judgement – a plague of scorpion-like locusts lead by Apollyon, is so horrifying that men try to kill themselves but are not allowed to die.

In *Assassins*, the Tribulation Force hurtles toward the four murders foretold in Scripture as Rayford and others vie for the privilege of being the tool that fulfils the prophecy that the Antichrist himself is to suffer a lethal head wound. The head of Enigma Babylon, the One World Faith, is in jeopardy, as are the two witnesses at the Wailing Wall as the due time approaches. As a supernatural horde of 200 million demonic horsemen slay a third of the remaining population, the Tribulation Force prepares for a future as fugitives. World history and prophecy collide in Jerusalem at the middle of the Tribulation. In the seventh novel, *The Indwelling*, the battle of the ages continues to rage until it spills to earth and hell breaks loose. Global Community forces launch a massive manhunt for the assassin of their fallen leader. The group's spiritual leader, Tsion Ben-Judah, keeps watch to see if prophecy will be fulfilled through Antichrist's resurrection, indwelt by Satan. Meanwhile the members of the Tribulation Force, face their most dangerous challenges. In this work the Beast takes possession as the world mourns the death of Nicolae Carpathia.

The next novel, *The Mark*, portrays the resurrected Nicolae Carpathia as the Antichrist and outlines his three and a half-year reign of terror over the earth. Ensconced in a new safe house, the

Tribulation Force suffers tragic loss at the dawn of the second half of the Great Tribulation. The Tribulation Force moles inside the palace in New Babylon face tragedy and danger; meanwhile Carpathia plans his attack on the Judahites while the Tribulation Force prepares for its most ambitious assault.

In *Desecration*, Rayford Steel and his rebels ready themselves to serve as agents of rescue for God's chosen people. Led by Chaim Rosenzweig, believers in Jerusalem must flee or take the mark of the beast. Nicolae Carpathia has ordered every Morale Monitor armed as he prepares to travel along the Via Dolorosa and then to the Temple. Buck Williams is uncertain whether he should take charge; Chloe fears for his safety; Tsion Ben-Judah prepares to meet with fellow believers in Petra. Here the lines are drawn between good and evil as God inflicts the first Bowl Judgement upon those who have taken the mark, while his chosen ones flee to the wilderness on the brink of Armageddon.

The tenth novel, *The Remnant*, depicts the events on the brink of Armageddon. The enemies of Nicolae Carpathia are massed at Petra. The earth is now a wasted shell and awaits future destruction. Rayford Steele, Buck Williams and all members of the Tribulation Force flee for their lives while trying to maintain their opposition to the Antichrist. Spiritual mentor Tsion Ben-Judah maintains that despite this travail, these dark days are a sign of God's grace and mercy as well as his wrath. Only miraculous interventions by heavenly forces give the believers hope against the assault of the Global Community. The planet hurtles towards Armageddon.

In the eleventh novel, *Armageddon*, the only safe place for believers is Petra, although the Tribulation Force is holding out in a San Diego safehouse. New Babylon is in a pillar of darkness that has incapacitated its population. The Tribulation Force is able to monitor Carpathia's inner circle and even take control of his broadcasting network for a special broadcast to the world. While the world focuses on the chaos in New Babylon, the Jezreel Valley is choked with troops and weapons. Like many of the battles in the Hebrew Bible, Armageddon will take place in a destructive form.

In the final novel, *Glorious Appearing*, the Antichrist has assembled the armies of the world in the Valley of Megiddo. The Tribulation Force has migrated to the Middle East. Jerusalem is falling to the Global Community's Unity Army and Tsion ben-Judah has been slain. It is now over seven years since the Rapture and almost seven years since Antichrist's covenant with Israel. Believers look to the heavens for the Glorious Appearance of Christ. All appears doomed, but God has another plan.

Messianic Jews and Premillennial Dispensationalism

Many Messianic Jews believe that during this period of Tribulation, which it is generally conceived will last for seven years, a powerful world leader who advocates peace for the world will be given unlimited control by the European countries, the United States and Israel. In the book of Daniel, this individual is referred to as the 'little horn' and the 'vile person'. In 2 Thessalonians, he is called 'the Son of Perdition', and in the Book of Revelation, he is 'the beast which rises out of the sea'.

This person will gain complete political authority because he has the answers: he has the solution to the crisis in the Middle East, and he will gain Israel's support because he will be able to guarantee the safety of the region. The world will be in such a critically terrible condition that its inhabitants will be willing to turn to this man to provide the much-needed unity of purpose in coping with its problems. This world leader will be joined by a religious leader who is referred to in the book of Revelation as 'the beast that rises out of the earth'. This individual never attempts to promote himself, but rather directs attention to the world's political leader. Like him, he will be charismatic and will imitate God's miracles. For example, he will cause fire to come down from heaven and imitate the miracles of Elijah to persuade the Jewish people that he is indeed 'Elijah' that the prophet Malachi predicted to come to them in Malachi 4:5–6. He will mould the religions of the world into one great brotherhood. Messianic Jews believe that the Bible declares that these two leaders are linked with Satanic forces and, like that of Satan, their impending destruction is foretold.

During the period of the Great Tribulation, Messianic Jewish theology predicts that the world political leader will consolidate his power in the same way that Hitler did. He will turn against Israel and the Jewish nation. Many Messianic Jews maintain that the last half of the period of Tribulation will be worse than what has already occurred. It will be a time of crisis for both the world as a whole and the Jewish people. Natural catastrophes will take place: there will be an increase in floods, famines, earthquakes and disease. The world religious leader will declare the world political leader to be God in the Temple that has been rebuilt for Jewish worship in Jerusalem. Those who do not believe in this world ecumenical religion will be accused of subversive activity against the brotherhood of all humanity. Both Jews and Christians who hold to their faiths will be persecuted and killed.

Eventually three coalitions of nations will converge on the Middle East to battle the world political leader who has firm control of Western countries. There will be a struggle for domination. The last battle between these coalitions and the Western political leader will be in a plain that stretches in north-central Israel ten miles south of Nazareth and fifteen miles inland from the Mediterranean seacoast. This is Armageddon. One coalition will include Russia and the North, the second will be from the Far East, and the third will be an Egyptian-African block. These coalitions battling against the world political leader in command of the Western block will devastate the world except for the fact that the Messiah will come back to earth at this stage. All of the coalitions and power blocks will forget their differences, and turn to fight against the Messiah, but he will triumph. Following his victory, there will finally be peace and a glorious future for Israel, the Jewish people, and all humanity. The Messianic Age will commence.

Owing to this eschatological picture, Messianic Jews are vigorous supporters of the Jewish state. Like Christian Zionists, they believe in the right of Israel to exist as a Jewish homeland and provide ample political support for the Jewish state. Given their understanding of the last days, many Messianic Jews wait in anticipation for the emergence of leaders who court the Jewish people and yet could easily turn against Israel and the Jewish nation. They are vociferous in their condemnation of groups that do not support the Jewish state and firmly believe that if the United States were to abandon the Jewish nation, the United States would be doomed. God only blesses those who bless his people. Such an attitude is reflected in one of the songs that Messianic Jews sing about the coming time:

> The Hebrews are back in their land to stay, No Arabs no Russians can chase them away, 'Cause God has His hand in the affairs of men, And just as the Bible says, things are coming to an end.[9]

Despite the common ground between Messianic Jewish theology and Christian dispensationalism, there are certain features of this eschatological scheme that distance Messianic followers from Christian dispensationalists. Messianic Jews insist that many elements of Torah Judaism are still applicable today. In this respect they are unlike Christian dispensationalists who consider the keeping of Torah a confusion of the present dispensation of the church with the time of the Great Tribulation where Jews will become prominent in God's plan for the world. Observance of the *mitzvot* is seen as a failure to distinguish between the dispensation of the law in the Hebrew Bible and that of grace in the New Testament. Against this position, Messianic

Jews assert the continued validity of keeping elements of the Torah to demonstrate that God's promises and covenant with Israel are still in effect. Hence, the Union of Messianic Jewish Congregations' Doctrinal Statement declares:

> As Jewish followers of Yeshua, we are called to maintain our Jewish biblical heritage and remain a part of our people Israel and the universal body of believers. This is part of our identity and a witness to the faithfulness of God.[10]

A further distinction between Messianic Jews and traditional Christian dispensationalists concerns the shift away from classical pre-Tribulation premillennialism in which all believers are 'raptured' up to heaven before the Tribulation, leaving behind all non-believers, including Jews. A number of Messianic Jewish thinkers adopt a mid-tribulationist or post-tribulationist stance – this is indicative of a theological trend that emphasizes Messianic Jewish solidarity with the Jewish community through the period of persecution.

There are some within the movement who go even further, and stress that eschatological speculation is of little consequence for Messianic believers. These writers are not preoccupied with end-time speculation or enthusiasm. Although they have a general sense of being in a new phase of history with the creation of Israel, they are not concerned with eschatological scenarios. Commenting on this development, Rich Nicol, a messianic rabbi, recounted his early encounter with premillennial dispensationalism:

> I was nineteen years old and I had read a book that changed everything for me. It was *The Late Great Planet Earth* by Hal Lindsey... Lindsey thrilled me and my friends with his predictions of Israel's soon-coming war with Russia, and other Eastern European nations... we were clearly in the end of the end of the age... Messianic Judaism has been more influenced – it has actually defined itself in terms of the end of the End Times. Almost a fundamental axiom of our faith, is the conviction that God raised up Messianic Judaism at this very period of human history because we figure prominently in His plans to rescue the world from itself.[11]

Yet, today he cautions against such end time speculation:

> By over focusing on the End Times, we can force people into an impossible bind... Too much emphasis on the End can become an excuse for not making life's hard choices... Just as overly optimistic utopianism is harmful to young people, so is the pessimism inherent in the End Times mentality.[12]

15

Christian Zionists and
the Middle East

In the United States a number of prominent dispensationalists have had a significant impact on the direction of political life. The practical impact of Christian Zionism is manifest at the highest levels of government in the United States. With religious fervour, premillennial dispensationalists press for renewed support for the Jewish cause. Outside the United States, the International Embassy in Jerusalem is arguably the most influential of all Christian Zionist organizations. Founded in 1980 by Jan Villem van der Hoeven, it was housed in West Jerusalem near the home of the Israeli Prime Minister.

American Evangelicals

Leading evangelicals in the United States include Jerry Falwell, the pastor of Thomas Road Baptist Church and the Founder and Chancellor of Baptist Liberty University. In addition to his other work, his Ministries sponsor the Liberty Broadcasting Network TV channel as well as the syndicated Old Time Gospel Hour programme, which is broadcast on 350 stations. Initially, Falwell was not interested in politics:

> Believing in the Bible as I do, I would find it impossible to stop preaching the pure saving gospel of Jesus Christ and begin doing anything else, including fighting communism, or participating in civil rights reform. Preachers are not called to be politicians but to be soul winners. Nowhere are we commissioned to reform the externals.[1]

Yet, after the Six Day War, Falwell became an ardent supporter of the Jewish state. The Israeli victory deeply influenced his thinking. Like other evangelical Americans, he gave full support to Israel's victory over Arab forces. In 1979 Falwell founded the Moral Majority; the same year the State of Israel gave him a Lear jet to help him in his work to encourage others to support a Jewish presence in the Holy Land. The next year, Falwell became the first non-Jew to be awarded the Vladimir Ze'ev Jabotinsky medal for Zionist excellence by Israel's Prime Minister Menachem Begin.

In 1981 when Israel bombed Iraq's nuclear plant, Begin phoned Falwell before he contacted President Reagan, intent on persuading him to explain the reasons for the bombing to the Christian public. Later, when Israel invaded Lebanon, Falwell gave his full support to the Jewish state. When during this onslaught the inhabitants of two Palestinian camps were massacred, he declared that the Israelis were not involved. Subsequently, when Falwell spoke to the conservative Rabbinical Assembly in Miami, he pledged to mobilize 60 million conservative Christians for Israel. When in January 1998 Benjamin Netanyahu visited Washington, his first meeting was with Falwell and with The National Unity Coalition for Israel, a gathering of more than 500 fundamentalist Christian leaders. Hailed as the 'Ronald Reagan of Israel', Falwell promised to contact 200,000 pastors and church leaders and ask them to encourage President Clinton to refrain from putting pressure on Israel to comply with the Oslo Accords.

A year later, in an interview with the *Washington Post*, Falwell described the West Bank as an integral element of the Jewish state. Pressing Israel to withdraw, he observed, would be like asking America to give Texas to Mexico. In 2000 Falwell revived the Moral Majority under the name People of Faith 2000, a movement which sought to reclaim America as one nation under God and which also adopts a pro-Israel position. More than any single leader, Falwell has managed to ensure that his followers recognize that it is their Christian duty to God to support the Jewish state in fulfilment of biblical prophecy.

Together with Jerry Falwell, Pat Robertson is one of the most important Christian supporters of Israel in the United States. His Christian Broadcasting Network was the first and remains the most influential Christian satellite TV network in the world with a budget in excess of 195 million dollars. The founder of CBN in 1960, he is also the Founder and Chancellor of Regent University as well as a number of educational, entertainment, political and humanitarian organizations, including the Christian Coalition with nearly two million members. The goal of this body is to take working control of the Republican Party and elect Christian candidates. At the same time it regularly lobbies the US government on pro-Israeli issues.

In 1990 Robertson founded International Family Entertainment Inc. as well as the Family Channel, a satellite cable-TV network with 63 million US subscribers. In 1997 Robertson sold IFE to Fox Worldwide Inc. for 1.9 billion dollars. Today, CBN is one of the world's largest television ministries and produces programmes seen in 180 countries and heard in 71 languages. The 700 Club, hosted by Robertson, is one of the longest running television programmes and reaches an audience of about seven million viewers. According to Robertson, its goal is to fulfil end-time prophecy:

> I will never forget the time, April 29 1977, when we had built the first earth station ever to be owned by Christian ministry in the history of the world, and we were the first ever to take a full-time transponder on a satellite... so we were pioneers in this area. I remember it was ten o'clock in the morning when we went on with the broadcast. We then cut to the Mount of Olives in Jerusalem, a little after five o'clock in the afternoon. There were some clouds forming over the Temple Mount... And when I saw the Mount of Olives, and I saw where my Saviour is going to put His foot down when He comes back to earth, I was thinking, 'I'm transmitting it!' The Bible says every eye is going to behold Him, and here it is happening! We see how it is going to be fulfilled right in front of our eyes!'[2]

Along with Jerry Falwell and Pat Robertson, Hal Lindsey has played a central role in the development of evangelical dispensationalism. The author of over 20 books spanning 27 years, he hosts his own radio and television programmes, leads pro-Israeli Holy Land tours, and publishes a monthly Christian journal *Countdown* as well as the International Intelligence Briefing. In addition, he hosts a weekly news programme, International Intelligence Briefing on the Trinity Broadcasting Network television station.

Lindsey's most famous book, *The Late Great Planet Earth*, has sold more than 18,000,000 copies in English and has been translated into 44 languages. Despite changes in the world events since it appeared in 1970, Lindsey argues that his prophetic and apocalyptic scenario is accurate. Determined that political events are the fulfilment of Scripture, he contends that the end of the world is imminent. Hence, later books such as *The Final Battle* (1994) and *Apocalypse Code* (1997) are revised versions of earlier works: *The Late Great Planet Earth* (1970), and *There's a New World Coming* (1973). Determined to demonize Russia, China, Islam and Arab nations, he encourages the economic funding of Israel by the United States. Israel, he insists, should resist any negotiation of land for peace; instead, the Occupied Territories should be incorporated within Israel.

These three figures – Falwell, Robertson, and Lindsey – are figureheads of a vast evangelical movement consisting of over 150 influential Christian leaders including Oral Roberts, Mike Evans, Tim LaHaye, Kenneth Copeland, Paul Crouch, James Dobson, Ed McAteer, Jim Bakker, Chuck Missler and Jimmy Swaggert. Together they reach an audience of over 100 million Americans weekly through their radio and television programmes. Determined to support the Jewish state, they have helped sustain the Christian Zionist agenda as envisaged by earlier premillennial dispensationalist thinkers such as Darby and Scofield. As a result, Christian Zionism has become a major force in American social and political life. As a consequence, some of the largest and most influential Christian Zionist organizations have redefined their message to that of blessing Israel and have set up headquarters in Jerusalem. Today there are over 250 pro-Israeli evangelical organizations in America. Thus, contemporary Christian Zionism has become a central factor in the West's support of the Jewish state.

Christian Zionism and Politics

As we have seen, Christian Zionists lobbied for a Jewish state in the late nineteenth century. Such figures as William Blackstone agitated for the creation of a homeland for the Jews on biblical grounds. In his bestseller, *Jesus is Coming*, he presented a premillennialist interpretation of the final days. Appealing to multimillionaire friends such as John D. Rockefeller, publisher Charles B. Scribner and industrialist, he was able to finance advertisements and a petition campaign. In addition to wealthy financiers, Blackstone also received support from members of the US Senate and the House of Representatives as well as the Chief Justice of the Supreme Court.

With the establishment of Israel in 1948, a number of premillennial dispensationalists began to assert themselves within the larger evangelical community. Israel and the Cold War were linked together by premillennial authors and preachers who interpreted world events in the light of biblical teaching. According to their view, the end of history was approaching, and an evil global empire was soon to emerge under the leadership of a world leader, the Antichrist. This would lead to an attack on Israel, and the climatic Battle of Armageddon. In the opinion of these conservative evangelicals, Israel would be at the centre of these cataclysmic events.

When Israel captured Jerusalem and the West Bank as well as Gaza, Sinai and the Golan Heights in June, 1967, these thinkers sensed that history had entered the final stages. Thus L. Nelson Bell, the father-in-law of Billy Graham and the editor of *Christianity Today*, wrote that for the first time in more than 2000 years Jerusalem was now in the hands of the Jews – giving students of the Bible a renewed faith in the accuracy of Scripture. Largely owing to Hal Lindsey's *The Late, Great Planet Earth*, such premillennialism gained a wide audience among a generation of Americans who had placed Israel at the centre of world history.

With the American bicentennial in 1976, a number of trends converged on the American scene. First, fundamentalist and evangelical churches became the fastest growing sector of American Christianity while mainstream Protestant and Roman Catholic movements saw a decline in their numbers. Second, Jimmy Carter, an evangelical from the Bible Belt, became president of the United States, thereby giving increased legitimacy to the evangelical movement. Third, Israel gained a larger share of the US foreign and military budgets, thereby becoming a pillar of the US strategic alliance against the Soviet bloc. Fourth, as support for Israel increased in the evangelical sphere, Roman Catholic and Protestant denominations began to develop a more balanced approach to the Middle East. This anti-Israel shift was perceived by the Jewish establishment as detrimental to Jewish interests. Finally, the election of Menahem Begin as Prime Minister of Israel evoked a positive response from the American Christian right.

These factors helped forge a fundamentalist Christian-Zionist alliance. Hence in March 1977, when President Carter inserted the clause 'Palestinians deserve a right to their homeland' into a policy address, the pro-Israel lobby and the Christian right took out full-page ads in major US newspapers, claiming that 'The time has come for evangelical Christians to affirm their belief in biblical prophecy and Israel's divine right to the land.' They went on to 'affirm as evangelicals our belief in the promised land to the Jewish people . . . We would view with grave concern any effort to carve out of the Jewish homeland another nation or political entity.'[3] This advertising campaign was one of the first signs of the Likud's and the pro-Israel lobby's alliance with the Christian right.

By the 1980 elections, the nature of life in the Middle East and in the US had changed. The Iranian hostage crisis led to President Carter's defeat. In addition, about 20 million fundamentalist and evangelical Christians voted for Ronald Reagan, who was an ardent supporter of Israel. As a consequence, pro-Israel Republicans gained a stronghold in the government. On at least seven public occasions President Reagan expressed his belief in a final Battle of Armageddon. At White House seminars organized by the administration and the Christian right along with the pro-Israel lobby, Christian Zionists including Hal Lindsey, Jerry Falwell, Pat Robertson, Tim LaHaye and Ed McAteer expressed their support for the Jewish state. Also working in the background was another Christian fundamentalist, Colonel Oliver North.

As we have noted, Menahem Begin enjoyed a close relationship with leading figures of the Christian Zionist movement, including Jerry Falwell. Nonetheless, late in the Reagan administration, a number of scandals in the Christian right evoked considerable discomfort. Pat Robertson's ineffective attempt to run for President led to a decline in fundamentalist political concerns. Yet, the pro-Israel lobby continued to assert itself with the election of Bill Clinton, a Southern Baptist president. During his two terms, President Clinton acted as the central negotiator of the Middle East conflict. However, Clinton proved to be more sympathetic to the Labour Party in Israel rather than Likud.

In Israel itself, Benjamin Netanyahu became a favourite of the Christian Zionists; frequently he spoke at Christian Zionists' functions, including the Feast of Tabernacles hosted by the International Christian Embassy in Jerusalem. Within a few months of his election as Prime Minister in May 1996 Netanyahu convened the Israel Christian Advocacy Council, bringing 17 American fundamentalist leaders to Israel. This tour concluded with a conference and a statement in line with Likud's political policy.

On their return to the United States, Christian Zionist leaders launched a national campaign with full-page advertisements in major newspapers under the banner: 'Christians call for a united Jerusalem.' Likud also sought Christian Zionist help in offsetting the decline in contributions to Israel from American Jews. As a result, the International Fellowship of Christians and Jews raised over 5 million dollars, largely from fundamentalist Christians. Later Christian Zionists worked with pro-Israel groups to mobilize constituencies to make telephone calls, and send emails and letters to President Bush encouraging him to stop putting pressure on Ariel Sharon to withdraw his forces from Palestinian areas.

Christian Zionist organizations and the pro-Israel lobby are among the special interest groups whose concerns have converged since Bush was first elected president. These interest groups include the right wing of the Republican Party; neo-Conservatives; multinational construction firms, the petroleum industry and the arms industry; the pro-Israel lobby and think tanks; and fundamentalist Christian Zionists. During the last 20 years, the conservative evangelical movement has been the fastest growing sector within American Christian circles. Estimates of the number of evangelicals range from 100 to 130 million. Most of these individuals are inclined to support the Christian Zionist position. A recent poll by the Pew Research Centre, for example, noted that 58 per cent of evangelicals believe in the Battle of Armageddon. Today, these Christian Zionists constitute the largest base support for pro-Israel interests in the United States. The alliance between such groups and the pro-Israel lobby is now of fundamental importance. As Don Wagner noted:

> Pro-Israel groups and fundamentalist Christian groups have brought significant political and economic pressures to bear on Congress and the Bush presidency. Their support for Sharon's militant Likud ideology is unquestioning and usually supported by selected Biblical footnotes. Policies such as increased Israeli settlements, the pre-emptive assassination of Palestinian leaders, Israeli sovereignty over all of historical Palestine... would find ready support within the Christian right.[2]

The International Christian Embassy

Initially the Embassy building was the home of Edward Said, the distinguished Palestinian–American scholar, before it was confiscated in 1948 and given to the Jewish philosopher, Martin Buber. It then became the Chilean embassy, before housing the International Christian Embassy. Describing its origin, van der Hoeven stated that it was created 'in direct response to the world's cowardice and especially the cowardice of those nations which, unable to stand up to Arab blackmail, moved their embassies to Tel Aviv'.[4]

In 1985, the ICEJ organized the first International Christian Zionist Congress in Basle, Switzerland, the same meeting place that was used by Herzl to launch the Zionist movement in 1897. The ICEJ claims to have staff in over 80 countries and to draw support from charismatic, evangelical and fundamentalist Christians, largely in the USA, Canada, and South Africa. In 1993, the ICEJ declared its principles, which have been widely accepted:

1. To show concern for the Jewish people and the reborn State of Israel, by being a focus of comfort.
2. To be a centre where Christians can gain a biblical understanding of Israel, and learn to rightly relate to the nation.

3. To present to Christians a true understanding of what is taking place in the Land today so that world events may be interpreted in the light of God's word.

4. To remind and encourage Christians to pray for Jerusalem and the Land of Israel.

5. To stimulate Christian leaders, churches and organisations to become effective influences in their countries on behalf of the Jewish people.

6. To encourage Jewish people to return to their homeland.

7. To be a channel of fulfilment of God's promise that one day Israel and her Arab neighbours will live in peace under the blessing of God, in the middle of the earth.

8. To begin or assist projects in Israel, including economic ventures for the well-being of all who live here.

9. To take part through these activities in preparing the way of the Lord and to anticipate His reign from Jerusalem.[5]

The main objectives of the ICEJ have been to encourage Soviet and Eastern European Jews to emigrate to Israel, provide assistance for Jewish immigrants and sponsor an annual Feast of Tabernacles celebration in Jerusalem as well as diplomatic banquets and receptions for church leaders and governmental officials. To convey its message, it has also created a news service which produces radio and TV programmes and a Middle East Intelligence Digest. Since 1980 every Prime Minister has addressed the Feast of Tabernacles celebration – this event which draws about 5000 delegates from 100 countries is the largest annual tourist event in the State of Israel.

At the third Christian Zionist Congress held in 1996 in Jerusalem under the auspices of the ICEJ, over 1000 delegates from over 40 countries affirmed a declaration which asserted the biblical basis for the Jewish return to Zion:

> God the Father, Almighty, chose the ancient nation and people of Israel, the descendants of Abraham, Isaac and Jacob, to reveal His plan of redemption for the world. They remain elect of God, and without the Jewish nation His redemptive purposes for the world will not be complete... Christian believers are instructed by Scripture to acknowledge the Hebraic roots of their faith and to actively assist and participate in the plan of God for the ingathering of the Jewish people and the restoration of the nation of Israel in our day... The Lord in His zealous love for Israel and the Jewish People blesses and curses peoples and judges nations based upon their treatment of the Chosen People of Israel... According to God's distribution of nations, the Land of Israel has been given to the Jewish People by God as an everlasting

possession by an eternal covenant. The Jewish People have the absolute right to possess and dwell in the Land, including Judea, Samaria, Gaza and the Golan.[6]

Convinced that once the Jewish nation is restored to the Holy Land it will acknowledge the true Messiah when he returns, the ICEJ has disavowed evangelism among Jews. In line with premillennial dispensationalism, the ICEJ embraces the belief that before the return of the Messiah there will be a final battle of Armageddon when the nations will fight against Israel. The theology of the ICEJ is thus consistent with traditional dispensationalism: Israel occupies a superior role over the Church in the future purposes of God.

To accomplish this goal, the ICEJ has staunchly supported the Israeli right-wing Likud political establishment. In 1997 at the ICEJ's annual Feast of Tabernacles celebration, Prime Minister Benyamin Netanyahu endorsed its support of his political aims:

> Now I don't have to tell you that the media isn't always scrupulously fair when it comes to Israel. You can counter those distortions. You can tell the story, our story in the world. All we need to triumph in this struggle, is for the truth to be told. You can do for us what no one else can do. I am counting on you. I am relying on you. I am relying on your friendship, on the constancy of your support, and I deeply appreciate it, in the name of my family, my wife, my children, but especially in the name of the Children of Israel, all of the People of Israel. We respect and appreciate and thank you for your continual love for the State of Israel.[7]

Given such support, the ICEJ has become the representative of a coalition of Christian Zionist bodies.

Not only is the ICEJ convinced that *Eretz Israel* belongs exclusively to the Jewish people by divine sanction; it regards Jerusalem as the eternal capital of Israel. In an address given in the presence of Teddy Kollek, the major of Jerusalem, at the opening ceremony of the ICEJ on 30 September 1980, Jan Willem van der Hoeven stated:

> Today, we open in this, your City, the International Christian Embassy and, because we believe in God, the God of Israel, and in the promises of His Book, the Bible, we will remain in Jerusalem to pray for its peace and work for its good, knowing that in the end, all shall be well. May this International Christian Embassy then, be a sign of hope; hope for your people, and hope for your City so that it may become what it was always destined to be under Israel – a new dawn for all mankind.[8]

The following amplifications of the resolutions passed at the ICEJ Third International Christian Zionist Congress in February 1996 illustrate its explicitly religious and political agenda:

We are persuaded by the clear action of our God to express the sense of this Congress on the following concerns before us this day.

Because of the sovereign purposes of God for the City, Jerusalem must remain undivided, under Israeli sovereignty, open to all peoples, the capital of Israel only, and all nations should so concur and place their embassies here.

As a faith bound to love and forgiveness we are appreciative of the attempts by the Government of Israel to work tirelessly for peace. However, the truths of God are sovereign and it is written that the Land which He promised to His People is not to be partitioned... It would be further error for the nations to recognise a Palestinian state in any part of *Eretz Israel*.

The Golan is part of biblical Israel and is a vital strategic asset necessary for the security and defense of the entire country...

The Islamic claim to Jerusalem, including its exclusive claim to the Temple Mount, is in direct contradiction to the clear biblical and historical significance of the city and its holiest site...

Regarding Aliyah, we remain concerned for the fate of imperilled Jewish People in diverse places, and seek to encourage and assist in the continuing process of Return of the Exiles to *Eretz Israel*. To this end we commit to work with Israel and to encourage the Diaspora to fulfil the vision and goal of gathering to Israel the greater majority of all Jewish People from throughout the world.[9]

16

Christian Zionism and
the Holy Land

As Christian Zionists propounded their theories about the restoration of the Jewish people, the conflict between Israelis and Palestinians continued in the Holy Land. Even though Christian Zionists have adopted a wide range of approaches to the return of the Jewish people to their ancestral home, they share a number of common political assumptions. Owing to their commitment to the Jewish state, some Christian Zionists regard Islam and the Palestinian people with mistrust and contempt. For a sizeable number of dispensationalist Christian Zionists, the rebuilding of the Temple is a vital step prior to the advent of the Second Coming.

Christian Zionism and the Temple

Prior to the creation of the Jewish state, dispensationalists looked for signs of the times and sought to predict what would occur in the future. Basing their views on biblical prophecy, they were determined to interpret world events and illustrate how they were leading to the Second Coming. As futurist premillennialists, they felt that they would be raptured before the end-times occurred, but they expected to live long enough to see history moving toward its predetermined end. However, with the establishment of Israel and the expansion of its borders dispensationalists became more politically active. Fearing for Israel's future, they organized themselves to offer support for the Jewish state and have forged strong relationships with its leaders. There is no doubt that many of these organizations have had a significant impact on the political scene. Israel is stronger as a result of the support of the Christian right, and the willingness of Christian fundamentalists to stand up for Israel has improved US–Israel relations.

One of the prime concerns of these dispensationalist groups has been the rebuilding of the Temple in Jerusalem. For over a century, they had predicted that once Jews gathered in the Holy Land, they would eventually build a Third Temple. In this regard, there are two stages to the rebuilding of the Jerusalem Temple. The Tribulation Temple is viewed as the creation of unbelieving Jews which will be desecrated by the Antichrist; the Millennial Temple, on the other hand, will be built by the Messiah and redeemed Jews, and as a sign of restoration, they will be assisted by Gentile nations. This Temple will be distinguished from the Tribulation Temple by the return of the *Shekhinah* and by Gentile worship.

Although not all dispensationalists agree on the details of this process, in general they view the rebuilt Temple as indispensable to the fulfilment of God's plans. According to a leading American dispensationalist, John F. Walvoord, not long after the Antichrist brings his false peace to the Middle East, he will assist the Jews in building the Temple on the Temple Mount, as a symbol of national security and the redemption of the Jewish nation. Grateful Jews will hail him as their Messiah and reinstitute the sacrificial system. After three and a half years, the Antichrist will betray Israel by entering the restored Temple, declaring himself to be God, and requiring worship.

However, many Jews will resist such blasphemy, and this will compel the Antichrist to launch the holocaust in Jewish history. During this phase of the great Tribulation, a missionary force of 144,000 converted Jews will spread the gospel of Jesus and the coming kingdom and will be martyred. Even though the Antichrist's power will be enormous, he will be ovecome. God will pour out his divine wrath on those who follow the Antichrist, who will finally be defeated by Christ at his Second Coming. Those Jews who survive will hail Jesus as their conquering and true Messiah. King Jesus will then establish his millennial throne in Jerusalem and construct the Millennial Temple, where Jews and Gentiles will gather together to worship in spirit and truth.[1]

Such a scenario is impeded by the existence of the Dome of the Rock and the Al-Aqsa Mosque where the Temple is to be rebuilt. Although a number of dispensationalists disagree about where the Temple will be sited, there is a strong feeling among many that the Dome of the Rock will have to be dismantled. Even though Jews do not share the convictions of dispensationalists, there have been a number of attempts in recent years to destroy the Dome and the Mosque. Such activities have been connected to a small movement on the far right of Israel politics: the Temple movement. In 1969 a Christian foreigner, Dennis Michael Rohan, entered the Al-Aqsa

Mosque and set fire to it. At his trial Rohan declared that he believed God had called him to rebuild the Temple and then rule over Jerusalem.

In 1979 an underground group of Israeli extremists led by Yehudah Etzion, Menachem Livni and Yehudah Ben-Shusha plotted to blow up the Dome. Most of their followers were from the Gush Emunim, a group founded in 1974 by religious Zionist settlers on the West Bank who believed that God had returned Judaea and Samaria and all of Jerusalem to the Jewish people. For these extremists, allowing Muslims to retain control of the Temple Mount was an abomination. Israel's redemption, they believed, depended on Jews regaining control of the mount on which the Temple stood. This group hoped that the destruction of the Dome would help to halt Israeli plans to vacate the Sinai Peninsula and encourage the Redemption Movement. Despite extensive planning, however, the Gush Emunim never carried out this attack.

Other Israeli groups conceived other schemes. In the 1980s the Temple Mount and Land of Israel Faithful was founded by Gershon Salomon, a soldier who had helped liberate the Temple Mount during the Six-Day War. Critical of Moshe Dayan, who had returned control of the Temple Mount to Muslims, Salomon and his followers were determined to seize control. Determined to achieve this end, Salomon sought the support of American dispensationalists who viewed him as a pious Jew who believed that God's plan for his people in the last days required the construction of the Temple on the Temple Mount in anticipation of Jesus' return. During the 1990s Salomon lectured to evangelical tour groups to Israel and raised money from American evangelicals.

Another important Jewish figure on the dispensationalist scene was Stanley Goldfoot, a South African immigrant to Israel who was connected to the Stern Gang and played a major role in the 1946 bombing of the King David Hotel and the murder of the UN Middle East emissary, Count Bernadotte. In the 1980s he and various dispensationalists founded the Jerusalem Temple Foundation to provide financial support for the Temple Movement in Israel. Anxious to locate the original Temple site, Goldfoot encouraged Lambert Dolphin, a dispensationalist and physicist at the Stanford Research Institute in California, to use an X-ray system to conduct tests on the Temple Mount. In 1983 Dolphin and his crew attempted to investigate the Temple Mount but were stopped by the police.

Another American group with ties to the Temple Mount Faithful is the Battalion of Deborah, a dispensational organization in Texas. According to its mission statement, this women's group declares:

We have dedicated our lives and hearts in service to the God of Israel in this most Holy cause, to the Mission of the Temple Mount and Land of Israel Faithful. In great Love and devoted Friendship, we support the Leadership of Adon Gershon Salomon in making these Godly events, God willing, a reality in the lifetime of this generation. We stand in agreement with the Temple Mount Faithful that 'the Temple in Jerusalem was, and will again be, a focus for godly, spiritual, moral and cultural values, not only for Israel, but also for all the world.' The Battalion of Deborah believes that it is a privilege and our duty to support the rebuilding of God's House in Jerusalem in anticipation for the Arrival of the *Moshiach* [Messiah] and the establishment of His Peace, as a real and eternal peace in the Land of Israel, the region, and the world, forevermore.[3]

Another right-wing Israeli group that has drawn on American dispensationalist support is the Temple Institute founded in 1986 by Rabbi Yisrael Ariel. Its aim is to educate Israelis about the significance of the Third Temple and to prepare for its creation. A veteran of the liberation of the Temple Mount during the Six Day War, Ariel believes that Israel's future depends on rebuilding the Temple. When this is achieved, God's original promises to Abraham will be fulfilled, including Israel's possession of the territories promised to Abraham's descendants.

In 1983 Ariel and a group of yeshivah students and members of the IDF devised a plan to tunnel under the Al-Aqsa Mosque to conduct Passover prayers. It appeared that his goal was to set up a small Israeli settlement there to create a Jewish presence on the Mount. Israel's forces, however, stopped the expedition. However in 1989 Ariel and Joel Lerner of the Sanhedrin Institute did manage to gain access to the Temple Mount, where they planned to have a Passover sacrifice. Yet, they were stopped by the authorities. As the leader of Tzifay, Ariel organized members of the Jewish underground who had been jailed after their attempt to blow up the Dome of the Rock. In his view, killing the enemies of Israel should not be the concern of the Israeli courts; in his journal, he condemned all Jews who did not support the creation of the Third Temple. In addition, he classified Christians as well as Muslims as idolaters, thereby making them unfit to live in the Holy Land. Dispensationalists are encouraged by such activities as well as the knowledge that under the institute's auspices, Israelis are sewing priestly vestments, manufacturing implements for animal sacrifice, and teaching Temple priests how to officiate.

One of the most important activities of dispensationalists has focused on the production of a red heifer. According to Numbers 19, it will serve to purify people who have come into contact with the dead. To accomplish this, a red heifer without any blemishes will be slaughtered and burned, and its ashes made into a liquid paste to be used in a ceremony that Jews believe they must undergo before they can enter the old Temple site. Since Herod's Temple was destroyed in 70CE, no such red heifer has been born within the biblical land of Israel. Given the significance of the red heifer, some American dispensationalist cattle breeders sought to produce the needed animal. In 1990 Clyde Lott, a Pentecostal cattleman from Mississippi, travelled to meet with Rabbi Yisrael Ariel to begin a cattle business. The original plan was to bring 200 pregnant cows to Israel via ocean liners; they believed that the new herd would eventually produce a red heifer. At the same time Gershon Salomon of the Temple Faithful also reported that he had been in contact with another concerned Christian in Texas who believed he could help to produce the required animal. Although these breeding programmes were not successful, in the summer of 1996 Melody, a red heifer from the dairy farm of the Orthodox Kfar Hasidim agricultural school, was born. However, eventually Melody produced white hairs on the end of her tail which disqualified her as a red heifer. But on 8 April 2002 another red heifer was produced. For dispensationalists, these events illustrate that the prophecies in Scripture are being fulfilled, and that the Second Advent is soon to come.

Christian Zionists and Palestinians

With the emergence of Arab nationalism and the growing aspirations of Palestinians, the polemic against Arabs has intensified. As Jan van der Hoeven of the ICEJ remarked regarding the Arab world, comparing the Nazis and the Arabs:

> The greatest hero (in the Arab world) is Hitler... Hitler's *Mein Kampf* is still required reading in various Arab capitals and universities... The only reason that the Arabs have not yet done to the Israeli Jews what Hitler did to their forefathers in Europe is that they have thus far lacked the military means and weapons of mass destruction which were at Hitler's disposal, to do so. Had there not been an Israeli Defense Force to defend the remnant of European Jewry that immigrated to Israel, the Arabs would have gladly fulfilled Hitler's dream a long time ago by finishing off those of the Jews the Nazi megalomaniac had left alive.[8]

Similarly, Hal Lindsey castigated the Arab world for its offensive against Israel:

> Long ago the psalmist predicted the final mad attempt of the confederated Arab armies to destroy the nation of Israel. The Palestinians are determined to trouble the world until they repossess what they feel is their land.[9]

For some Christian Zionists, Yasser Arafat was perceived as the Antichrist. In February, 1999, Arafat was invited to attend the 47th annual Congress-sponsored National Prayer Breakfast in Washington. Regarding this event, the ICEJ declared that attending the breakfast with Arafat would be like praying with Satan himself. Respecting Palestinian claims to the Holy Land, Christian Zionists are anxious to counter the arguments of those who support the Palestinian cause. Ramon Bennett, for example, denied that there ever was a Palestinian people:

> Central to the Middle East conflict today is the issue of the so-called Palestinian people... Palestinians? There never was a Palestinian people, nation, language, culture, or religion. The claim of descent from a Palestinian people who lived for thousands of years in a land called Palestine is a hoax! That land was Canaan, inhabited by Canaanites, whom God destroyed because of their wickedness. Canaan became the land of Israel given by God to His people. Those who today call themselves Palestinians are Arabs by birth, language, and culture, and are close relatives to Arabs in surrounding countries from whence most of them came, attracted by Israel's prosperity.[10]

Frequently Islam is also demonized, particularly after the events of 11 September 2001. Various dispensationalist authors have described America's war against Islamic terrorism following this event. Hal Lindsey's writings, for example, are characterized by Arab negative stereotypes:

> All Muslims see Israel as their enemy.... The Arab nations are united in their fanatical obsession to destroy Israel... Agreements in the Arab nations don't mean the same thing they mean in the Judeo-Christian world. Islam not only has a track record of re-interpreting, denouncing and reversing settlements, such actions are actually encouraged if they further the cause of Allah... The movement seeks not only to destroy the State of Israel but also the overthrow of the Judeo-Christian culture – the very foundation of our western civilisation... They have, like the Communists, at their philosophic core the sworn duty to 'bury us'.[11]

In February 2002 Pat Robertson described Islam as a violent religion determined to dominate the world. In his view, American Muslims had formed terrorist cells in order to destroy the United States. On the Christian Broadcasting Network's 700 Club, he alleged that Islam is not a peaceful religion. In this light, Christian Zionists oppose Palestinian aspirations to self-determination. Not surprisingly, a number of Christian Zionists are critical of the peace process since it threatens to legitimize Palestinian claims to Jerusalem and other parts of Israel. Dismissive of the peace process, Clarence Wagner of the BFP has been dismissive of the peace negotiations:

> We need to encourage others to understand God's plans, not the man-inspired plans of the UN, the US, the EEC, Oslo, Wye, etc. God is not in any plan that would wrestle the Old City of Jerusalem, including the Temple Mount area and the Mount of Olives, and give it to the Moslem world. Messiah is not coming back to a Moslem city called Al-Quds, but to the ingathered, restored Jewish city of Jerusalem.[12]

According to some Christian Zionists, those who support the Arab world against Israel are acting against God. As David Brickner cautioned:

> Peril awaits those who presume to say that God is finished with his chosen people... Just as God judged the nation of Egypt for her ill treatment of His people, so will He judge nations today. Evangelicals who would understand the Middle East must pay close attention to the teaching of Scripture, and take note of the cosmic forces that now do battle in the heavens but will soon do battle on earth.[13]

While demonizing Islam, Christian Zionists have sanctioned the relationship between Israel and the United States. Continually they take the side of Israel in its negotiations with the Arab world, recognizing that they share a common war against Islamic terrorism. Israel has the right, they believe, to live securely within expanded borders of the Jewish state. In their view God has granted sovereignty to his people to rule exclusively over the land that was promised to the patriarchs. Many of these Christian believers are convinced that there will eventually be an apocalyptic war between God and evil in the near future: as a consequence, there can be no peace between Jews and Arabs.

Critical of such an uncompromising stance, Palestinians have been anxious to repudiate the claims made against them. Typical of such reactions is the response by Jonathan Kuttab, a Palestinian Christian, to a speech by the Archbishop of Canterbury to the International Sabeel Conference which took place in Jerusalem in April, 2004:

Palestinian Christians had suffered much at the hand of theologies and interpretations of scripture that provided a mantle of divine legitimisation to the ideology of Zionism and the political movement that worked for their displacement from their homeland, and built a Jewish state on the basis of their exile, and oppression. One of our constant complaints was that Christian Zionism ignores our national rights. The creation of the state of Israel was done on our land and the ingathering of Jews from all the world came at the price of exiling and scattering our people throughout the world. All this was supported by Christian theologies that ignored or delegitimized us as a people, claiming a divine imperative based on scripture for the creation of the state of Israel.

Such views generally side-stepped or totally ignored the Palestinian people on whose land the state was created. While the Jewish people were seen to hold a divinely mandated right to peoplehood, and even chosenness, as well as a promise to ownership of the land, by its creator and ultimate sovereign, the Palestinian people had only individual and transient rights at best, as strangers in the midst of God's people. These issues were not of passing theological or academic interest to us, but had direct tangible consequences for us of life and death, as well as of faith.[14]

Steps toward Peace

In December 1991 a conference took place in Washington dealing with the procedures for future talks. Israel insisted that it was not willing to discuss territorial concessions; instead it desired to focus on Palestine autonomy. The Palestinians, however, were not content with such a limitation. After these talks, Jews and Arabs met in a number of cities to explore various practical issues. Such collaborative ventures were interrupted by the Israeli election in which Labour became the largest party, forming an alliance with the left-wing party Meretz and the Arab Democratic Party as well as Shas. As Prime Minister, Yitzhak Rabin was committed to continuing the peace process.

In July 1992 James Baker arrived in the Middle East to seek a solution to the conflict between Israel and its neighbours, and two days later went to Cairo to renew negotiations for a peace settlement. Despite such political activity, tension mounted in the West Bank and Jerusalem. The effort to renew the peace process inflamed members of Hamas and Islamic Jihad. Despite a series of acts of violence, talks between Israel and the PLO began on 20 January 1993. At a villa outside Oslo representatives met for three days; this gathering was followed by further meetings. Eventually the Oslo Accords were approved by both the Israelis and the Palestinians and a ceremony took place in Washington on 13 September 1993 with Yitzhak Rabin and Yasser Arafat as the main representatives.

The Oslo Accords served as the framework for the peace process and a basis for Israeli-Arab co-operation. The form of self-government authorized at Oslo and the withdrawal plans provided a basis for eventual Palestinian statehood. In an effort to thwart these steps toward a settlement, an Israeli gunman, Baruch Goldstein, opened fire on Palestinian Arabs inside a mosque in Hebron in February 1994. This massacre disrupted negotiations, yet they were soon resumed. On 3 May, Rabin and Arafat met in Cairo to finalize a peace agreement. Negotiations continued, and on 4 July 1995 Shimon Peres met with Arafat in Gaza to finalize Oslo II; this was followed on 22 September by a meeting with Peres and Arafat at an Egyptian resort to discuss Palestinian rule in the West Bank. The next week Rabin flew to Washington, where he signed the Oslo II agreement.

In Israel right-wing demonstrators protested against the government, and the leader of Likud, Benjamin Netanyahu, attacked Rabin. At a rally in Jerusalem on 28 October 1995, Rabin was denounced as a traitor to the Jewish state. The next week, he and Shimon Peres appeared at a rally in Tel Aviv in support of the peace process. At the end of the rally Rabin left the platform and was shot dead by a religious Jew, Yigal Amir, a student at Bar-Ilan University. This incident derailed the peace process, and an election took place on 29 May 1996. Labour had the largest number of seats in the Knesset, but in the vote for Prime Minister, Benjamin Netanyahu won the election.

Together with parties opposed to the Oslo peace process, as well as the religious bloc, a new Russian immigrant party and the centrist Third Way Party, Netanyahu was able to form a coalition government. Despite his defeat, Peres pressed forward with his peace plans. However, Netanyahu delayed completing the arrangements for Israel's withdrawal from the Occupied Territories. Conflict continued during this period, and further settlement took place in the West Bank. Adopting a different approach to the Palestinian problem, the government altered the maps from the Oslo Accords under which the vast majority of the West Bank would be transferred to the Palestinians.

In October 1998 Prime Minister Netanyahu and Yasser Arafat met in Washington to discuss the peace process. After prolonged argument, Israel and the Palestinians agreed to embark on a new stage of co-operation. According to the Wye agreement, Israel would effect a further West Bank redeployment. Arafat agreed that the Palestinian authorities would take all measures necessary to prevent acts of terrorism, crime and hostilities. They further agreed to apprehend, investigate and prosecute individuals suspected of violence. The summer of 1999 witnessed a change of government with the election of Ehud Barak as Prime Minister of Israel.

On 28 September 2000 violence erupted when Ariel Sharon made a visit to the Temple Mount in Jerusalem; nonetheless, in January 2001 peace talks were held at Taba, an Egyptian resort town. Determined to continue the peace process, the United States sought to persuade Palestinians and Israelis that a negotiated settlement was vital to security in the Middle East. In April 2001 the Mitchell report was published, which made a series of recommendations. On September 11, however, al Qaeda terrorists hijacked airliners and flew them into the World Trade Centre in New York and the Pentagon outside Washington. A fourth plane, apparently heading for the White House, crashed into a field in Pennsylvania.

Following this attack, Arab and Islamic countries stressed the need for their co-operation in the war against terrorism in order to obtain concessions from Israel. However, many Americans began to lose sympathy for the Palestinian cause: Palestinians were criticized for their apparent support of Bin Laden. Against this background, the US and the EU appeared to give Israel wider latitude for actions against the Palestinians. Israel continued to make incursions into Palestinian areas, and confined Yasser Arafat to his compound in Ramallah. In the wake of such actions, Palestinians increased attacks on soldiers and civilians.

The Israeli onslaught, referred to as Operation Defensive Shield, began on 28 March 2002; its goal was to dismantle the terrorist infrastructure developed by the Palestinian Authority. The operation consisted of moving Israeli forces into the West Bank and Gaza for the purpose of arresting terrorists, finding and confiscating weapons, and destroying explosives. Eventually Yasser Arafat signed into law the Basic Law or constitution of the Palestinian transitional state. This law guaranteed basic rights, but stated that Palestinian legislation will be based on the principles of Islamic law. In June 2002 Israeli forces reoccupied the West Bank. In August and September attempts were made to bring about Palestinian cease-fire initiatives, but these were opposed by extremist groups.

In Israel a further election took place in 2003 and Ariel Sharon became Prime Minister. In March 2003 the United States and Britain attacked Iraq, overthrowing Saddam Hussein. Prior to this conflict President Bush reiterated his desire for a solution to the Palestinian problem in the Middle East, a theme which was reinforced after his election for a second term in November, 2004. With the death of Yasser Arafat in the same year and the subsequent election of Muhammad Abbas as the new President of the PLO, hopes have been raised for an eventual settlement of the problems facing this region.

The Political Agenda of Christian Zionism Today

Most importantly, Christian Zionists maintain that the Jewish nation remains God's chosen people in some ways separate from the Church. As a consequence, Christian Zionists are determined to support Israel against charges of racism and apartheid. Frequently they have lobbied Western governments on behalf of the Jewish State; in addition, they promote Israeli products, host pro-Israeli events, and participate in solidarity tours.

A CMJ resource pack produced in 1996 typifies such unqualified support of the Jewish nation. In a section entitled: 'The State of Israel: Why should we support it?', CMJ asserted:

> In the biblical worldview one cannot... divorce the issue of Israel's rela-
> tionship with God from their relationship to their delegated sover-
> eignty in the land of Israel... It seems to us that God is undoubtedly
> behind the recreation of the Jewish state in the modern world.[3]

In this regard the International Christian Zionist Centre (ICZC) is anxious to express solidarity with Israel by organizing the annual Feast of Tabernacles celebration in Jerusalem, which draws thousands of Christian Zionists to the city in order to bless Israel. This feast, they assert, is a prophetic celebration for the end-times, when all the nations of the earth will be welcomed to celebrate this Feast with Israel. Many Christian Zionists believe that when the world stands against Israel and economic support from the United States disappears, the Jewish state will need to turn to Christian friends for assistance.

As we have seen, in the United States the Christian right came to prominence following the election of Ronald Reagan as president. His presidency ushered in the most pro-Israel administration in history and provided an opportunity for Christian Zionists to occupy influential political positions. Figures such as Attorney General Ed Meese, Secretary of Defense Caspar Weinberger, and Secretary of the Interior James Watt, came to play an influential role in shaping American foreign policy. White House seminars were a feature of Reagan's administration, and Christian Zionists including Jerry Falwell, Mike Evans and Hal Lindsey came into personal contact with political figures.

In 1991 at a National Prayer Breakfast, the Christian Israel Public Affairs Committee was launched, which has lobbied on behalf of the Israeli Likud Party. The aim of this body is to encourage Christian support for Israel. More recently, the United Coalition for Israel (UCFI), which comprises a coalition of 200 different Jewish and Christian members, has lobbied the US media and political establishment to challenge what they perceive as distortions about Israel. This organization includes three of the largest Christian Zionist bodies: Bridges for Peace, the International Christian Embassy Jerusalem, and Christians for Peace.

Alongside such political activity, Christian Zionists have become allies of the Israeli government in promoting solidarity tours and pilgrimages to the Holy Land. Recently, Israeli tourism minister Benny Elon honoured Pat Robertson at the national Association of Broadcasters Convention in Charlotte, North Carolina, praising his leadership, which has saved Israel's tourism from bankruptcy by promoting pilgrimages to the Holy Land: 40,000 evangelicals, he said, had travelled to Israel in 2003, thereby contributing millions of dollars to the economy.

Jerry Falwell's Friendship Tour of Israel is typical of such programmes. Taking over 600 pilgrims, Falwell's itinerary has included:

1. An Israeli American Friendship Banquet in Jerusalem with Jerry Falwell and Prime Minister Menahem Begin.
2. Meetings with Israeli administration officials and Knesset members.
3. Luncheon with Major Saad Haddad, Commander of Christian forces in Southern Lebanon.
4. Participating in transatlantic, live TV satellite programmes.
5. On-site tour of modern Israeli battlefields.
6. Official visit to an Israeli defence installation.
7. A Bibleland tour.[4]

The primary aim of such visits to the Holy Land is to bring a blessing to the Jewish people, especially for settlers in the Occupied Territories. As Sizer notes:

> They seek to show solidarity with the State of Israel and witness the literal fulfilment of biblical prophecy. The presence of an indigenous Palestinian Christian community is an unwelcome complication either demonized as Muslim fundamentalists or cast as recent economic migrants, drawn by the wealth of Israel. With greater contact occurring between Western Christians and the State of Israel, Christian Zionists return home galvanized in their support for

agencies encouraging Jewish people to make aliyah and claim their inheritance.[5]

Regarding the borders of Israel, Christian Zionists are anxious to put the territorial claims of Israel into a wider context than the Middle East. David Allen Lewis, president of the Christians United for Israel, argued that it is not acceptable that the Arabs have 99.5 per cent of the land: Derek Prince of the Christian Friends of Israel complained that Israel has only 22 per cent of their original inheritance; Jan Willem van der Hoeven of the International Christian Embassy, Jerusalem asserted:

> God wanted to give His people that part of the land which they did not receive in 1948 and by hardening the hearts of the different Arab leaders... He impelled Israel to react. The result of what became known as the Six Day War was that Judea and Samaria – heartland of biblical Israel – and the ancient city of Jerusalem – King David's capital – were returned to their original owner... Thus, the Lord, by hardening the hearts of the Arab leaders, caused His people Israel to inherit the rest of the land, especially their ancient city, in a war of self defence! Until then, since 1949, Jordan had illegally held and occupied the 'West Bank' and Jerusalem. Thus, when Israel recaptured Judea, Samaria and Jerusalem, they did not even take over a territory that legally belonged at that time to any nation![6]

At the First International Christian Zionist Conference in 1985 sponsored by the ICEJ, a resolution calling for the judaization of Palestine was passed. At the Third International Zionist Congress held in Jerusalem in February 1996, over a thousand delegates from over 40 countries affirmed a declaration of Israeli sovereignty. The belief that the entire West Bank is integral to the Jewish state has led many Christian Zionists to adopt Jewish settlements to strengthen their ties to the region. The Christian Friends of Israeli Communities, for example, was founded in response to the Oslo Process, which returned land to the Palestinian Authority. The purpose of this organization is to forge links between Jewish settlements in the Occupied Territories and churches and Christians internationally. Christian Zionists are also active in funding Jewish settlements on the West Bank. At the 1991 ICEJ Feast of Tabernacles celebration, for example, representatives from 12 countries presented cheques to Prime Minister Yitshak Shamir to help finance these communities.

It is also a central principle of Christian Zionism that Jerusalem must remain the exclusive and undivided capital of Israel. Some Christian Zionists claim that God has decreed that Jerusalem become the capital of the Jewish people and will bless or curse nations on the basis of how they view this issue. As Clarence Wagner of Bridges of Peace stated:

> Despite the peace process, the idea of Jerusalem as the undivided capital of Israel is still far from accepted by the nations of the world or the Moslems... The nations can plot and plan what they will regarding the division of the land of Israel and the city of Jerusalem. Yet they will not succeed. In the end, God will be faithful to His prophetic word.[7]

Amongst Christian Zionists the determination to ensure that Jerusalem is the capital is unceasing. Their efforts have focused on persuading American presidents to authorize the transfer of the American embassy to Jerusalem; in their view, such a move would ensure Israel's claim to the city as their eternal capital.

17
Conclusion

As we have seen, there are various strands of Christian Zionism that have evolved through the centuries. With the emergence of Protestantism, there was increased interest in the Bible: this led to renewed preoccupation with the role of the Jewish people in God's providential plan. Amongst the Puritans in particular, a number of writers believed that the Jewish people must return to their ancient homeland prior to the Second Coming. Pre-eminent among these thinkers, Sir Henry Finch, an eminent lawyer and member of the English Parliament published a work entitled *The World's Great Restoration or Calling of the Jewish, (and with them) all the Nations and Kingdoms of the Earth, to the Faith in Christ.* In this tract, Finch encouraged Jews to reassert their claim to the Holy Land. According to Finch, the Jewish community will eventually convert to Christianity.

Premillennial restorationism was embraced by a wide variety of writers including the Dutch pietist Holger Paulli, who maintained that the Jewish return to the Holy Land was a precondition of the Second Coming. Writing in the late eighteenth century, the Anglican Bishop Richard Hurd stressed that God would gather the Jewish people in their ancient land. At the same time the evangelist Edward Witaker published a dissertation on the final restoration of the Jews. There will be a literal restoration, he believed, since God had promised to Abraham all the land which he could see – this promise was absolute and everlasting. At the end of the century Charles Jerram maintained that the title of the Jews to the land was inalienable.

For these early Christian Zionists, the role of the Jewish people in the final days was of paramount importance. The distinguished preacher Charles Haddon Spurgeon argued that the Church and Israel would eventually be united spiritually and face tribulation together. The millennial kingdom on earth would thus be made up of Jews and gentiles. All this would be preceded by a restoration of Israel. Jesus will then come upon Mount Zion with his ancients and the days of the millennium will dawn. Like Spurgeon, other thinkers, including Henry Drummond, a city banker and High Sheriff of Surrey, were preoccupied with the role of the Jewish people in the millennial kingdom. Through Drummond's influence, figures such as Edward Irving, Lewis Way and James Hatley Frere met together to discuss the nature of biblical prophecy concerning the Second Coming. In the United States, the return of the Jews to the land of their fathers was also promoted by such groups as the Mormons. According to Joseph Smith, the restoration of the Jews to Palestine must precede the coming of the Messiah.

Alongside such theological reflection, various groups were created to foster the return of the Jewish people to their ancestral home. In Britain, the London Society for Promoting Christianity Amongst the Jews was created by Joseph Frey in the late eighteenth century. Early in his ministry, he proposed the creation of a meeting house of Hebrew Christians as well as a boarding school; later Frey and his followers created the London Jewish Society (LJS), which was supported by leading British Christians. Later the LJS leased the old French Protestant Church in Spitalfields in London, which they renamed 'The Jews Chapel', and formed a society 'Benei Avraham', which met for prayer. Supported by such figures as Lewis Way, the Society subscribed to the belief in the eventual return of the Jews to the Holy Land and the eventual conversion of Jewry. By the end of the nineteenth century, the LJS supported missionary stations in 46 places outside Britain. In 1841 one of Way's followers, Michael Solomon Alexander, became the first Anglican bishop in Jerusalem.

The development of Christian Zionism within Anglicanism was influenced by Charles Simeon who was dedicated to the work of the LJS: he, too, looked for a full restoration of the Jewish people prior to the Second Coming. In his view, the future restoration of the Jews and their union with the gentiles will take place together, and for this reason he sought to convert Jews to the true faith. Through their conversion, he believed, all nations will be drawn to Christ. A student of Simeon, Joseph Wolff, who had converted to Roman Catholicism and then to Anglicanism, went to Jerusalem, where he distributed New Testaments and Christian literature to Jews.

During the mid-nineteenth century, Christian statesmen began to take an interest in the Holy Land. The first leading Christian to express concern about those Jews living in Palestine was Lord Palmerston, the British foreign secretary. In 1840 he wrote to the British Ambassador in Constantinople, encouraging a Jewish settlement in the Holy Land. Lord Ashley (later Lord Shaftesbury) was another who was convinced that the return of the Jews to Palestine was linked to the Second Coming. Determined to see this event come about, he presented a formal document to Lord Palmerston for the recall of the Jews to Palestine. Alongside such political aspirations, Christian missionaries championed the cause of Jewish restoration. In their view, the prophecies concerning the Second Coming were linked with guilt concerning the harsh treatment of Jews through the centuries.

In Palestine, Christian missionaries sought to draw Jews to the Christian faith. Through the efforts of the Dutch missionary John Nicolayson of the LJS, steps were taken to establish an ongoing Protestant presence in the Holy Land. By the middle of the nineteenth century, Nicholayson sought to purchase property for the Church, and made plans for the creation of a mission house and chapel. At this time the LJS sent out two more Hebrew Christians to re-establish medical work. Later the LJS established other institutions to care for the Hebrew Christian community.

Unlike the early Christian Zionists, however, secular Jewish Zionists were in no respect concerned about the coming of the Messiah. Instead, secular proponents of Jewish nationhood were convinced that the Jewish community must create a homeland in which they would be able to protect themselves from persecution. Although some Orthodox Zionists, such as Zwi Hirsch Kalischer and Yehuda Hai Alkalai, did believe that the creation of a Jewish commonwealth in Palestine would hasten the coming of the Messiah, the majority of Zionists were unconcerned about eschatology.

By the middle of the nineteenth century, a number of Christian writers championed the idea of Jewish restoration. Following the Damascus Affair, a German Lutheran, C.F. Zimpel, published a work, *Israelites in Jerusalem*, in which he argued that it is necessary to bring about the return of the Jews to their original homeland. In the United States, Zimpel promoted his plan to establish Jewish farming villages in Palestine. The return of Jews to their ancestral home, he believed, would be a realization of biblical prophecy. In Britain, similar practical steps were undertaken to restore the Jews to Palestine, such as the creation of the British and Foreign Society for Promoting the Restoration of the Jewish Nation to Palestine. During this period Laurence Oliphant, an officer in the British Foreign Office, became increasingly interested in the Holy Land. Eventually he sought to persuade the Sultan in Constantinople to grant lands to the Jewish people.

In the United States, William E. Blackstone, a Christian evangelical missionary, published *Jesus is Coming* and pressed for the return of the Jews. In this work, he envisaged the Jewish restoration to Palestine as the fulfilment of biblical prophecy. In 1891 he presented a petition – 'Palestine for the Jews' – which advocated the return of Palestine to the Jewish nation. Leading Jewish secular Zionists, too, sought the return of the Jewish people to Palestine. Theodor Herzl, for example, sought to persuade co-religionists of the necessity of a Jewish State. In this quest, he was supported by William Hechler, an Anglican priest who was convinced that the return of the Jews to the Holy Land would be the fulfilment of biblical prophecy. Anxious to achieve this aim, Hechler introduced Herzl to leading political figures, including the Duke of Baden.

Within the Jewish community Zionists differed about the nature of the Jewish state and its spiritual aspirations. Simultaneously, ultra-Orthodox critics of Zionism united in their opposition to the creation of a Jewish state. In their view, Zionism was a betrayal of the Jewish faith, since they maintained it is forbidden to accelerate divine redemption through human efforts. Paralleling this critique, liberal opponents assailed Zionism as misguided utopianism. Christian Zionists, however, continued to support the creation of a Jewish homeland in Palestine. Pre-eminent among Christian enthusiasts were Lord Salisbury, William Hechler and Laurence Oliphant, who were actively involved in the LJS. In Palestine itself, the LJS helped early Jewish immigrants to the country.

In the early decades of the twentieth century, Christian Zionists continued to press for Jewish settlement in Palestine. Initially Lieutenant Colonel John Henry Patterson, a Protestant Irishman, became the commander of the Jewish Legion. When the Balfour Declaration was issued in 1917, he believed that the return of the Jews to their ancestral land would be the fulfilment of biblical prophecy. Lord Balfour himself was deeply influenced by Scripture, as was Lloyd George. Both recognized that their upbringing had influenced their attitude toward Zionism.

Just as Christian Zionists had supported the Balfour Declaration, they were dedicated to the establishment of the Jewish homeland in Palestine under the Mandate. Pre-eminent among such figures was Josiah Clement Wedgwood, who proposed a scheme for the creation of a Jewish national home. The LJS (renamed the CMJ) was also active in Palestine in the post-Balfour era. Determined to ensure the return of the Jewish people to the Holy land, it reaffirmed its belief in the restoration of the Jewish people and opposed any attempt to limit immigration. In Britain, a number of leading politicians were also supportive of Zionist ambitions, including Winston Churchill; similarly, in the United States leading statesmen, including President

Woodrow Wilson were also in favour of creating a Jewish presence in Palestine. Alongside politicians who supported Zionism, a number of American Christians also lent their support for a Jewish state in the Holy Land.

Parallel with such developments, a separate stream of Christian eschatology – different from premillennial restoration – had deeply influenced a wide range of supporters of the restoration of the Jews to the Holy Land. In the first half of the nineteenth century Christian thinkers came to view the return of the Jewish people as inaugurating the end of the world in which humanity would endure terrible sufferings. Beginning with the writings of Edward Irving, premillennial dispensationalism came to influence a wide range of thinkers. Like Irving, John Nelson Darby rejected the optimism of earlier theologians. Concerned about current events, Darby employed the term 'dispensation' to refer to a series of failed attempts by humankind to find acceptance with God. In Darby's opinion, the Church was only one more dispensation that had failed, and only a small remnant would be saved.

According to Darby, there could be no future earthly hope for the Church, and it will soon be replaced in God's purposes by Israel. The promises made to the Jewish people, he believed, were unfulfilled and would find their eventual consummation in the reign of Jesus Christ on earth during the millennium. This eschatological scheme served as the foundation for later dispensational doctrines in which the Church was understood as a parenthesis to God's continuing covenantal relationship with the Jewish nation. In Darby's view, the Jews will serve as the primary instrument of God's rule on earth during the millennium. The Jews, he argued, will rule on earth in league with Satan, but a remnant of the Jews will be delivered and the Antichrist destroyed. For Darby, there will be two stages to Christ's return. First, believing Christians will be raptured and meet Christ in the air. This Rapture will then be followed by seven years of Tribulation; this will end when Jesus will return to Jerusalem to set up his kingdom.

Although Darby's influence in Britain waned, his ministry continued in the United States where he influenced such evangelistic figures as James H. Brookes, Dwight L. Woody, William Blackstone, and C.I. Scofield as well as the emerging Bible Schools and prophecy conferences. Amongst Darby's followers, C.I. Scofield had a profound impact on the development of premillennial dispensationalism. Determined to write a commentary on Scripture, Scofield eventually composed the *Scofield Reference Bible* in which he argued that dispensations should be understood as periods of time during which human beings are tested in relation to their obedience to God. Influenced by Darby, he argued that the Church age will end in failure and apostasy and be replaced by a revived national Israel who will experience the blessings of the final kingdom dispensation.

Following Darby, Scofield explained that God has a separate plan for Israel and another for the Church – Israel's destiny is on earth while the Church's is in heaven. During the great Tribulation on earth a remnant of Israel will turn to Jesus as the Messiah and become his witnesses after the removal of the Church. Like Darby, he taught that God seeks to bring the Jewish people back to Palestine, reconstitute the priesthood and rebuild the ancient Temple. In his reference Bible, he reiterated that terrible events will take place during the period of Tribulation. Following its publication, *Scofield's Reference Bible* had an enormous impact. By the 1950s half of all conservative evangelical student groups were using *Scofield's Reference Bible* and it became the primary document of fundamentalism.

In time other leading dispensationalists championed the theories expounded by Darby and others. Such figures as Arno C. Gaebelein, Harry Ironside, M.R. DeHann, and Reuben A. Torrey were committed to a biblical basis for the restoration of the Jews to their ancestral home. Dispensationalism was also popularized by such writers as Hal Lindsey, whose books portrayed the period of Tribulation in graphic terms. His most famous work, The *Late, Great Planet Earth*, depicts the dangers facing humanity. In his view, the battle of Armageddon is unavoidable. Only by believing in Jesus can the faithful be saved and avoid a global holocaust. In presenting his predictions, Lindsey was sympathetic to Israel. Like other dispensationalists, he stressed that the promises made to Abraham is eternal.

For Lindsey, God will not forsake the Jewish people, and all nations will receive blessings through Israel. Biblical prophecy demands a national restoration of the Jewish people. However, in his view many Israelis will die in the holocaust of Armageddon, but the Church will be replaced by Israel as the people of God on earth. Within this framework, Lindsey maintains that the incorporation of the Occupied Territories into Israel is essential. Further, the occupation of Jerusalem must also continue, since it will become the spiritual centre of all the world. All peoples will come to worship Jesus there, and he will rule from the holy city. In The *Late, Great Planet Earth*, Lindsey describes Armageddon, although he insists that Christians who embrace a dispensational theology will be raptured before the Tribulation commences. In this way believers will escape the terrible events of the holocaust.

This picture of the final days is graphically portrayed in the series of novels by Tim LaHaye. Along with Lindsey, LaHaye has become a successful popularizer of premillennial dispensationalism. Implicit in his works is a fatalistic view of the future. LaHaye's mission has been to gain support for the political agenda of the religious right. His *Left Behind* series reinforces the fear that there is a sinister group at work creating a one-world socialist gulag for those who have not been saved. According to LaHaye, his novels are true to the literal interpretation of biblical prophecy. Beginning with *Left Behind*, the series depicts the period of Tribulation and the final Armageddon. In the final novel, *Glorious Appearing*, believers look to heaven for the appearance of Christ, who will return and rule over all the world.

Such millennial predictions have influenced millions of Christian believers as well as many Messianic Jews who have embraced premillennial dispensationalism. In their view, all believers in Yeshua will be raptured at the beginning of the great Tribulation. During this period, a powerful world leader who advocates peace for the world will gain unlimited control. Seeking to solve the Middle East crisis, he will gain Israel's support. But eventually there will be a final Armageddon in which the world will be devastated. Yet, the Messiah will return to vanquish his enemies and rule over all Israel. In this vision of the future, the Jewish people will have a central place in the Messianic age. Although some Messianic Jews seek to distance themselves from this view, Messianic Jews – like Christian Zionists – are active supporters of the Jewish state.

As we have noted, premillennial dispensationalism in its various forms has had a profound impact on the Christian right. Today, it is the most prevalent form of Christian Zionism, with millions of followers worldwide. A variety of authors and preachers have predicted that an evil global empire will emerge under the leadership of a mysterious world leader, the Antichrist, and attack Israel, and eventually there will be a climactic Battle of Armageddon. In the view of these believers, after seven years of Tribulation Jesus will return as the Jewish Messiah and king to reign in Jerusalem for a thousand years, and the Jewish people will enjoy a privileged status and role in history. When Israel captured Jerusalem and the West Bank plus the Gaza Strip and the Golan Heights in 1967, many Christian Zionists believed that the latter days were imminent, and that in their support of Israel seeking to hasten the coming of the Messiah, they would usher in a new age of fulfilment and glory.

Despite their differences, both premillennial restorationism and premillennial dispensationalism have a number of common features.

Christian Zionists – no matter what their theological orientation – believe that the prophecies in Scripture concerning the Jewish nation are being fulfilled in our own time. The aim of Christian Zionism is to support the Zionist aim of the sovereign state of Israel. As apologists for Israel, Christian Zionists are critical of those who are opposed to the Jewish homeland in *Eretz Israel*, particularly in the Arab world. From a religious perspective, they envisage God's hand in current events. As Grace Halsell explains:

> What is the message of the Christian Zionist? Simply stated, it is this: every act taken by Israel is orchestrated by God, and should be condoned, supported, and even praised by the rest of us.[1]

In certain respects, Christian Zionists share the same religious agenda as Jewish Zionists. As Stephen Sizer explains:

> Whether consciously or otherwise, Christian Zionists subscribe to a religious agenda best expressed by Rabbi Shlomo Aviner, who claims: 'We should not forget... that the supreme purpose of the ingathering of exiles and the establishment of our State is the building of the Temple. The Temple is at the very top of the pyramid.' Another rabbi, Yisrael Meida, explains the link between politics and theology within Jewish Zionism: 'It is all a matter of sovereignty. He who controls the Temple Mount, controls Jerusalem. And he who controls Jerusalem, controls the land of Israel.' This paradigm may be illustrated by way of three concentric rings. The land represents the middle ring and the Temple is the centre ring. The three rings comprise the Zionist agenda by which the Land was claimed in 1948, the Old City of Jerusalem was occupied in 1967 and the Temple site is being contested. For the religious Zionist, Jewish or Christian, the three are inextricably linked.[2]

Today, millions of these fundamentalist Christians have become a massive lobby, actively involved in Middle East affairs. Some, like Pat Robertson and Jerry Falwell, have played an important role in the highest levels of American political life. Yet, the Christian community is divided as to whether Christian Zionism is true to the teaching of the Church. In the Christian world, those who are offering support for the Jewish state are being delegitimized and demonized by a growing chorus of critics. Frequently, they are accused of blocking the way to peace in the Middle East, or of having some end-time agenda that seeks to hasten the Apocalypse.

In the media Christian Zionists are often portrayed as dangerous and deluded. Thus the British commentator Robert Fisk charged in an *Independent* column that President George Bush had legitimized terrorism by 'giving way to the crazed world of Christian Zionism.

The fundamentalist Christians who support Israel's theft of the West Bank on the grounds that the state of Israel must exist there according to God's law until the Second Coming, believe that Jesus will return to earth and the Israelis ... will then have to convert to Christianity or die in the Battle of Armageddon.'[3]

A range of popularized books dealing with Christian Zionism have followed a similar line. In her study of Christian Zionism, *Prophecy and Politics*, for example, Grace Halsell argues that Christian Zionists practise the same form of muscular Christianity that their forefathers once followed when they slaughtered Indians to win the West. The American fundamentalists, she claimed, see Armageddon as an event most earnestly to be desired. In the Arab world, the Palestinian scholar Edward Said stated in the Egyptian weekly *Al-Ahram* that the vast number of Christian fanatics in the US, who form the core of George Bush's support ... are in my opinion, a menace to the world and furnish Bush's government with its rationale for punishing evil while righteously condemning whole populations to submission and poverty'. In his view, the Christian right is rabidly pro-Israel and deeply anti-Semitic for believing that Jews who do not convert at the Messiah's coming will be doomed to perdition.[4]

Alongside such criticism, a number of Christian scholars have been anxious to illustrate that Christian Zionism does not correspond to traditional Christian teaching. Pre-eminent among such writers, Stephen Sizer in *Christian Zionism: Road Map to Armageddon* outlines a number of objections to its central characteristics:

1. A literalist and futurist reading of prophecy is the foundation upon which the other six tenets are based. However... this method of interpretation is no more consistent or free of presuppositional influence than any other, and is at times inconsistent, contradictory and arbitrary.

2. A belief that the Jews remain God's chosen people, and separate from the church, flows from this literalist hermeneutic. While covenantal and dispensational Christian Zionists view the relationship between the church and Israel somewhat differently, the consequences of both are essentially the same: Israel is elevated to a status above the church; for dispensationalists at least, Israel will replace the church on earth; while Christians, and indeed whole nations, will be blessed through their association with, and support of, Israel. This view is entirely at variance with the New Testament which universalizes the concept of the people of God and makes chosenness conditional on faith in Jesus Christ.

3. Belief in a final restoration of the Jews to Zion is also based on a literal and futurist reading of selective Old Testament prophecies. However, the texts themselves indicate that such a return occurred under Ezra and Nehemiah and that no further return is to be anticipated. It may be argued that Jesus repudiated any such expectation. New Testament writers apply such Old Testament promises to both believing Jews and Gentiles.

4. It is also an article of faith that *Eretz* or greater Israel, extending from the River of Egypt to the Euphrates, is the Jewish inheritance originally promised unconditionally to Abraham and his descendants for ever. The progressive revelation of Scripture shows that such promises were actually conditional and, from a New Testament perspective, have been universalized to embrace the entire cosmos.

5. Jerusalem, or Zion, lies at the heart of Christian Zionism. The city is seen as the eternal, undivided and exclusive Jewish capital. Nothing in the New Testament, however, substantiates this claim. Instead Christians are called to break with any dependency upon an earthly city and by faith to recognize that they are already citizens of the heavenly Jerusalem.

6. Most controversially, many believe the temple must be rebuilt and sacrifices re-instituted in order that it can be desecrated by the Antichrist before Jesus returns. The New Testament is emphatic that after the death of Christ, the temple, priestly caste and sacrificial system became obsolete and their perpetuation apostate.

7. For virtually all Christian Zionists, the immediate future is intrinsically pessimistic. The battle of Armageddon will, they claim, lead to the death of two-thirds of the Jewish people before Christ returns to save a remnant. He will judge the world on the basis of how the nations have treated the Jews... Christian Zionism's particular reading of history and contemporary events, sustained by the dubious exegesis of selective biblical texts, sets Israel and the Jewish people apart from other peoples in the Middle East. In so doing, however unintentionally, it justifies the endemic racism intrinsic to Zionism, exacerbates tensions between Jews and Palestinians and undermines attempts to find a peaceful resolution of the Palestinian–Israeli conflict.[5]

In Israel itself, Palestinian Christians have also been determined to refute the claims made by Christian Zionists. At the April 2004 conference of opponents to Christian Zionism convened by the Palestinian Christian Sabeel Ecumenical Liberation Theology Centre, a press statement was made which alleged that Christian Zionism is detrimental to a just peace in the Holy land. A conference document attached to the press release claimed:

In its extreme form [Christian Zionism] places an emphasis on apocalyptic events leading to the end of history rather than living Christ's
love and justice today... We categorically reject Christian Zionist doctrines as false teaching that undermines the biblical message of love,
mercy, and justice... We reject the heretical teachings of Christian
Zionism that facilitate and support [Israel and US] extremist policies
as they advance a form of racial exclusivity and perpetual war rather
than the gospel of universal love, redemption and reconciliation
taught by Jesus Christ.[6]

Determined to refute such charges, Christian Zionists claim that their
views are based on biblical principles and promises, which are backed
up by biblical prophecies and New Testament truths. Their position,
they believe, looks beyond the evolving concerns of political Zionism
and views both the Jewish people and the land of Israel as chosen by
God for the purpose of redeeming the world. Whatever one makes of
this debate, there is no doubt that Christian Zionism has become a
massive and influential movement. Dispensational premillennialism
in its various forms, in particular, continues to arouse passionate
devotion to the Jewish state and generates both political and financial support for a Jewish homeland in the Middle East. In our
war-torn world it will inevitably play a significant role as Jews and
Palestinians seek to find a solution to the crisis in the Middle East.

Notes

Preface

1. Dale Crowley, in Grace Halsell (ed.), *Forcing God's Hand* (Amana Publications, 2003), p. 5.

2. Ibid., p. 4.
3. Ibid., p. 6.
4. Ibid., p. 9.
5. Ibid., pp. 9–10.
6. Ibid.

Chapter 1

1. Franc Kobler, *The Vision was There* (London: Lincolns–Prager, 1956), p. 16.

2. Mayir Verete, 'The Restoration of the Jews in English Protestant Thought, 1790–1840', *Middle Eastern Studies* (1972), p. 14.

3. Kobler, *The Vision was There* p. 37.

4. Mayir Verete, 'The Restoration of the Jews in English Protestant Thought 1790–1840' p. 20.

5. Ibid., p. 22.
6. Ibid., p. 23.
7. Ibid., p. 25.
8. Ibid., p. 27.

9. Michael J. Pragai, *Faith and Fulfilment: Christians and the Return to the Promised Land* (London: Vallentine Mitchell, 1985), p. 23.

10. George Eliot and *Daniel Deronda* in Pragai, *Faith and Fulfilment*, pp. 23–24.

11. Charles Haddon Spurgeon, 'The Form of Godliness Without the Power', Metropolitan Tabernacle Puplit, Vol. 2, (London: Passmore and Alabaster, 1862–1917), p. 249 quoted in Stephen Sizer, *A Promised Land* (unpublished PhD thesis), 2002, p. 37.

12. Charles Haddon Spurgeon, 'The Restoration and Conversion of the Jews', Metropolitan Tabernacle Puplit, Vol. 10 (London: Passmore and Alabaster, 1892–1917), p. 426 quoted in Sizer, *A Promised Land*, p. 38.

13. Charles Haddon Spurgeon, 'The Harvest and Vintage', Metropolitan Tabernacle Pulpit, Vol. 50 (London: Passmore and Alabaster, 1862–1917), p. 533; Charles Haddon Spurgeon, 'The Church of Christ', New Park Street Pulpit, Vol. 1 (London: Passmore and Alabaster, 1856–1861), pp. 213–214 quoted in Sizer, *A Promised Land*, p. 39.

14. Edward Miller, *The History and Doctrines of Irvingism*, Vol. 1 (London: Kegan and Paul, 1878), pp. 44–45 quoted in Sizer, *A Promised Land*, p. 45.

15. Edward Irving, *The Last Days: A Discourse on the Evil Character of These Our Times, Proving them to be the 'Perilous Times' and the 'Last Days'*. Cited in Stephen Sizer, *Edward Irving, The Rapture and Rupture Between Israel and the Church*, www.christchurch-virginiawater.co.uk/articles/irving1.html

Chapter 2

1. J.N. Darby, 'Progress of Evil on the Earth', *The Collected Writings, Prophetic*,

Vol. 1, pp. 471, quoted in Stephen Sizer, 'John Nelson Darby (1800–1882) The Father of Premillennial Dispensationalism', www.christchurch-virginiawater.co.uk/articles/darby1.html

2. J.N. Darby, 'The Apostasy of the Successive Dispensations', *The Collected Writings of J.N. Darby*, Vol. 2, Ecclesiastical No. 1, ed. William Kelly (Kingston on Thames: Stow Hill Bible and Trust Depot, 1962), pp. 124–130 quoted in Sizer, 'John Nelson Darby (1800–1882)', www.christchurch-virginiawater.co.uk/articles/darby1.html

3. J.N. Darby, 'The Character of Office in the Present Dispensation', *The Collected Writings*, Eccl. I, Vol. I, p. 94 quoted in Sizer, 'John Nelson Darby (1800–1882)', www.christchurch-virginiawater.co.uk/articles/darby1.html

4. *The Christian Witness*, April, 1838, p. 164 quoted in Sizer, 'John Nelson Darby (1800–1882)', www.christchurch-virginiawater.co.uk/articles/darby1.html

5. J.N. Darby, 'The Hopes', *The Collected Writings, Prophetic I*, Vol. II, pp. 372–373 quoted in Sizer, 'John Nelson Darby (1800–1882)', www.virginiawater.co.uk/articles/darby1.html

6. J.N. Darby, 'The Hopes', *The Collected Writings, Prophetic I*, Vol II, p. 379 quoted in Sizer, 'John Nelson Darby (1800–1882)', www.virginiawater.co.uk/articles/darby1.html

7. J.N. Darby, 'The Rapture of the Saints and the Character of the Jewish Remnant', *The Collected Writings, Prophetic I*, Vol. II, pp. 153–155 quoted in Sizer, 'John Nelson Darby (1800–1882)', www.virginiawater.co.uk/articles/darby1.html

8. Michael Pragai, *Faith and Fulfilment* (London: Vallentine Mitchell, 1985), p. 30.

9. Preface to 'The Book of the Laws and Liberties Concerning the Inhabitants of the Massachusetts' quoted in Pragai, *Faith and Fulfilment*, p. 31.

10. Ibid., p. 34.

11. Ibid., p. 34.

12. Ibid., p. 34.

13. Ibid., p. 35.

14. Kelvin Crombie, *For the Love of Zion: Christian Witness and the Restoration of Israel* (London: Hodder and Stoughton, 1991), p. 17.

15. Pragai, *Faith and Fulfilment*, p. 41.

16. Ibid., pp. 43–44.

17. Charles Simeon, 'The Millennial Period Fast Appraching', *Horae Homileticae*, Vol. VIII (London: Samuel Holdsworth, 1836), p. 24.

Chapter 3

1. Barbara Tuchman, *Bible and Sword* (New York: Funk and Wagnalls, 1950), p. 155.

2. Ibid., p. 190.

3. Ibid., p. 191.

4. Michael Pragai, *Faith and Fulfilment* (London: Vallentine Mitchell, 1985), p. 46.

5. Tuchman, *Bible and Sword*, p. 29.

6. *Jewish Expositor*, 1834, p. 137 quoted in Kelvin Crombie, *For the Love of Zion: Christian Witness and the Restoration of Israel* (London: Hodder & Stoughton, 1991), p. 22.

7. Ibid., p. 51 quoted in Crombie, *For the Love of Zion*, p. 24.

8. LJS Report, 1839, p. 75 quoted in Crombie, *For the Love of Zion*, p. 25.

9. Foreign Office, 78/368, no. 8, quoted in Crombie, *For the Love of Zion*, p. 26.

10. Crombie, *For the Love of Zion*, p. 28.

11. Yehudai Hai Alkalai, 'The Third Redemption', in Arthur Hertzbeg (ed.), *The Zionist Idea: A Historical Analysis and Reader* (New York, 1959), p. 105.

12. Ibid., p. 106.

13. Ibid.

14. Ibid.

15. In Hertzberg, (ed.) *The Zionist Idea*, pp. 109–110.

16. Zwi Hirsch Kalischer, *Derishat Zion*, in S. Avineri, *The Making of Modern Zionism* (New York, 1981).

17. Zwi Hirsch Kalischer, 'Seeking Zion', in Hertzberg (ed.), *The Zionist Idea*, p. 113.

Chapter 4

1. *Jewish Intelligence* (1845), p. 112 quoted in Kelvin Crombie, *For the Love of Zion: Christian Witness and the Restoration of Israel* (London: Hodder and Stonghton, 1991), p. 32.
2. Foreign Office, 78/390, no. 134 quoted in Crombie, *For the Love of Zion*, p. 33.
3. *Jewish Intelligence*, (1841), pp. 390–1, quoted in Crombie, *For the Love of Zion*, p. 43.
4. *Jewish Intelligence*, (1843), p. 17 quoted in Crombie, *For the Love of Zion*, p. 50.
5. Foreign Office, 78/540, quoted in Crombie, *For the Love of Zion*, p. 55.
6. Franc Kobler, *The Vision was There*, p. 56, quoted in Pragai, *Faith and Fulfilment*, p. 49.
7. Lawrence Oliphant, The Land of Gilead, p. 32 in Pragai, *Faith and Fulfilment*, p. 54.
8. Pragai, *Faith and Fulfilment*, p. 55.
9. William E. Blackstone, *Jesus is Coming*, (Chicago, 1908), p. 107ff., quoted in Pragai, *Faith and Fulfilment*, p. 56.
10. Reuben Fink, *America and Palestine* (New York: American Zionist Emergency Council, 1945), pp. 20–21 quoted in Stephen Sizer, 'The Historical Origins of Christian Zionism', www.christchurch-virginiawater.co.uk/articles/history1.html.
11. Moses Hess, *Rome and Jerusalem*, in Hertzberg (ed.), *The Zionist Idea*, p. 119.
12. Leon Pinsker, *Autoemancipation*, (London, 1932), p. 6.
13. Leon Pinsker, *Autoemancipation* quoted in Hertzberg (ed.), *The Zionist Idea*, p. 196.

Chapter 5

1. *LJS Report*, (1855), p. 61 quoted in Kelvin Crombie, *For the Love of Zion*, p. 91.

2. J. Finn, *Stirring Times*, (London, 1878), p. 120 quoted in Crombie, p. 93.
3. Foreign Office, 78/1294, Pol no. 36 quoted in Crombie, *For the Love of Zion*, pp. 93–4.
4. Hess, *Rome and Jerusalem* (New York: Bloch Publishing Company, 1945), pp. 132–137, quoted in Pragai, *Faith and Fulfilment*, pp. 65–66.
5. Mark Twain, *Innocents Abroad*, Vol. II, p. 357, quoted in Crombie, *For the Love of Zion*, p. 66.
6. Finn, *Reminiscences of Mrs. Finn*, p. 64, quoted in Crombie, *For the Love of Zion*, p. 67.
7. Finn, *Reminiscences of Mrs. Finn*, p. 123, quoted in Crombie, *For the Love of Zion*, p. 67.
8. Finn, *Reminiscences of Mrs. Finn*, p. 134, quoted in Crombie, *For the Love of Zion*, p. 68.
9. Kelvin Crombie, *For the Love of Zion*, pp. 69–70.
10. Kelvin Crombie, *For the Love of Zion*, p. 73.
11. Martin Gilbert, *Israel: A History*, (London: Black Swan, 1999), p. 6.
12. Ibid., p. 8.

Chapter 6

1. Theodor Herzl, 'First Entry in his Diary', in Hertzberg (ed.), *The Zionist Idea*, p. 204.
2. Theodor Herzl, 'The Jewish State', in Hertzberg (ed.), *The Zionist Idea*, p. 209.
3. Ibid., pp. 225–6.
4. Theodor Herzl, *The Diaries of Theodor Herzl* (New York, 1956) quoted in Sizer, *A Promised Land*, p. 63.
5. Harry Zohn, 'Herzl, Hechler, The Grand Duke of Baden and the German Emperor', in *Herzl Year Book*, Vol. 4, (New York: Herzl Press, 1961–62) pp. 210ff., quoted in Pragai, *Faith and Fulfilment*, p. 59.
6. Ibid., p. 59.
7. Ibid., p. 60.

8. '22 April, Diaries', in David Vital, *The Origins of Zionism* (Oxford: Oxford University Press, 1990), p. 285.

9. Ibid., p. 285.

10. Paul Merkley, *Christian Attitudes towards the State of Israel* (Kingston, London: McGill-Queen's University Press, 2001), pp. 16–17, quoted in Sizer, *A Promised Land*, p. 63.

11. Zohn, quoted in Pragai, *Faith and Fulfilment*, p. 60.

12. Paul Merkley, *Christian Attitudes towards the State of Israel*, p. 16, quoted in Sizer, *The Promised Land*, p. 64.

Chapter 7

l. Ahad Ha-Am, *Nationalism and the Jewish Ethic*, (New York, 1962), pp. 74–5.

2. Ibid., pp. 78–9.

3. Ibid., p. 80.

4. S. Avineri, *The Making of Modern Zionism* (New York, 1981), p. 122.

5. Ibid., p. 123.

6. Aharon David Gordon, 'Some Observations', in Hertzberg (ed.), *The Zionist Idea*, p. 376.

7. Ibid., p. 376.

8. Aharon David Gordon, 'Labour' in S. Avineri, *The Making of Modern Zionism*, p. 155.

9. Ibid., p. 155.

10. Ibid., p. 156.

11. Ibid., p. 156.

12. Ibid., p. 157.

13. Walter Laqueur, *A History of Zionism* (New York, 1972), p. 388.

14. Ibid., p. 394.

15. Ibid..

Chapter 8

1. *Jewish Intelligence* (March 1882), p. 53 quoted in Crombie, *For the Love of Zion*, p. 109.

2. *Jewish Chronicle* (28 July 1882), p. 4.

3. *Jewish Record* (July 1883), pp. 26–7.

4. *First Report of the JRAS* (1884), p. 5.

5. Ibid., pp. 9–10.

6. Ibid., p. 11.

7. *LJS Report* (1884), p. 101, quoted in Crombie, *For the Love of Zion*, p. 119.

9. 'West to Kennaway', 31 January, 1888, Bodleian Library, dept CMJ, d. 55/1 quoted in Crombie, *For the Love of Zion*, p. 125.

10. Kelvin Crombie, *For the Love of Zion*, p. 131.

11. Ibid., p. 132.

12. *Jewish Missionary Intelligence* (1897), p. 154, quoted in Crombie, *For the Love of Zion*, p. 139.

13. R. Sanders, *The High Walls of Jerusalem: A History of the Balfour Declaration and the Birth of the British Mandate for Palestine* (New York: 1984), pp. 37–38.

14. 'Balfour Declaration' in Paul Mendes-Flohr and Jehuda Reinharz (eds.), *The Jew in the Modern World* (Oxford University Press, 1995), p. 582.

Chapter 9

1. Michael Pragai, *Faith and Fulfilment*, pp. 76–77.

2. Ibid., p. 79.

3. John Patterson, *With the Judeans in the Palestine Campaign*, (London: Hutchinson and Company, 1922), p. viii, quoted in Pragai, *Faith and Fulfilment*, p. 81.

4. John Patterson, *with the Judeans in the Palestine Campaign*, p. 17, quoted in Pragai, *Faith and Fulfilment*, p. 82.

5. John Patterson, ibid., p. 18, quoted in Pragai, ibid. p. 82.

6. Michael Pragai, *Faith and Fulfilment*, p. 87.

7. Ibid., pp. 87–88.

8. J.H. Patterson, *With the Judeans in the Palestine Campaign*, 276, quoted in Pragai, *Faith and Fulfilment*, p. 88.

9. D.L. Moody, *To All People: Comprising Sermons, Bible Readings, Temperance Addresses and Prayer-Meeting Talks* (Boston: The Globe Publishing Company, 1877), p. 354, quoted in Sizer, *A Promised Land*, p. 73.

10. William E. Blackstone, *Jesus is Coming* (Chicago: Fleming Revell, 1916),

p. 240, quoted in Sizer, *A Promised Land*, p. 74.

11. Reuben Fink, *America and Palestine*, (New York: American Zionist Emergency Council, 1945), pp. 20–21, quoted in Sizer, *A Promised Land*, p. 76.

12. Stephen Sizer, *A Promised Land*, p. 77.

13. Anro C. Gaebelein, *Moody Monthly*, **43**, 1943, p. 278, quoted in Stephen Sizer, 'Cyrus Ingerson Scofield (1843–1921) The Author of the Scofield Reference Bible', www.christchurch-virginiawater.co.uk/articles/scofield1.html.

14. C.I. Scofield, *The Scofield Reference Bible* (New York: Oxford University Press, 1917), p. iii, quoted in Sizer, 'Cyrus Ingerson Scofield (1843–1921)' www.christchurch-virginiawater.co.uk/articles/scofield1.html.

15. C.I. Scofield, *New Scofield Study Bible*, New York: Oxford Univ Press, 1984, fn. 1, p. 922, quoted in Sizer, 'Cyrus Ingerson Scofield (1843–1921)' www.christchurch-virginiawater.co.uk/articles/scofield.html.

16. C.I. Scofield, *The New Scofield Reference Bible* (New York: Oxford Univ Press, 1967), fn. 1, p. 795, quoted in Sizer, 'Cyrus Ingerson Scofield (1843–1921)' www.christchurch-virginiawater.co.uk/articles/scofield.html.

17. C.I. Scofield, *Truth*, No. 19, p. 385, quoted in Sizer, 'Cyrus Ingerson Scofield (1843–1921)' www.christchurch-virginiawater.co.uk/articles/scofield.html.

18. C.I. Scofield, *Scofield Reference Bible* (1917) quoted in Sizer, 'Cyrus Ingerson Scofield (1843–1921)' www.christchurch-virginiawater. co.uk/articles/scofield.html.

19. C.I. Scofield, *The New Scofield Reference Bible* (1984), fn 1, p. 1148, quoted in Sizer, 'Cyrus Ingerson Scofield (1843–1921)' www.christchurch-virginiawater.co.uk/articles/scofield.html.

Chapter 10

1. S. Avineri, *The Making of Modern Zionism*, p. 162.

2. Ibid., p. 164.
3. Ibid., p. 167.
4. Ibid., p. 169.
5. Ibid., p. 170.
6. Ibid., p. 180.
7. Ibid., p. 181.
8. *Jewish Missionary Intelligence* (1915), p. 46, in Crombie, *For the Love of Zion*, p. 150.
9. *Jewish Missionary Intelligence* (1915), p. 26, ibid., p. 155.
10. *Jewish Missionary Intelligence* (1917), pp. 129–30, ibid., p. l60.
11. *Jewish Missionary Intelligence* (1918), p. 38, ibid., pp. 164–5.

Chapter 11

1. Norman and Helen Bentwich, *Mandate Memories 1918–1948* (London: Hogarth Press, 1965), p. 69 quoted in Pragai, *Faith and Fulfilment*, p. 94.

2. Bentwich, *Mandate Memories 1918–1948*, pp. 69–70, ibid., p. 95.

3. Bentwich, *Mandate Memories 1918–1948*, p. 32, ibid., p. 96.

4. *Congressional Record* (30 June, 1922), quoted in Pragai, *Faith and Fulfilment*, p. 97.

5. Norman Bentwich, *Sir Wyndham Deeds, A Christian Zionist* (Jerusalem: Keren Ha'yessod, 1954), p. 11, quoted in Pragai, *Faith and Fulfilment*, p. 100.

6. Richard Meinertzhagen, *Middle East Diary 1917–1956* (New York: Thomas Yoseloff, 1960), pp. 202–203, quoted in Pragai, *Faith and Fulfilment*, p. 105.

7. Meinertzhagen, *Middle East Diary 1917–1956*, p. 16, ibid., p. 106.

8. *Zionist Review* (July 1918), quoted in Pragai, *Faith and Fulfilment*, p. 117.

9. *Jewish Missionary Intelligence* (1919), p. 87, quoted in Crombie, *For the Love of Zion*, p. 167.

10. *Jewish Missionary Intelligence* (1921), pp. 81–82, ibid., pp. 170–171.

11. *Bread Cast Upon the Waters*, (1920/21), p. 56, quoted in Crombie, *For the Love of Zion*, p. 171.

12. *Jewish Missionary Intelligence* (1921), p. 109, quoted in Crombie, *For the Love of Zion*, p. 175.

13. *Jewish Missionary Intelligence* (1922), p. 125, ibid., p. 176.

14. *Jewish Missionary Intelligence* (1929), p. 147, ibid., p. 187.

15. *Jewish Missionary Intelligence* (1930), ibid., p. 191.

16. *Jewish Missionary Intelligence* (1933), p. 147, ibid., p. 193.

Chapter 12

1. Christopher Sykes, *Orde Wingate* (New York: World Publishing Co, 1959), p. 112, in Pragai, *Faith and Fulfilment*, p. 113.

2. Sykes, *Orde Wingate*, p. 201, ibid., p. 114.

3. *Zionist Review*, (July 1918), in Pragai, *Faith and Fulfilment*, p. 118.

4. *Parliamentary Debates, House of Lords*, Vol. 113, No. 165, Columns 113–118, in Pragai, *Faith and Fulfilment*, pp. 121–122.

5. *Book of Documents: Submitted to the General Assembly of the United nations, relating to the establishment of the National Home for the Jewish People*, The Jewish Agency for Palestine, New York, May 1947, p. 218, in Pragai, *Faith and Fulfilment*, p. 123.

6. *Book of Documents*, p. 218, ibid., p. 124.

7. *Book of Documents*, p. 219, ibid., p. 124.

8. Ibid.

9. *Book of Documents*, p. 220, ibid., p. 126.

10. *Proclamation of the State of Israel*, eds. Paul Mendes-Flohr and Jehuda Reinharz, (eds.), *The Jew in the Modern World*, p. 629.

11. *Pro-Palestine Herald*, Vol. 3, Nos 3–4 (1934), in Pragai, *Faith and Fulfilment*, p. 128.

12. *Book of Documents*, pp. 339–340, in Pragai, *Faith and Fulfilment*, p. 132.

13. *Joint Anglo-American Committee, Hearings Washington, D.C., Jan. 12, 1946*, pp. 101ff., in Pragai, *Faith and Fulfilment*, p. 138.

14. Michael Pragai, *Faith and Fulfilment*, p. 140.

15. *UN Security Council*, December 17, 1948, in Pragai, *Faith and Fulfilment*, p. 189.

16. *UN General Assembly*, (May 10, 1949), in Pragai, *Faith and Fulfillment*, p. 189.

17. *UN General Assembly*, (May 11, 1949), ibid., p. 189.

18. *UN General Assembly*, (May 11, 1949), ibid., p. 190.

Chapter 13

1. Memorandum to the Anglo-American Committee of Inquiry by the Rt. Rev. W.H. Stewart, Bishop of Jeruslaem, Bodleian Library, dept, CMJ, c. 218, quoted in Crombie, *For the Love of Zion*, p. 207.

2. H. Hurnard, *Watchment on the Walls*, (London, 1950), pp. 11–12, quoted in Crombie, *For the Love of Zion*, pp. 212–20.

3. Hurnard, quoted in Crombie, *For the Love of Zion*, pp. 116–118

4. Jones to Gill, 23 December 1947, Bodleian Liberary, dept. CMJ, c. 218, quoted in Crombie, *For the Love of Zion*, pp. 229–230.

5. Arno C. Gaebelein, *Our Hope*, 27 April 1921, p. 601, quoted in Sizer, *A Promised Land*, p. 83.

6. David Rausch, 'Fundamentalism and the Jew: An Interpretive Essay, *Journal of the Evangelical Theological Society*, **23** (2) June, 1980, pp. 107–112, quoted in Sizer, *A Promised Land*, p. 83.

7. Arno C. Gaebelein, 'Has God Cast Away His People? (1905) in Sizer, *A Promised Land*, p. 83.

8. M.R. DeHann, *Daniel the Prophet, 35 Simple Studies in the Book of Daniel*, (Grand Rapids, MI: Zondervan, 1947),

pp. 169–172, quoted in Sizer, *A Promised Land*, p. 90.

9. Donald Wagner, 'Evangelicals and Israel: Theological Roots of a Political Alliance', *The Christian Century*, November 4, 1998, pp. 1020–1026, quoted in Sizer, *A Promised Land*, p. 90.

10. Lyndon B. Johnson, www.us-israel.org/jsource/US-Israel/bpeace1.html, quoted in Sizer, *A Promised Land*, p. 90.

11. Grace Halsell, *Prophecy*, pp. 5, 45 quoted in Sizer, *A Promised Land*, p. 92.

12. Larry Jones and Gerald T. Sheppard, 'Ronald Reagan's "Theology" of Armageddon' in Hassan Haddad and Donald Wagner (eds.), *All in the Name of the Bible*, (Battleboro, Vermont: Amana, 1986), pp. 32–33, quoted in Sizer, *A Promised Land*, p. 92.

13. Ronnie Dugger, 'Does Reagan Expect a Nuclear Armageddon?', *Washington Post*, 18 April, 1984, quoted in Sizer, *A Promised Land*, p. 94.

Chapter 14

1. Hal Lindsey, *The 1980's: Countdown to Armageddon* (New York: Bantam, 1981), quoted in Sizer, 'Hal Lindsey: Father of Apocalyptic Christian Zionism', p. 11 www.christchurchvirginiawater.co.uk.

2. Lindsey, *The Final Battle* (Palos Verdes, California: Western Front, 1995), p. xxi, quoted in Sizer, 'Hal Lindsey: Father of Apocalyptic Christian Zionism,' p. 11.

3. Lindsey, *There's a New World Coming, A Prophetic Odyssey* (Santa Ana, California: Vision House, 1973), p. 115, quoted in Sizer, 'Hal Lindsey: Father of Apocalyptic Christian Zionism,' p. 12.

4. Lindsey, *The Apocalypse Code*, (Palos Verdes, California: Western Front, 1997), p. 121, quoted in Sizer, 'Hal Lindsey: Father of Apocalyptic Christian Zionism', p. 16.

5. Lindsey, *The Late, Great Planet Earth* (London: Lakeland, 1970), pp. 243–244, quoted in Sizer, 'Hal Lindsey:

Father of Apocalpytic Christian Zionism', p. 30.

6. Hal Lindsey, *The Late, Great Planet Earth*, p. 284, ibid., p. 34.

7. Hal Lindsey, *There's a New World Coming*, p. 237 ibid., p. 34.

8. Hal Lindsey, *There's a New World Coming*, p. 121, ibid., p. 35.

9. David Rausch, *Messianic Judaism: Its History, Theology and Polity*, (New York: Edwin Mellen, 1982), p. 130.

10. Doctrinal Statement, para. 8.

11. Rich Nichol, 'Are We Really at the End of the End Times: A Reapprisal', in ed. Dan Cohn-Sherbok, *Voices of Messianic Judaism*, (Baltimore: Lederer, 2001), p. 204.

12. Ibid., p. 208–9.

Chapter 15

1. James Price and William Goodman, *Jerry Falwell, An Unathorized Profile*, cited in Grace Halsell, *Prophecy and Politics, Militant Evangelicals on the Road to Nuclear War*, (Westport, Connecticut: Lawrence Hill, 1986), pp. 72–73, cited in Sizer, *A Promised Land*, p. 95.

2. Skipp Porteous, 'Road to Armageddon', http://www.ifas.org/fw/9512/robertson.html, cited in Sizer, *A Promised Land*, p. 98.

3. Don Wagner, 'The History of Christian Zionism,' *SocialistViewpoint*, 4(1), January 2004, p. 10, www.socialistviewpoint.org/jan_04-04.html.

4. Stephen Sizer, 'The International Christian Embassy, Jerusalem: A Case study in Political Christian Zionism,' in Michael Prior (ed.), *Speaking the Truth About Zionism and Israel* (London: Melisende, 2004), p. 105.

5. ICEJ, 1993:5, cited in Sizer, 'The International Christian Embassy, Jerusalem', p. 106.

6. Sizer, 'The International Christian Embassy, Jerusalem', p. 107.

7. Ibid., pp. 112–113.

8. Ibid., p. 116.

9. Ibid., pp. 113–114.

Chapter 16

1. Timothy Webber, 'On the Road to Armageddon', p. 2, www.christiancounterculture.com/articles/armageddon.html.
2. Ibid., p. 6.
3. CMJ, 'The State of Israel: Why should we support it', in Always Be Preparedto Give an Answer, resource pack, (St. Albans: CMJ, l996) cited in Stephen Sizer, *Christian Zionism: Road Map to Armageddon?* (Leicester: IVP, 2004), p. 2ll.
4. Sizer, *Christian Zionism: Road Map to Armageddon?*, pp. 216–217.
5. Ibid., p. 2l7.
6. Ibid., p. 226.
7. Clarence Wagner, 'Jerusalem 3000 Celebration, Bridges for Peace' in Sizer, *Christian Zionism: Road Map to Armageddon?*, p. 23l.
8. Jan Willem van der Hoeven, 'Hitler and the Arabs', 200l, in Sizer, *Christian Zionism: Road Map to Armageddon?*, p. 242.
9. Hal Lindsey, *Israel and the Last Days*, (Eugene OR: Harvest House, 1983) pp. 38–39, cited in Sizer, *Christian Zionism: Road Map to Armageddon?*, p. 243.
10. David Hunt, 'O Jerusalem, Jerusalem', September, 2000, in Sizer, *Christian Zionism: Road Map to Armageddon?*, p. 245.
11. Sizer, *Christian Zionism: Road Map to Armageddon?*, p. 248.
12. C. Wagner, 'Driving the Nations Crazy', p. 9, in Sizer, *Christian Zionism: Road Map to Armageddon?*, p. 250.
13. David Brickner, 'Don't Pass Over Israel's Jubilee' in Sizer, *Christian Zionism: Road Map to Armageddon?*, p. 250.
14. Jonathan Kuttab, 'An Open letter to the Archbishop of Canterbury from a Palestinian Christian', christianzionism.org/fulltext.asp?ID=23

Chapter 17

1. Grace Halsell, 'Israelil Extremists and Christian Fundamentalists: The Alliance', *Washington Report*, Dec. 1988, p. 31, cited in Sizer, *Christian Zionism: Road Map to Armageddon?*, p. 21.
2. Stephen Sizer, *Christian Zionism: Road Map to Armageddon?*, p. 21.
3. Robert Fisk, 'By endorsing Ariel Sharon's plan George Bush has legitimised terrorism', *The Independent*, 16 April, 2004.
4. David Parsons, 'Swords into Ploughshares', Jerusalem, International Christian Embassy Jerusalem, p. 9.
5. Stephen Sizer, *Christian Zionism: Road Map to Armageddon?*, p. 202–205.
6. Sabeel Press Statement, cited in David Parsons, *Swords into Plowshares*, p. 14.

Biographies

Sheikh Izz al-Din al-Qassam: 20th-century Palestinian leader and supporter of the Palestinian cause.

Michael Solomon Alexander: 19th-century Anglican bishop in Jerusalem.

Yehuda hai Alkalai: 19th-century Jewish religious Zionist.

Ahad Ha-Am: 19th-century Russian essayist and supporter of spiritual Zionism.

Hayyim Amzalak: 19th-century Jewish settler in Palestine who bought the land on which Petah Tikvah had been built and gave it to Bilu settlers.

Aaron Aaronsohn: 20th-century organizer of a Jewish undergound intelligence organization (Nili) in Palestine.

Yasser Arafat: 20th-century leader of the Palestine Liberation Organization.

Yisrael Ariel: 20th-century founder of the Temple Institute.

Chaim Arlosoroff: 20th-century Zionist and head of the Political Department of the Jewish Agency.

Clement Attlee: 20th-century British Prime Minister.

Grand Duke of Baden: 19th-century supporter of Jewish settlement in Palestine.

James Baker: 20th-century American Middle East negotiator.

Arthur Balfour: 20th-century British statesman and author of the Balfour Declaration.

Thomas Baring: 19th-century President of the London Jews Society.

Menahem Begin: 20th-century head of the Irgun and Prime Minister of Israel.

Nelson Bell: 20th-century editor of *Christianity Today*.

David Ben-Gurion: 20th-century Prime Minister of Israel.

Yehudah Ben-Shusha: 20th-century leader of a group of extremists who plotted to blow up the Dome of the Rock.

Eliezer Ben-Yehuda: 19th-century founder of a society to spread Hebrew language in Palestine.

William E. Blackstone: 19th-century American evangelist and author of *Jesus is Coming* who presented a petition, Palestine for the Jews, to President Harrison.

George Francis Popam Blyth: 19th-century Anglican bishop in Jerusalem.

Andrew Bonar: 19th-century supporter of the Society for the Propagation of the Gospel Amongst the Jews.

Samuel A. Bradshaw: 19th-century author of *Tract for the Times, Being a Plea for the Jews*.

Louis Brandeis: 20th-century American Supreme Court Justice and Zionist.

Thomas Brightman: 16th-century author of *Apocalypsis Apocalypseos*.

James H. Brookes: 19th-century minister of the Walnut Street Presbyterian Church in St Louis, Missouri, and father of American dispensationalism.

Thomas Burnet: 18th-century writer who believed that the Bible made the promises of the Messiah and his kingdom first to the Jews and hence they have a title to the Land of Israel.

George W. Bush: 21st-century President of the United States of America.

Jimmy Carter: 20th-century President of the United States.

Ebenezer Cartwright: 17th-century Puritan who petitioned the English Parliament to allow Jews to settle in the Holy Land.

Joanna Cartwright: 17th-century Puritan who petitioned the English Parliament to allow Jews to settle in the Holy Land.

Edward Cazalet: 19th-century British economist and author of *England's Policy in the East: Our Relations with Russia and the future of Syria*.

Victor Alexander Cazalet: 20th-century British politician and chairman of the Pro-Palestine Committee.

Joseph Chamberlain: 20th-century British politician who was sympathetic to Zionist aspirations.

Neville Chamberlain: 20th-century British Prime Minister.

Winston Churchill: 20th-century British Prime Minister.

Claude Regnier Conder: 19th-century co-author with H.H. Kitchener of *The Survey of Western Palestine*.

Constantine: 4th-century Roman emperor.

Henry Crawford: 19th-century Head of Mission for CMS in Jerusalem.

Stafford Cripps: 20th-century British supporter of the partition plan.

Nathaniel Crouch: 18th-century author of *Two Journeys to Jerusalem*.

John Nelson Darby: 19th-century founder of Premillennial Dispensationalism.

M.R. DeHann: 20th-century Christian Zionist and supporter of the Jewish return to the Holy Land.

Diocletian: 3rd-century Roman emperor.

Meir Dizengoff: 20th-century first mayor of Tel Aviv.

Henry Drummond: 19th-century British publisher of *Morning Watch*.

Blanche Dugdale: 20th-century niece of Lord Balfour and supporter of Zionism.

Jean Henry Dunant: 19th-century Swiss Calvinist and founder of the Palestine Colonization Society.

Yehudah Etzion: 20th-century leader of an undergound group of Israeli extremists who plotted to blow up the Dome of the Rock.

Mary Ann Evans: Known as George Eliot, she was the 19th-century author of *Daniel Deronda*.

Joseph Eyre: 18th-century author of *Observations upon the Prophecies relating to the Restoration of the Jews*.

Jerry Falwell: 20th-century pastor of Thomas Road Baptist Church and founder of Baptist Liberty University.

Emir Feisel: 20th-century head of the Hedjaz Delegation.

Henry Finch: 17th-century author of *The World's Great Restoration or Calling of the Jews (and with them) all the Nations and Kingdoms of the Earth, to the Faith in Christ*.

Elizabeth Finn: Wife of James Finn, the 19th-century British consul in Jerusalem, and author of *Remniscences*.

James Finn: 19th-century British consul in Jerusalem and supporter of Jewish population in Palestine.

Giles Fletcher: 16th-century English ambassador who argued that the Ten Lost Tribes of Israel along with other tribes would re-establish their kingdom in the Holy Land.

Felix Frankfurter: 20th-century American Supreme Court Justice and Zionist.

Joseph Frey: 19th-century founder of the London Jews Society.

Dr Fuller: 18th-century author of *A Pisgah Sight of Palestine*.

Arno Gaebelein: 19th-century Christian Zionist and author of the prophetic notes for *Scofield's Reference Bible*.

Gamaliel II: 1st–2nd-century CE rabbinic scholar.

John Cox Gawler: 19th-century soldier who encouraged Jewish settlements in *Eretz Israel*.

Samuel Gobat: 19th-century Anglican bishop in Jerusalem.

Stanley Goldfoot: 20th-century founder of the Jersualem Temple Foundation.

Baruch Goldstein: 20th-century Israeli who opened fire on Palestinian Arabs in a mosque in Hebron.

Moritz Goldstein: 20th-century writer and supporter of Zionism.

Aharon David Gordon: 19th-century Jewish settler in Palestine and supporter of spiritual Zionism.

Hajj Amin: 20th-century Grand Mufti of Jerusalem.

Warren Harding: 20th-century American President and supporter of Zionism.

William H. Hechler: 19th-century British clergyman and supporter of Jewish settlements in Palestine.

Theodor Herzl: 19th-century author of The Jewish State.

Moses Hess: 19th-century German Jewish Zionist and author of *Rome and Jerusalem*.

Samson Raphael Hirsch: 19th-century advocate of neo-Orthodoxy.

Jan Willem van der Hoeven: 20th-century founder of the International Christian Embassy.

Herbert Hoover: 20th-century President of the United States.

Richard Hurd: 18th-century Anglican who argued that the Jewish people would be gathered to their ancient land.

King Hussein: 20th-century King of Jordan.

Naphtali Herz Imber: 19th-century Romanian author of *Hatikvah*.

Edward Irving: 19th-century author of *The Last Days: A Discourse on the Evil Character of These Our Times, Proving them to be the 'Perilous Times' and the 'Last Days'.*

Vladimir Jabotinsky: 20th-century Zionist and founder of the Revisionist movement.

Jerry B. Jenkins: 20th-century co-author of the *Left Behind* series of novels.

Charles Jerram: 18th-century scholar who wrote about the future restoration of the Jewish people.

Lyndon B. Johnson: 20th-century President of the United States.

Zwi Hirsch Kalischer: 19th-century Jewish religious Zionist.

John Kennaway: 19th-century president of London Jews Society (LJS).

H.H. Kitchener: 19th-century co-author with Claude Regnier Conder of *The Survey of Western Palestine*.

Teddy Kollek: 20th-century mayor of Jerusalem.

Manuel Lacunza: Spanish author of *The Coming of the Messiah in Glory and Majesty*.

Ernest Laharanne: 19th-century author of *The New Eastern Question: The Egyptian and Arab Empires: The Reconstitution of the Jewish Nation*.

Tim LaHaye: 20th-century co-author of the *Left Behind* series of novels.

Lord Lansdowne: 19th-century British Foreign Secretary.

Johannes Lepsius: 19th-century German Lutheran pastor and author of *Armenians and Jews in Exile, or the Future of the East with Reference to the Armenian Question and the Zionist Movement*.

W. D. Lewis: 19th-century missionary to the Holy Land.

Hal Lindsey: 20th-century author of *The Late, Great Planet Earth*.

Lord Lindsey: 19th-century author of *Letters from Egypt, Edom, and the Holy Land*.

Ernst Lissauer: 20th-century supporter of assimilation.

Menachem Livni: 20th-century leader of a group of Israeli extremists who plotted to blow up the Dome of the Rock.

David Lloyd George: 20th-century British Prime Minister and supporter of the Jewish restoration in Palestine.

Ramsay Macdonald: 20th-century British Prime Minister.

Robert Murray M'Cheyne: 19th-century supporter of the British Society for the Propagation of the Gospel Amongst the Jews.

Ed Meese: 20th-century American Attorney General.

Richard Meinertzhagen: 20th-century chief political officer in the British post-war administration and supporter of Zionism.

Adam Mickiewicz: l9th-century Catholic poet.

Moses Montefiore: l9th-century Jewish leader who supported Jewish settlement in the Holy Land.

Dwight L. Moody: l9th-century evangelist and founder of the Bible Institute for Home and Foreign Missions of the Chicago Evangelization Society.

Benedetto Musolino: l9th-century author of *Gerusalemme ed il Popolo Ebrea.*

Gemal Abdul Nasser: 20th-century President of Egypt.

Benyamin Netanyahu: 20th-century Prime Minister of Israel.

Charles Netter: l9th-century French educator who founded a school for agriculture at Mikveh Israel.

B.W. Newton: John Henry Darby's assistant in Plymouth who opposed Darby's views and became the leader of the Open Brethren.

Rich Nichol: 21st-century Messianic rabbi.

John Nicholayson: l9th-century Dutch missionary to Jerusalem.

Richard Nixon: 20th-century President of the United States.

Manual Noah: l9th-century Jew who sought to create a city of refuge for Jews on Grand Island in the Niagara River, New York.

Max Nordeau: l9th-century Zionist leader.

Leo Oczeret: l9th-century missionary to Palestine.

Laurence Oliphant: l9th-century British officer in the Foreign service who sought to persuade the Sultan to grant land to the Jewish nation.

Lord Palmerston: British Foreign Secretary who supported the return of the Jewish people to Palestine.

Jemal Pasha: 20th-century Turkish military commander.

John Henry Patterson: 20th-century Protestant Irishman and commander of the Jewish Legion and author of *With the Judeaeans in the Palestine Campaign.*

Holger Paulli: l7th-century Dutch pietist who believed that the Jewish return to the Holy Land was a precondition of the Second Coming.

Shimon Peres: 20th-century Prime Minister of Israel.

Mr Pieritz: l9th-century Hebrew Christian on the staff of the London Jews Society in Palestine.

Leon Pinsker: l9th-century Jewish Zionists and author of *Autoemancipation.*

Pope Pius X: l9th-century pope who insisted that the Jewish people embrace the Christian faith if he were to support the return of Jewry to Palestine.

V.K. Plehve: l9th-century Russian Minister of the Interior who was supportive of Zionism.

Baron Plumer of Messines: 20th-century British High Commissioner in Palestine.

Lady Powerscourt: l9th-century sponsor of prophetic conferences held near Dublin.

Yitzhak Rabin: 20th-century Prime Minister of Israel.

Ronald Reagan: 20th-century President of the United States.

Pat Robertson: 20th-century evangelical preacher who built the Christian Broadcasting Network.

Franklin Delano Roosevelt: 20th-century President of the United States.

Edmond de Rothschild: l9th-century supporter of Jews in Palestine.

Arthur Ruppin: 20th-century head of the Palestine Office of the Zionist Executive.

Anwar Sadat: 20th-century President of Egypt.

Gershon Salomon: 20th-century founder of the Temple Mount and Land of Israel Faithful.

Abdul Aziz Ibn Saud: 20th-century King of Saudia Arabia.

Herbert Samuel: 20th-century British politician and High Commisoner in Palestine.

C. Schwartz: 19th-century minister of Trinity Chapel, Edgware Road, London who sought to unite all Jewish Christians through the creation of the Hebrew–Christian Alliance.

Cyrus Ingerson Scofield: 20th-century author of the *Scofield Reference Bible*.

Charles Prestwich Scott: 20th-century editor of the *Manchester Guardian* and supporter of Zionist aspirations.

Lord Shaftesbury: 19th-century politician and supporter of the Jewish return to Palestine.

Moshe Sharett: 20th-century Israeli statesman and Prime Minister of Israel.

Ariel Sharon: 21st-century Prime Minister of Israel.

Charles Simeon: 19th-century supporter of the London Jews Society (LJS) who believed in the restoration of the Jewish people to Palestine.

Stephen Sizer: 20th-century author of *Christian Zionism: Road Map to Armageddon?*

George A. Smith: 19th-century Mormon who reported on the trip to the Mount of Olives.

Joseph Smith: Founder of the Mormons.

Charles Haddon Spurgeon: 19th-century preacher who argued that the there will be a restoration of Israel.

Nathan Strauss: 20th-century Jewish philanthropist who provided funds to establish a Jewish hospital in Jerusalem.

Ahmed Tevfik: 20th-century Ottoman ambassador to Berlin.

John Thomas: 19th-century founder of the Christadelphians and author of *Elpis Israel*, in which he argued that the restoration of the Jewish nation to Palestine could be realized with the political assitance of Great Britain.

John Toland: 18th-century author of *Reasons for Naturalizing the Jews in Great Britain and Ireland on the Same Footing with all Other Nations*.

Harry S. Truman: 20th-century President of the United States.

Joseph Trumpeldor: 20th-century Zionist who sought to protect Jewish settlements in Palestine.

Mark Twain: 19th-century American author of *Innocents Abroad*.

Shabbatai Tzevi: 17th-century false Messiah.

Menachem of Ussishkin: 19th-century convenor of a conference at Zichron Yaakov.

Otto Warburg: 20th-century philanthropist who founded the Bezalel art school.

Charles Warren: 19th-century author of *Land of Promise*.

James Watt: 20th-century American Secretary of the Interior.

Lewis Way: 19th-century supporter of the London Jews Society who believed that Israel would return to its ancient homeland.

Joseph Clement Wedgwood: 20th-century British soldier and supporter of Zionist aspirations.

Josiah Clement Wedgwood: 20th-century British supporter of Zionism.

Caspar Weinberger: 20th-century former American Secretary of Defense.

Chaim Weizmann: 20th-century Zionist and President of the State of Israel.

W.N. West: 19th-century chairman of the London Jews Society.

Kaiser Wilhelm II: 19th-century German emperor who was sympathetic to Zionism.

Charles Wilson: 19th-century British topographer and explorer.

Woodrow Wilson: 20th-century President of the United States.

Charles Orde Wingate: 20th-century British soldier and supporter of Zionism.

Edward Witaker: 18th-century writer who published a dissertation on the final restoration of the Jews.

Joseph Wolff: 19th-century Jewish missionary to the Holy Land.

John F. Wolvoord: 20th-century head of the Dallas Theological Seminary and author of *The Final Drama*.

William Tanner Young: 19th-century British consul in Jerusalem.

Zadok of Lublin: 19th-century critic of Zionism.

Johanan ben Zakkai: 1st-century CE rabbinic scholar.

C.F. Zimpel: 19th-century author of *Israelites in Jerusalem*.

Organizations

Bridges for Peace (BFP) www.bridgesforpeace.com

Christian Broadcasting Network (CBN) www.cbn.com

Christian Friends of Israel (CFI) www.cfi-usa.org

Christian Witness to Israel (CWI) www.cwi.org.uk

Churches Ministry Among Jewish People (CMJ) www.cmj.org.uk

Dallas Theological Seminary www.dts.edu

Evangelicals for Middle East Understanding www.emeu.net

Friends of Israel Gospel Ministry www.foigm.org

International Christian Embassy Jerusalem (ICEJ) www.icej.org

International Messianic Jewish Alliance (IMJA) www.imja.com

Middle East Council of Churches (MECC) www.mec-churches.org

Palestine Academic Network www.planet.edu

Sabeel www.sabeel.org

The National Unity Coalition for Israel www.israelunity.org

Watch Jerusalem www.watchjerusalem.org

Further Reading

Abanes, Richard, 1998, *End-Times Vision: The Doomsday Obsession*, Nashville, TN, Broadman and Holman.

Alnor, William M, 1989, *Soothsayers of the Second Coming*, Old Tappan, NJ, Fleming H. Revell.

Ateek, Naim, 1990, *Justice and Only Justice: A Palestinian Theology of Liberation*, Maryknoll, NY, Orbis.

Bass, Clarence, 1960, *Backgrounds to Dispensationalism*, Grand Rapids, MI, Eerdmans.

Blackstone, W.E., 1916, *Jesus is Coming*, Chicago, Fleming H. Revell.

Blaising, Craig, and Bock, Darrell (eds), 1992, *Dispensationalism, Israel and the Church: The Search for Definition*, Grand Rapids, MI, Zondervan.

Boston, Robert, 1996, *The Most Dangerous Man in America? Pat Robertson and the Rise of the Christian Coalition*, New York, Prometheus.

Brickner, David, 1999, *Future Hope: A Jewish Christian Look at the End of the World*, San Francisco, Purple Pomegranate.

Brookes, James, 1985, *Till He Come*, New York, Fleming H. Revell.

Burge, Gary, 2003, *Whose Land? Whose Promise?* Carlisle, Paternoster.

Canfield, Joseph, 1988, *The Incredible Scofield and his Book*, Vallecito, CA, Ross House Books.

Chacour, Elias, 1984, *Blood Brothers: A Palestinian's Struggle for Reconciliation in the Middle East*, Eastbourne, Kingsway.

Chacour, Elias, 1990, *We Belong to the Land*, London, Marshall Pickering.

Chafer, Lewis, 1936, *Dispensationalism*, Dallas, Dallas Seminary Press.

Chafer, Lewis, 1947, *Systematic Theology*, Dallas, Dallas Seminary Press.

Chapman, Colin, 2002, *Whose Promised Land, Israel or Palestine?* Oxford, Lion.

Cohn-Sherbok, Dan and El-Alami, Dawoud, 2001, *The Palestine–Israeli Conflict*, Oxford, Oneworld.

Cragg, Kenneth, 1997, *Palestine, the Prize and Price of Zion*, London, Cassell.

Dallimore, Arnold, 1983, *The Life of Edward Irving, The Fore-runner of the Charismatic Movement*, Edinburgh, Banner of Truth.

Darby, John Nelson, 1962, *The Collected Writings of J.N. Darby*, Kingston on Thames, Stow Hill Bible and Trust Depot.

Davenport, Rowland, 1970, *Albury Apostles*, London, Free Society.

Davies, W. D., 1974, *The Gospel and the Land: Early Christianity and Jewish Territorial Doctrine*, Berkeley, CA, University of California.

Davies, Uri, 1987, *Land, An Apartheid State*, London, Zed.

DeMar, Gary, 1997, *Last Days Madness: Obsession of the Modern Church*, Atlanta, GA, American Vision.

Dolan, David, 1991, *Holy War for the Promised Land: Israel's Struggle to Survive*, London, Hodder and Stoughton.

Dyer, Charles, 1991, *The Rise of Babylon: Signs of the End Times*, Wheaton, IL, Tyndale House.

Falwell, Jerry, 1981, *The Fundamentalist Phenomenon*, New York, Doubleday.

Frazer, T.L., 1999, *A Second Look at the Second Coming*, Ben Lomond, CA, Conciliar Press.

Freuchtenbaum, Arnold G., 1989, *Israelology: The Missing Link in Systematic Theology*, Tustin, CA, Ariel Ministries Press.

Fuller, Daniel, 1980, *Gospel and Law, Contrast or Continuum? The Hermeneutics of Dispensational and Covenant Theology*, Grand Rapids, MI Eerdmans.

Gaebelein, Arno, 1991, *The History of the Scofield Reference Bible*, Spokane, WA, Living Words Foundation.

Gerstner, John, 1982, *A Primer on Dispensationalism*, Phillipsburg, NJ, Presbyterian and Reformed.

Gorenberg, Gershom, 2000, *The End of Days: Fundamentalism and the Struggle for the Temple Mount*, Oxford, Oxford University Press.

Grenz, Stanley, 1992, *The Millennial Maze: Sorting out Evangelical Options*, Downers Grove, IL, IVP.

Grier, W.J., 1970, *The Momentous Event: A Discussion of Scripture Teaching of the Second Advent*, London, Banner of Truth.

Haddad, Hassan and Wagner, Donald, 1986, *All in the Name of the Bible: Selected Essays on Israel and American Christian Fundamentalism*, Brattelboro, VT, Amana Books.

Halsell, Grace, 1986, *Prophecy and Politics: Militant Evangelists on the Road to Nuclear War*, Westport, CA, Lawrence Hill.

Halsell, Grace, 1999, *Forcing God's Hand: Why Millions Pray for a Quick Rapture and Destruction of Planet Earth*, Washington, Crossroads.

Harrison, John Fletcher Clews, 1979, *The Second Coming: Popular Millenarianism 1780–1850*, London, Routledge and Kegan Paul.

Hindson, Edward, 1997, *Approaching Armageddon: The World Prepares for War with God*, Eugene, OR, Harvest House.

Hunt, Dave, 1990, *Global Peace and the Rise of Antichrist*, Eugene, OR, Harvest House.

Irving, Edward, 1827, *The Coming of Messiah in Glory and Majesty, by Juan Josafat Ben-Ezra a converted Jew*, London, L.B. Seeley and Sons.

Jeffrey, Grant, 1991, *Messiah: War in the Middle East and Road to Armageddon*, Toronto, Frontier Research Publications.

Jorstad, Erling, 1970, *The Politics of Doomsday: Fundamentalist of the Far Right*, Nashville, TN, Abingdon.

Kraus, C. Norman, 1958, *Dispensationalism in America*, Richmond, VA, John Knox.

Ladd, George Eldon, 1956, *The Blessed Hope: A Biblical Study of the Second Advent and the Rapture*, Grand Rapids, MI, Eerdmans.

LaHaye, Tim, Jenkins, Jerry B., 1999, *Left Behind*, Wheaton, IL, Tyndale House.

LaHaye, Tim and Ice, Thomas (eds), 2003, *The End Times Controversy: The Second Coming Under Attack*, Eugene, OR, Harvest House.

Lindsey, Hal, 1970, *The Late, Great Planet Earth*, London, Lakeland.

Lindsey, Hal, 1973, *There's a New World Coming*, New York, Vision House.

Lindsey, Hal, 1981, *The 1980's: Countdown to Armageddon*, New York, Bantam.

Lindsey, Hal, 1983, *Israel and the Last Days*, Eugene, OR, Harvest House.

Lindsey, Hal, 1989, *The Road to Holocaust*, New York, Bantam.

Lindsey, Hal, 1994, *Planet Earth 2000 AD*, Palos Verdes, CA, Western Front.

Lindsey, Hal, 1995,*The Final Battle*, Palos Verdes, CA, Western Front.

Lindsey, Hal, 1997, *The Apocalypse Code*, Palos Verdes, CA, Western Front.

MacPherson, Dave, 1983, *The Great Rapture Hoax*, Fletcher, NC, New Puritan Library.

Mathison, Keith, 1995, *Dispensationalism: Rightly Dividing the People of God?* Phillipsburg, NJ, Presbyterian and Reformed.

Merkley, Paul, 1998, *The Politics of Christian Zionism 1891–1948*, London, Frank Cass.

Newton, Benjamin Wills, 1859, *Antichrist, Europe and the Middle East; The Antichrist Future*, London, Houlston and Sons.

Noe, John, 2000, *Shattering the 'Left Behind' Delusion*, Bradford, PA, International Preterist Association.

O'Neill, Dan, Wagner, Don, 1993, *Peace or Armageddon? The Unfolding Drama of the Middle East Peace Accord*, Grand Rapids, MI, Zondervan.

Pragai, M.J., 1985, *Faith and Fulfilment: Christians and the Return to the Promised Land*, London, Vallentine Mitchell.

Prince, Derek, 1982, *The Last Word on the Middle East*, Fort Lauderdale, FL, Derek Prince Ministries International.

Prince, Derek, 1992, *The Destiny of Israel and the Church*, Milton Keynes, Word.

Prior, Michael, 1997, *The Bible and Colonialism: A Moral Critique*, Sheffield, Sheffield Academic Press.

Rantisi, Audeh, 2003, *Blessed are the Peacemakers: A Palestinian Christian in the West Bank*, Swindon, Eagle.

Riggans, Walter, 1988, *Israel and Zionism*, London, Handsell.

Robertson, Pat, 1992, *The Secret Kingdom: Your Path to Peace, Love and Financial Security*, Dallas, Word.

Ruether, Rosemary Radford, and Ruether, Herman J., 1989, *The Wrath of Jonah: The Crisis of Religious Nationalism in the Israeli-Palestinan Coflict*, San Francisco, Harper.

Schlissel, Steve, Brown, David, 1990, *Hal Lindsey and the Restoration of the Jews*, Edmonton, Alberta, Still Waters Revival Books.

Scofield, Cyrus Ingerson, 1917, *The Scofield Reference Bible*, London, Oxford University Press.

Simon, Merrill, 1984, *Jerry Falwell and the Jews*, Middle Village, NY, Jonathan David.

Sizer, Stephen, 2004, *Christian Zionism: Road-Map to Armageddon*, IVP.

Tuchman, Barbara, 1957, *Bible and Sword: How the British Came to Palestine*, London, Macmillan.

Wagner, Donald, 1995, *Anxious for Armageddon*, Scottdale, PA, Herald Press.

Walvoord, John, 1957, *The Rapture Queston*, Findlay, OH, Dunham.

Walvoord, John, 1998, *End Times: Undersanding Today's World Events in Biblical Prophecy*, Waco, TX.

Index